DECADENT DINNERS & LASCIVIOUS LUNCHES

(X-rated Recipes for Sensuous Cooks and Their Friends)

by Norma Ewalt

as digested by

Tom Huth

Illustrated by Kathy Sherman

CREDITS

To Ann Deahl Shaffer, my dear mother, for her tolerant understanding. To Steve Elliott and Alan Martin for ongoing inspiration—(no 55-year-old man came forth to inspire me; so I opted for these two 30-year-olds.) To the Pulis family and their friends, of Ottumwa, Iowa, for creating the "family" dinner. To Kay Simms for mouthing the phrase: "Decadent Diners Get Oral Satisfaction". To Jean Lovell for formulating the massage oil. To R.J.E., a wonderfully creative Gemini, for motivating me in a unique way. Almost last, but not least to Todd, Jill, Beth and Brian for indulging and helping me during this latest idiosyncracy.

The authors and publisher are grateful to Norma Millay Ellis for her permission to reprint excerpts from: the translation from French by Edna St. Vincent Millay, of Charles Baudelaire's *Flowers of Evil,* Harper & Row. Copyright 1936, 1963 by Edna St. Vincent Millay and Norma Millay Ellis.

RENAISSANCE HOUSE PUBLISHERS
A Division of Jende-Hagan, Inc.
541 Oak Street • P.O. Box 177
Frederick, Colorado
80530

Library of Congress Cataloging-in-Publication Data

Ewalt, Norma.
Decadent dinners & lascivious lunches.

Includes index.
1. Cookery. I. Title.
TX652.E925 1985 641.5 85-25622
ISBN 0-939650-43-6

Book production and cover design by Three Friends Studio

ISBN 0-939650-43-6

DEDICATION

This book is dedicated to the memory

of my husband, Jerre,

who for 25 years made

my wildest dreams come true.

FABLE OF CONTENTS

CHARITABLE CONTRIBUTIONS

The proceeds realized from the sale of **DECADENT DINNERS AND LASCIVIOUS LUNCHES,** will go in part to the charity of your choice. From the list below, please indicate the charity or charities you wish to support: (If no choice is indicated the proceeds will go to The Center for the Permanent Eradication of Horrid Age Spots.)

I wish my contribution to go to:

- _____The Linda Looselace Home for Tired Trollops
- _____The Sunkissed Institute for the Study of the Sectional Performance of Navel Oranges
- _____The Annual Agronomy Award for the Improvement of a Strain of Wild Oats
- _____The Union for Stiffening the Resolve
- _____The League for the Prolongation of Connubial Bliss

AUTHOR KNEADS DILL DOUGH...

FOREPLAY

If your idea of decadent dining is to invite a friend over, dress up like Betty Crocker and the Pillsbury Doughboy, and do funny things to each other with rolling pins, just remember two pieces of advice. Pull the shades before you begin. And if the police show up, don't say you got the idea from me.

As far as I'm concerned there are no rules for what I call decadent dining (or lascivious lunching). The idea is simply to invite romance to your table, to turn a dinner date into an excuse to act out your most delicious fantasies, to allow your taste buds to whisk you away on a foreign intrigue.

Not many of us can afford to jet off to Tokyo for the weekend, but what's to prevent you from turning your living room into a Japanese tea house for the evening? If you and your spouse always dreamed of spending a week in the Caribbean but were afraid the natives might be restless, why not bring the Caribbean to you?

A good many people, I realize, might be reluctant to dress up as a belly dancer or a samurai warrior, even in front of their lifelong mates. Some people might have a hard time pretending that they're dining on an Aegean island when in fact they're sitting in a studio apartment in Cleveland, Ohio. But I think it's a wonderful tonic, to risk being foolish now and then: to crawl out of your tired old skin and try somebody else's on for size, if only for the laughs. If you're single, it's a dramatic way to meet someone new. If you're married, it's just what the therapist ordered for the seven-year itch.

The following chapters suggest how you might arrange for your strangest flights of fancy to come to life. Party ideas and recipes in a dozen international flavors are offered for summer and winter affairs, and for both gala ("Avec Argent") and budget ("Sans Argent") occasions. But keep in mind that they are only suggestions, and at best they will inspire readers to design their own menus for sensuous home entertainment. My aim is to get you into the mood. When I think of getting decadent myself, I imagine being alone with a man, and so the ideas in this book tend to favor intimate dinner parties for two. But they are easily adaptable to other circumstances, whether you're planning a full-blown bacchanalian orgy or a PTA social. I've attended my share of each, and it seems perfectly plausible to me that the Ladies' Aid Society of the Methodist

Church would embrace my suggestions about table settings and menus while politely skipping over the passages about massage oils and hot tubs.

Likewise, the book is written not only for women, but just as equally for men who would like to entertain their lady friends — or their boyfriends, for that matter. Decadent dining is too much fun to be restricted to any one clique, such as bored housewives.

I thought it might be helpful to explain, at the outset, how my passions became so intricately involved with cooking and eating good food in the first place.

A large helping of the blame has to go to my Pennsylvania Dutch ancestors. As strict as they were in avoiding other worldly pleasures, those old Swiss-Germans sure could lay out a lusty banquet. Most of the agreeable memories of my childhood, in fact, are involved with the gathering and preparation and consumption of food.

All of the people on my mother's side of the family were Pennsylvania Dutch who had followed a long and circuitous route to settle in Iowa. One branch came from the Williamsburg area of Tidewater Virginia, where my great-grandmother-twelve-times-over, Elizabeth James, died in 1621. Over the next couple of hundred years her descendents moved west to the Roanoke area, where they were joined by another clan that had migrated down from Pennsylvania. In 1852, when they saw the Civil War coming, these people left Virginia en masse and traveled halfway across the continent in a wagon train of 151 families to make their homes in the more peaceful pastures of Iowa.

Just after the turn of the century, my grandfather pushed farther west and settled in Denver, and that's where I was born a generation later. But then in the depths of the Depression our relatives persuaded my mother to move back to Iowa. A least, these farmers reasoned, we'd always have enough to eat there. So we ended up in a little town named Centerville, and it was in Iowa, during summers on the farm, that I was introduced to the fine arts of churning butter, making sorghum, plucking chickens, tending gardens, picking gooseberries, canning, pickling, and preserving.

Those are fond recollections now. At the time, however, I hated every minute of it. After being raised in a city (Denver had 128,000 people then), I couldn't believe that life could be so rural. My horse-and-buggy Brethren uncles eschewed all modern conveniences, and so I spent those summers on the farm without electricity, running water, radios and telephones. My escapes were daydreaming and reading, and my favorite books were the Perkins Twins series—about a brother and sister who traveled to exotic countries and ate exotic foods and who'd never heard of Iowa.

I questioned everything around me. I wondered, for example, why we always had oyster dressing on Thanksgiving and Christmas and at weddings and funerals. My relatives were incorrigibly frugal, and I couldn't figure out why, here in the middle of the prairie, they were motivated to buy a delicacy like oysters on those certain days. It was this sort of idle speculation that led me to put together my family's genealogy—and to discover the branch from the Tidewater where there'd been oysters by the boat load.

Traditions like that seem to live forever. I like to think of my great-great-grandmothers, who brought their distinctive traditions of hearty home cooking to Roanoke and then to Iowa, as the homelier successors to Catherine de'Medici, who a century or two earlier had introduced Florentine cuisine into the more innocent kitchens of Paris. In both cases, the best of the old traditions became part of the new one.

My curiosity has never ceased. It gives me a sense of myself to know where my appetites came from—and those appetites, I should mention, weren't only for food. Because it turned out that those old Pennsylvania Dutch who could lay out the lusty banquets were just as lusty in their bedchambers. They didn't smoke, drink, dance, wear jewelry, or go to the movies, so it must have been them that Mark Twain had in mind as he made the observation: "When you're looking for pleasure, you can't beat sex."

Sex was not a casual act among the unmarried but they married young and got on with it. There was a wedding-night custom in my family called the shivaree. Relatives and friends gathered with pots and pans and other kitchen utensils and proceeded to create a hellish din by banging them together. At the time I didn't give much thought to why they were doing this, but it occured to me later in life that it might have been a polite way to drown out the sounds coming from those old rope-sprung beds.

I had a crash course in sex when I was 12. While my parents were away at the Chicago World's Fair that year, I noticed a strange squarish lump under a corner of the carpet in my parents' bedroom. Upon investigation I made the most amazing discovery—a stash of pornographic comic books. They evidently belonged to my father, and what a revelation they were! I hadn't known that Tillie the Toiler and her friend Mac did *that* sort of thing! Nor had I imagined that Popeye needed a wheelbarrow to help him cart around a certain overdeveloped muscle. But I knew one thing—that I'd stumbled upon a source of magical power and wealth. With the help of a girl friend, I set up a peep show under her back porch and charged the neighborhood kids a penny a page to inspect those comic books. This was in the Depression, and I seldom had a nickel for a candy bar or a dime for the movies. Neither did my friends, but I did a lively business under that porch in the few days my folks were gone. By the time I had to put the books back under the corner of the carpet, my penny jar was full enough for Butterfingers and Ginger Roger movies for the rest of the summer.

Summertime was also when we journeyed into the Iowa countryside to visit my aunts and uncles. We always showed up unannounced, since these people never had phones. Furthermore, my aunts had to cook on wood-burning stoves and didn't have refrigerators. Nevertheless, whenever we stopped in to see my great-aunt Flo (who died in 1981 at the age of 102), she always served up a feast.

It was the proverbial "seven sweets and seven sours," and consisted of three kinds of meat, three or four salads, three or four vegetables, many kinds of pickles and relishes and a couple choices of dessert.

In those days Aunt Flo was nimble enough to lead me down the nearly perpendicular steps to her cellar so that I could help her carry up the fixin's for the noontime dinner. There in the dark damp recesses of the cellar lay earthy-smelling bags of potatoes, parsnips, turnips, carrots, and onions. On the shelves above them were cabbages, crocks full of pickles, and jars of eggs in waterglass. There were bushel baskets of apples and pears and nuts and, above those, row upon row of canned meat, vegetables, preserves, relishes, and yet more pickles.

Just as we had been promised, our family never went hungry during the Depression. My father's side of the family, in Denver, was quite different from my mother's. They first arrived in Denver at about the same time as my mother's people, but from the more anglicized precincts of Suffield, Connecticut. My grandfather Dibble was descended from Englishmen who had come to America on the *MAYFLOWER* and the *MARY AND JOHN*. Ancestors of ours surveyed the original city of Boston and then moved on to settle what is now Windsor, Connecticut, but my grandfather sought his fortune in the West.

The woman he married, my grandmother, was the daughter of immigrants from Northern Ireland. Consequently, her kitchen was rooted in Ireland and New England, and she was determined to keep the faith. Even when lamb was almost a bootleg commodity because of the range wars, my grandmother served leg of lamb on Sunday.

I spent a lot of time with my grandma Dibble before I moved to Iowa. I recall most vividly a time when I was in kindergarten and recuperating from the whooping cough, and it was decided that she would build me up to good health again. How I cherished those memories of my Irish grandma so cheerfully tempting my appetite, not only with good food, but with its irresistible presentation as well. One day she would arrange a tea party for me, with toast and lemon curd, and put it out in my grandpa's grape arbor on a table set with fresh violets. Another day I'd have eggnog and shortbread served on my doll dishes on my own tiny table, with three of my dolls for company. Sometimes my lunch tray would be adorned with little homemade dolls that my grandma had fashioned out of clothespins and hollyhocks. At other times she'd let me put on her best hat and her furs and jewels and I'd pretend I was a lady friend coming for lunch.

I didn't ever want to grow up (and some people might claim I never have). But anyway that is where I first got the notion, at the age of 5, that mealtime was not just for eating.

It was a time to play dress-up, to go off into a world of make-believe, to be somebody else. In each of their own ways, both sides of my family taught me that to eat well was to celebrate oneself, even while taking flight from it.

Against the good wishes of most of my Iowa relatives, who believed that women didn't need an advanced education, I went off to the rather avant-garde Grinnell College and studied, of all things, "liberal arts." When I left Iowa altogether in 1944, to take a job in Oak Ridge, Tennessee, they must have figured I was lost forever. And they were right.

I got married—to a city boy, naturally—and as fate would have it, Jerre was an adventuresome eater. He encouraged me to experiment in the kitchen, and his strongest complaint was a gentle,"Let's not have *this* again." Over the years, the two of us learned to treat certain special dinners as centerpieces for our most romantic encounters, turning mere meals into experiences that stimulated all of the senses.

Our "decadent dinners," we called them.

Jerre traveled in his work, every Monday through Friday, and I had a keen old-fashioned sense of wanting to make his life at home more exciting than his life on the road. Thus some of our most extravagant dinner dates were on Friday nights, and my husband never knew quite what to expect when he walked through the door.

One weekend he came home from Chicago to report that he had been to a new place called the Playboy Club where the waitresses dressed up like half-naked bunny rabbits. This seemed to have impressed him, and so when he left on another trip the next week I started planning for that Friday's reunion. I studied the Playboy Club brochure that Jerre had left and began putting a costume together. I went out and bought some black fishnet tights to go with my merry-widow bra, then whipped up some rabbit ears and a sassy little tail. What difference did it make if I was eight months pregnant? When my husband came home that Friday evening he was welcomed by the biggest, bounciest bunny rabbit he'd ever get a chance to lay his hands on.

Another time I sent all of our furniture out to be reupholstered and our rugs out to the cleaners, and then transformed our house into a Mexican cantina. Since I ran a Mexican-import business at the time, it was easy to round up the props. That weekend we had a Mexican dinner party for 50 friends followed by a Mexican brunch for another 50. People came dressed as matadors and senoritas, and we had mariachi music, and everybody drank too many margaritas, and then on the next day the cantina was closed, the props were returned to the import shop, our furniture came back from the reupholsterers—and Jerre was back on the road, wondering, "Where have I seen that woman before?"

This was at a time when my marriage was in its 20th year and I was resting on my laurels as a cook. My canned and baked goods had won ribbons at county fairs and I'd taken first place in a cooking contest, but my home was still the setting for what I considered my greatest culinary triumphs. Then in December 1972, after sharing 24 years of fantasies with a most willing partner, I became a widow.

After I got my life in order I moved for a while to Mexico, and it was there that I had a rude awakening as a cook. After dreaming about foreign cultures all my life I had finally settled into the middle of one, and, faced with the delicious variety of real Mexican cooking, I was forced to see how parochial my own tastes were. The same thing happened when I spent three months in Europe studying classic cuisines and their presentations: My education consisted mainly of finding out how much I still had to learn.

But that thought doesn't discourage me; it challenges me. Learning to cook better and with ever-more variety is a constant adventure and satisfaction. I like the idea that I could begin tomorrow and never have to repeat the same combination of foods even if I lived as long as my dear Aunt Flo.

Putting it into larger context, I believe that a lot of our frustration and unhappiness these days come from knowing (or believing) that there are certain conditions of our lives that we can't change. We take mates until death do us part; we lock ourselves into mortgages that run far into the 21st century; we cling to the security that our jobs seem to offer; we buy our clothes for their durability; we pay our annual dues at the club; we seek re-election.

Where is the variety—the spice—in our lives?

Well, it's a modest suggestion, to be sure, but I propose that at least we have a choice about what we're going to have for dinner tonight. From one day to the next, the easiest thing in our lives to change is how we're going to fix that leftover chicken. Food certainly can't offer us much in the way of security. No matter how expensive or mouthwatering it is, once we've popped it into our mouths it's gone. The everlasting truth is that we can't have our cake and eat it, to, so we'd better revel in it while it's here.

I'm not talking about gulping down a hot-fudge sundae to make yourself feel better after you've bashed in the fender of your Audi. I'm talking about creating an entire evening around a meal and sharing it with someone special—an evening so sumptous in its conception that you can gorge yourself in the anticipation almost as joyously as in the event itself, and still again in the memories left over.

That is what this book is about.

I want to emphasize again that there are absolutely no rules for decadent dining. Your own instincts are the best ones to follow. Don't worry if your foreign affairs aren't authentic in every detail. Nobody's going to stop you from coming to your own Egyptian dinner party as Lawrence of Arabia or a Turkish harem dancer. Remember that nothing kills the mood of a romantic early dissertation on the ethnic origins of one's flatware pattern.

As for me, I'm not quite ready yet to pass the torch on to the next generation. I am doing serious research for a sequel: Illegitimate Son of Decadent Dinners and Lascivious Lunches.

WAY-OUT WEST

WANTED
. . .for the pleasure of your company
for the crimes of reckless flirtation
and second degree mischief

WAY-OUT WEST

Summer Menu
(Avec Argent)

Chili Cheese Nuggets
Cream of Zucchini Soup
Barbecued Chili-Steak
Corn on the Cob
Mushroom Salad • Corn Muffins
Buñuelos with Ice Cream and Wine Sauce

Summer Menu
(Sans Argent)

Cheese Log
Cream of Pumpkin Soup
Fried Chicken and Gravy
Baked Tomatoes
Apple Slaw • Biscuits
Fruit Shortcake

Winter Menu
(Avec Argent)

Bacon Pinwheels • Cheese Soup
Game Sauerbraten
Baked Sweet Potatoes
Apple-Date Salad
Sourdough Bread
Brandied Peach Cheesecake

Winter Menu
(Sans Argent)

Beef Jerky and Cheese Ball
Chili Con Carne • Accompaniments
Tex-Mex Salad
Tortilla Chips • Pecan Pie

A lady friend asked me the other day after she'd returned from the National Western Rodeo in Denver: "How come cowboys think they're such great lovers when they consider eight seconds a good ride?"

Frankly, I don't understand it either. As a native Coloradan, I've gotten to know some cowboys personally—maybe too personally—because I'm left wondering why they've become the very embodiment of American masculinity.

Despite periods of womanizing, cowboys are generally loners— alone on the range with their horses, that is. Occasionally a cowboy will come to town on Saturday night to "get his buckle shined" (A euphimism for dancing belly to belly), but women play secondary roles in his life...his horse gets kissed first. If a cowboy does have a woman back at the ranch, she is there to keep the home fires burning while he is out herding cattle or boozing it up with the boys.

There's your real cowboy.

Let that be a warning to the contemporary urban cowgirl! If she should ever get into a passionate wrestling match with a *real* working cowboy, she'd better ask him to clean his fingernails before he explores much more than her earlobes, because he probably just got done picking his horse's hooves. A real cowboy won't be wearing Frye boots, either; he'll be wearing *genuine* shit-kickers, with those telltale white lines above the soles from sloshing around in a urine soaked corral. A real cowboy wouldn't be caught dead or alive in a Ralph Lauren shirt, but creates his own fashions,instead—such as long-johns turned a ghastly grey from being laundered too many times with his Levis. A real cowboy probably isn't a Marlboro man, but can be distinguished by the worn white ring on his hip pocket made by his can of "chew". A real cowboy, alas, will not be tanned from head to toe. His is a scratchy business, handling hay and working around barbed wire, and so the cowboy has to work under cover and is often tanned only in the face and above the shirt collar— whence the term *redneck.* Nor will the cowpoke of today be wearing a ten gallon hat—except for dress occasions—but rather a tractor cap that says something like BUD'S SEED AND FEED.

However, most of us are fortunate enough not to have to deal with reality. We live in an age of synthetics, and the new-model cowboys coming off the assembly line are superior to the originals in terms of cleanliness, reliability, versatility, colorfastness, and trade-in value. There are so many guys posing as cowboys nowadays that it's easy to find one who is housebroken. This new generic cowboy is much easier to handle, too: He's not overly horny from rubbing against a saddle all day long, but simply mighty agitated from sitting in commuter traffic in his four-wheel-drive pickup. The generic cowboy comes in all standard shapes and sizes, a variety of attractive colors, and is suitable for everyday ropin' and ridin'. So let's suppose that, regardless of whether you are a man or a woman, you want to arrange a dinner date, and you'd like to make it a Wild West party. Let's also assume that you and the pardner of your choice might enjoy getting into some role-playing to make the fantasy really come alive. The popular folklore, then — as schmalzy and sexist as it is — offers us a barrelful of plausible scenarios:

* He is the gambler and she is the dance-hall girl. He has a pencil-thin mustache, narrowed eyes, and a black Stetson. His name is Jack Kincaid, and he knows a crooked deal when he sees one. She has net stockings, garters, and rouge on her cheeks, and she knows a few tricks that even Jack hasn't seen. Or here's a variation: He is Marshall Dillion and she is Miss Kitty, and they have a few hours alone while Chester is away being rolfed.

* He is the outlaw—the gunslinger who's been shot in the stage holdup—and she is the skittery schoolmarm who tends to his wounds. He asks her, ''You ain't afixin' to turn me into the sheriff, are you ma'am?'', and she replies, ''It's not 'ain't' it's 'aren't'... and besides, I can't let you go until that strange swelling has abated,'' and he says, moving closer, ''Can I show you the cure for it ma'am?''

* He is the new hired hand; she is the rancher's daughter. He is a mite bashful, hanging his head and kicking the dust like the young John Wayne. She tells him she's bored with the wide open spaces. She'll scream if she hears one more lonely refrain of "Red River Valley" coming from over by the old bunkhouse. She tells the hired hand that she wants to run away, at least as far as to the hayloft.

* He is the young bronc-rider who has been thrown off his steed in the middle of the Sonora Desert, and she is the Indian maiden who chances upon him. Or he is the legendary Indian chief and she is the young anthropologist who has been sent from Boston to learn about the ancient ways.

* Going further back into history, he is the trapper and she is the missionary's wife. He has come to the West in search of beaver pelt. She hasn't seen another human being since her husband left to live among the heathens, and she tells the trapper about her unspeakably sinful dreams.

* Going even further back, to the Spanish conquistadores who first brought the horse to the West, the gentleman can be the gaucho and the lady the senorita, with an old-world grace to it all.

* Bringing it up to date, he can be the modern young buckaroo who patrols the streets of Longmont in his Chevy pickup filled with empty Bud cans, and she can be the chick in the supercharged Ford V-8 with a bottle of Ten High under the seat who leaves him standing in the dust. One way or another, the West is the setting for our most

romantic and sentimental images of ourselves as Americans. The movie that we've seen so many times under so many titles—The Winning of the West—is our only enduring (if somewhat tarnished) national myth, heralding the triumph of rugged individualism over an uncompromising land.

Your own romantic involvements might not be quite as majestic, but they probably won't be as trying, either, and you can always blame the lack of nobility on the 20th Century in general. Maybe it's enough to simply ride off into the sunset in a condominium elevator with your generic cowboy and celebrate the triumph of fertile imagination over uncompromising boredom.

INVITATIONS:

If you have a photograph of your guest, or if you're a good enough artist to sketch his or her face, you can make a "Wanted" poster. It could say something like: "Wanted: for crimes of reckless flirtation, second degree mischief, conspiracy to commit lewd and indecent exposure...and for the pleasure of his company at a Way-Out West dinner party..."

A similar idea would be to draw up a handbill of "Coming Attractions", as if for an Old West theater or opera house.

Or take a wood-burning tool and brand the invitation into a piece of cowhide (Available at leatherworking stores) or a small slab of barnwood.

SCENTS:

Oil lamps are decidedly Western—and so is the smell of kerosene. I'd suggest sacrificing a bit of authenticity and burning scented oil instead, in such fragrances as Bayberry, Pine, or Cinnamon.

If you happen to live in the West and can pick up some wild sage, it can be burned in a saucer or simply placed on the surface of a stoked up wood stove, and the resulting aroma is truly enchanting. You can get a similar, if lesser, effect by using sage that has been packaged.

TABLE SETTINGS:

For sitting around the old campfire (or new fireplace), you'll want some cowboy cookware, which is to say tin pie pans. These can often be found at second hand stores, or new at supermarkets. While you're shopping, look for tin cups or those heavy earthenware coffee mugs that would bounce if you dropped them from a second-story window. Maybe you'll even come across some three-tined forks. For napkins, what could be more appropriate than the sleeve of an old denim shirt?—but if that's too cute, then a bandana would do just as well.

If you want a more elegant setting, go Hollywood and pretend that you'll be dining in a private parlor at the Long Branch Saloon, with a damask tablecloth, fine china, pressed-pattern glass tumblers or goblets, Victorian napkin rings, and an oil lamp.

Any Southwestern table setting could include Mexican pottery in addition to other tableware. To lend an even heavier Spanish influence—especially if you're doing a patio party—try setting out luminarias. These are votive candles placed inside small brown paper bags that have been filled with an inch or two of sand as ballast. Fold the tops of the bags down to give them some stiffness and keep them away from the flame. Luminarias are often placed along the edges of driveways or paths, or on porches and balconies, and they give off a very ambient ochre glow. When you're lighting luminarias, a pair of needle-nose pliers comes in handy for holding matches.

For a patio party you might want to sit on bales of hay instead of chairs—unless of course, you're wearing shorts. And if you've got an old grain barrel around, that's the traditional place to stash the swiggin' bottle of Ten High. More local color can be added by decorating the scene with saddles, harness, lariats and whips, according to taste and prudence.

CLOTHING:

We all have enough images of Western get-ups to be able to choose a style that fits us. For men, blue jeans are almost obligatory, and might best be worn with a Western style shirt, perhaps a leather vest, and a Western felt or straw hat. Women can decide from among vintage gingham, dance-hall costumes square dance dresses, Levis or designer jeans.

MUSIC:

No matter where you live these days, you can turn your radio dial and probably come across at least a dozen country stations, where you'll hear Tom T. and Loretta and Mel and Tammy and Willie and Waylon and the boys wailin' about the hard-drinking, hard-fighting, hard-loving people who still live home on the range. One recent song I heard went, "My wife has a drinking problem and that drinking problem is me," and another one went, "She wipes the gravy off my vest, and drives me home when I'm too drunk to see." Romantic stuff like that.

After an hour or so of this, it might be better—especially if you can play the guitar—to arrange your own serenade. You might even do some parodies, such as "Please Wean Me Off the Bottle and Back Onto You", or, "If You Won't Leave Me Alone, I'll Find Somebody Who Will," or "How Can I Miss You If You Won't Go Away?"

CHILI CHEESE NUGGETS — Serves 2-4

- ½ C. soft butter
- ½ tsp. dry mustard
- 2 C. cheddar cheese, grated
- ½ tsp. salt
- 1 T. green chilies, canned, minced
- ½ tsp. Worcestershire sauce
- 1½ C. flour
- ½ tsp. onion salt

Blend the butter, cheese, mustard, salts, chilies, and Worcestershire together until completely mixed. Add the flour and mix to make a stiff dough. Take a heaping teaspoon in the hands and roll into a ball. Place on ungreased cooky sheet and press down lightly with the tines of a fork. Bake at 350 degrees about 15 minutes or until lightly browned. Can be served hot or cold.

Beer is a compatible beverage with spicy foods such as chilies and barbecues, and the amount of beer consumed with these Western foods may account for the "wild" in Wild West. If you consult a bar-tenders' guide, you'll find such appropriate drinks for a Western party as: The Western Rose, The Cowboy, The Whip, The Broken Spur, and on the following pages are drink cartoons inspired by some observations I've made.

CREAM OF ZUCCHINI SOUP — Serves 2-4

- 1 medium zucchini
- 1 C. chicken broth or bouillon
- 2-3 green onions, minced
- ½ C. buttermilk
- ½ tsp. dill weed
- Sour cream

Combine the zucchini, chicken broth, onions, salt and pepper to taste and simmer until the zucchini has all but lost its shape. Put mixture into a blender and blend about 15 seconds. Return to pan and add the buttermilk and dill if you are going to serve hot. If serving cold, add dill to mixture after blending then let cool before adding buttermilk. To serve, place in serving dishes, garnish with sour cream and paprika if desired.

BARBECUED CHILI STEAK — Serves 2

- 1½ lbs. rib eye steak, about 1½" thick
- 2 chilies chipotle, canned or 1 4 oz. can green chilies
- ¾ C. catsup
- 1 T. wine vinegar
- ½ tsp. garlic salt
- Freshly ground pepper

Blend chilies, tomato catsup, wine vinegar and part of the liquid from the canned chilies. (Chipotles are hot. Be sure to wash hands thoroughly after handling.) Place meat in glass container and cover with the blended chili mixture. Let stand 2 or 3 hrs. Lift meat out of marinade and drain well. Sprinkle with garlic salt and pepper. Broil over hot coals to desired doneness. To serve, slice in thin slices and serve with sauce.

CORN ON THE COB

Serves 2

2 ears corn
Butter
Salt
Chili powder

Husk corn and remove silks. Trim ends. Spread with soft butter and sprinkle with salt and chili powder. Seal ears firmly in double thickness of foil. Cook to the back of grill, turning frequently, about 30 minutes.

MUSHROOM SALAD

Serves 2-4

¼ lb. fresh mushrooms, trimmed and sliced
½ C. vegetable oil
2 T. wine vinegar
1 stalk celery, sliced
¼ C. green pepper, diced
¼ C. green olives chopped
Salt and Pepper
Lettuce leaves

Clean mushrooms with damp paper towel, and slice. Marinate in the oil and vinegar for several hours. Do not add salt to marinade. To serve, stir celery, peppers, and green olives into the mushroom marinade. Salt and pepper to taste. Drain salad and arrange on lettuce leaves. Garnish with olives, hard cooked eggs, etc....

BUÑUELOS WITH WINE SAUCE

2 C. flour
1 T. sugar
½ tsp.baking powder
½ tsp. salt
1 egg lightly beaten
½ C. milk
2 T. melted butter
Cinnamon Sugar

Combine dry ingredients in bowl and set aside. Beat egg with fork and add milk while continuing to beat. Add milk mixture to dry ingredients all at once and mix until dough holds together in a ball. Lift ball out onto floured surface and knead gently a few times. Divided into 12 equal parts and form each into a ball. Roll out with a rolling pin to form 6" circles. Fry in 2" deep fat at 375 degrees until buñuelos puff up and rise to surface and edges brown on the bottom side.

Sprinkle with cinnamon sugar (1 C. sugar plus 1 tsp. cinnamon) while still warm. Keep warm in shallow pan in warm oven or warm up in microwave.

Sauce:

1 C. red wine
¼ C. sugar
1 T. cornstarch
5 T. water
1 T. Kirsch or other cherry liqueur

Mix the cornstarch with the water. Combine with wine and sugar in the top of a double broiler. With a whisk stir mixture while cooking over boiling water. When mixture thickens and becomes clear, add liqueur, blend in and remove from heat. Hold warm or reheat to serve.

To serve: Top bũnuelos with scoop of vanilla ice cream and spoon wine sauce over all.

COWBOY'S DREAM
1½ oz. Wild Turkey Liqueur
1 c. coffee
Top with whipped cream

COWBOY'S DREAM (2)

$1\frac{1}{2}$ oz. Wild Turkey Liqueur
1 c. coffee
Top with whipped cream
Garnish with cherry

CHEESE LOG

- 1 8 oz. pkg. cream cheese
- ½ lb. Kaukauna Klub cheddar cheese
- ½ cube butter softened
- ¼ tsp. dry mustard
- ½ tsp. Worcestershire
- 1 drop Tabasco
- 1 T. Sherry or Port
- 1 T. horseradish, cream style
- Chili powder
- Minced pecans

Have all cheese and butter at room temperature. Mix all ingredients together thoroughly. Chill. On a wax paper, sprinkle a generous coating of chili powder and minced pecans. When cheese is chilled enough to handle, form a log and roll in chili-nut mixture, including ends. Wrap in plastic and chill until ready to serve. Serve with crackers. (This keeps well refrigerated for long periods.)

My search for "Shades of the Pioneers' " recipes turned up the following beverages: Bull's Milk, Bull's Eye, Bull Shot and the Apple Pie Cocktail. My adaptation of the Bull Shot would be good with this cheese log. In a tall glass, pour Mott's Beefamato over ice. Add a shot of vodka and stir. Another lighter summer drink is: half Beefamato and half beer, both chilled.

CREAM OF PUMPKIN SOUP

Serves 2-4

- 2 T. onion chopped
- ½ tsp. curry powder
- 1 T. butter
- ½ C. canned pumpkin
- 1 C. chicken consommé
- Salt to taste
- ½ C. cream or evaporated milk

Cook onion and curry powder in butter in a covered saucepan over low heat until tender. Add pumpkin, consommé and salt. Blend briefly, then put in blender and purée. Put back into the saucepan and add evaporated milk and heat slowly. To serve, ladle into individual serving bowls. Can be chilled and served cold. Garnish with parsley. (After measuring out ½ C. pumpkin, put remainder in plastic container and freeze for later use.)

APPLE SLAW

Serves 2-4

- 2 C. cabbage shredded
- ¼ C. dates pitted and chopped
- 1 apple with red skin
- ½ C. celery sliced thinly
- ½ C. sour cream
- 2 T. mayonnaise
- 1 T. sugar
- 1 tsp. lemon juice

Blend the sour cream, mayonnaise, sugar, and lemon together and let stand for enough time to let the sugar dissolve. Combine the rest of the ingredients in a bowl, and dress with the dressing. Add salt to taste. Chill until serving time. Serve on individual plates or in a relish dish garnished with apple.

FRIED CHICKEN AND GRAVY

Choose either a cut fryer or chicken parts to meet the needs of your party. In a clean brown paper bag, put ½ C. flour, 1 tsp. salt, pepper to taste and a dash of paprika. (This will coat 6-8 pieces.) Wipe the chicken pieces, then shake 2 at a time in the bag of seasoned flour. Use a skillet large enough to allow all pieces to lie flat or cook in batches. A heavy, thick-walled skillet is best. Heat enough shortening to have at least ½ inch depth in the bottom of skillet. Heat until it just begins to smoke, then carefully lay chicken in with tongs, taking care not to get splattered. Cover the skillet with an inverted colander to keep from being splattered, but to allow the steam to escape. Watch the chicken carefully, and when it is nicely browned on one side, turn and brown the other side. Fryers should cook in 25 to 30 minutes. You may want to reposition the pieces during cooking so they all cook evenly. Remove chicken to a shallow pan and keep warm while making gravy.

Gravy: Pour off all but about 2 T. shortening after removing chicken from skillet. Add the flour left in the bag, and work it into the shortening. (There should be about 2 T. seasoned flour.) Scrape all the browned bits loose from skillet and add 1 cup liquid . . . water or milk . . . stirring constantly. If too thick, add more liquid. Stir over low heat until thick and relatively smooth . . . the lumps should only be bits from the fried chicken. Serve with biscuits.

BAKED TOMATOES

Serves 2

- **2 medium to large firm tomatoes**
- **Salt and pepper**
- **¼ C. Parmesan cheese, grated**
- **⅛ tsp. each oregano and basil finely crumbled**
- **½ C. sour cream**
- **¼ C. mayonnaise**

Rinse and core the tomatoes. Cut in half crosswise and arrange in a buttered casserole. Sprinkle with salt and pepper. Blend the herbs and cheese with sour cream and mayonnaise. Spoon on top of each tomato. Spread evenly. Bake uncovered at 375 degrees until lightly browned, about 15 to 20 min. Serve in casserole.

A depraved shepherd from Boulder
Kept an un-"ewe"-sual mate, but told her,
"You are really great lookin'
But I can't stand your cookin'."
And with that he up and sold her.

Adapted from the old joke that the Lord made women because ewes can't cook.

BACON PINWHEELS

Serves 2-4

6-8 slices bacon cut in two
1 C. biscuit mix
¼ C. Parmesan cheese, grated
½ C. cheddar cheese, grated
⅓ C. milk

Fry bacon slowly to brown but do not crisp. Reserve. Blend all the rest of the ingredients together until a ball is formed. Add a bit more liquid if necessary. Turn out onto a floured surface and knead about 6 to 8 turns. Pat into rectangular shape and roll with a rolling pin into a long rectangle 6" X 16". You will then cut in strips 1" wide by 6" long. Put a piece of bacon on each strip. Roll up like a pinwheel, secure with a toothpick and bake on a cooky sheet in hot, 450 degree oven for about 8 to 10 min. or until nicely browned. Reheat if necessary.

CHEESE SOUP

Serves 2-4

¼ C. green onion minced
2 T. butter
1 T. flour
1 C. chicken bouillon
1 C. milk or cream
½ C. cheddar cheese, grated
1 tsp. brandy or cognac
Salt and pepper

Sauté the onions carefully in the butter, being sure they do not take on color. Blend in the flour and gradually add the liquid, and stir until the mixture thickens. Add the cheese a bit at a time being sure each addition is incorporated before adding the next. Add the brandy and season to taste. Do not boil. Serve hot. Garnish with seasoned croutons.

For this dinner entitled, "The Gambler and the Fallen Angel", you might look in the bar-tenders' guide for Fallen Angel, Floradora Cooler, Casino or Poker, but a nice red wine should accompany the sauerbraten.

BAKED SWEET POTATOES

Serves 2

Scrub two sweet potatoes (or you can use yams). Cut off the pointed ends, keeping the potatoes about equal size. Cutting off the ends keeps them from bursting in the oven. As an added precaution, you may want to pierce them with a fork along in the cooking process. Put the potatoes into a preheated 400 degree oven. Bake for about 40 minutes then test. Use a sharp, long pronged fork and it will release some of the built up steam. When done, the potatoes will pierce easily. Remove from oven when done and brush skins with butter. To serve, treat them as you would other baked potatoes, or you may want to serve them with a bit of honey in addition to butter and salt.

GAME SAUERBRATEN

2-3 lb. rump, chuck or other meaty cut of game such as elk...or use beef
1 C. red wine vinegar
1 C. red wine
2 C. water
1½ C. sliced onions
1 clove garlic, peeled
2 bay leaves
5 cloves
10 peppercorns
5 whole allspice
1½ tsp. salt
¼ C. sugar
6 slices bacon if using game

Additions

1 C. onions sliced
6 cloves
6 peppercorns
2 T. margerine
2 T. flour
6 gingersnaps crushed, (optional)
1 C. sour cream

The bacon should be placed 3 strips each side of roast and tied to keep in place during marinating process. Put all the rest of the above ingredients in a saucepan and bring to boil. Reduce heat and simmer about 5 min. Cool completely, then pour over the roast which has been put in a glass or stainless steel container. Cover and refrigerate. You will want to turn the roast morning and evening for two to four days.

To cook: Remove meat from marinade, reserving marinade. Pat the roast dry with paper towel, then dredge with flour, salt and pepper. Heat a Dutch Oven with enough lard or oil to brown roast on both sides. Strain marinade and add enough to half cover the meat. Using fresh onion, put 1 C. sliced onion and 6 fresh cloves and peppercorns on top of meat. Cover. Bring to a boil, then reduce heat and simmer 3½ hrs. Test for doneness at this point. It is done whe pierced easily with a long-pronged fork. Remove from pan and put on heated platter. Keep warm.

Make gravy as follows: Strain the liquid from the Dutch Oven and reserve. In the Dutch Oven melt margerine and blend in the flour and gingersnaps if desired. Then with a whisk, stir in about 2 cups of the reserved marinade. Stir constantly while thickening. Correct seasoning. Stir in sour cream just before serving. Serve gravy over meat or in a seperate bowl.

APPLE DATE SALAD

Serves 2

2 large, crisp eating apples
1 T. lemon juice
¼ C. celery thinly sliced
½ C. pitted dates, chopped
¼ C. mayonnaise
2 T. sour cream
1 T. sugar
Chopped nuts

Peel, core and dice apples, and sprinkle them with lemon juice to prevent discoloration. Add the celery and dates. Mix the dressing by blending the mayonnaise, sour cream and sugar together with a whisk. Dress the salad, arrange in a fruit dish or on a lettuce leaf and garnish with chopped nuts.

BRANDIED PEACH CHEESECAKE

Serves 2

1 C. fresh or frozen peaches, sliced
¼ C. butter
¼ C. brown sugar
¼ C. brandy

2 servings of cheesecake

If using frozen peaches, thaw and pat dry. Meanwhile melt butter in small skillet and add peaches. Stir-fry over low heat until peaches are tender. Add sugar and blend until sugar dissolves. When ready to serve, warm the brandy, ignite and pour over the peaches, letting it burn out. Spoon peaches over cheesecake.

CHILI CON CARNE

I am not going to get in the middle of a big controversy. The West is full of chili buffs, who even have their own "cook-offs". Much of the chili concocted at these events is so hot it is not pleasing to less seasoned palates. I am making no claim to authenticity for my recipe, but remember that, literally translated, "chili con carne" means chili with meat. It was just that, until Texans started adding tomatoes, beans, onions. etc... I am not going to include my personal recipe for chili because I'm acclimated to "hot stuff", but many aren't. Don't despair if you like it hot because this recipe allows you to build your own bowl of red.

To accompany the bowls of chili in the following recipe, set out separate bowls of:

Red beans
Chopped onions
Crumbled bacon
Cooked rice
Sour cream
Tortilla chips
Grated cheese
Crushed red peppers
Minced green peppers (even jalapeños)

1 lb. beef, coarsely ground or cubed
Piece of suet
1 small onion chopped
1 bay leaf
2-3 T. Gebhardt's Chili Powder
1 tsp. unsweetened cocoa
1 8 oz. can tomato sauce
3 cans water
Salt and Pepper

Render out the suet over low heat so it does not burn. When you have sufficient fat, remove suet bits and add the beef to the hot fat. Stir-fry to brown on all sides. Remove from heat but while still hot stir in the onion so it will wilt without browning. Put pan back on stove on low heat and stir in the chili powder and cocoa. Add the tomato sauce and the water. Put in the bay leaf and simmer over low heat for about 2 hours or until meat is very tender. Serve hot with the accompaniments previously listed.

TEX-MEX SALAD

Serves 2-4

1 large pink grapefruit
1 large orange
1 large avocado
2 T. lime juice
1 T. salad oil
1 tsp. sugar
Dash salt
Fresh mint

Peel the fruits, remove membranes and cut in bite size chunks. Peel avocado, remove seed, cut into bite size pieces and sprinkle with lime juice to prevent discoloration. Combine the fruits then make dressing of the 2 T. lime juice, salad oil and sugar. Blend dressing and fruit. Chill. To serve toss again and spoon into serving dish and garnish with mint.

NEVER FAIL PIE CRUST

If you are a pie lover, the pie crust recipe herein is worth the price of the book. I have shared this recipe infrequently, but I am including it here because even the novice cook can turn out a beautiful pie.

You will notice that this makes 8 single crusts. I consider this a distinct advantage because it takes no more work to make 8 than it does to make one, and you have frozen crust on hand for use anytime. Use it for quiches, pasties and turnovers as well as for pies. It is so short that some special care must be taken when baking just a pie shell. Use two pie tins; one to hold the crust, and one to sit inside the crust to keep it in place; or use the special pellets designed for this purpose. Always roll this pastry out between two pieces of waxed paper. Turn over from time to time and loosen paper to get rid of wrinkles.

1 lb. lard of best quality, (must be lard!) Chilled
5 C. flour
2 tsp. salt
1 egg
Milk
2 tsp. white or cider vinegar

Break the egg into a liquid measuring cup and beat with a fork. add enough milk to make 1 cup, and add vinegar to this mixture. Set aside where it will clabber. In a large bowl put the cold lard and add the salt and flour and cut with a pastry blender until it is pea sized granules. Make a well in the center and add the liquid all at once. Mix quickly until dough balls up. Add a bit more liquid if too stiff or a bit more flour if too sticky. Divide into 8 portions and package in plastic Baggies. Freeze reserve crusts, chill crust before immediate use.

Pecan Filling:

3 eggs
¼ C. butter melted
2 T. flour
½ tsp. vanilla
1 C. dark corn syrup
½ C. sugar
1 C. pecans
Dash salt

Beat the eggs and sugar until light and lemony looking. Blend in the melted butter, salt, flour, vanilla and corn syrup. Sprinkle pecans over the bottom of the pastry lined pie tin. Carefully pour filling over pecans. Bake at 425 degrees for 10 min. then at 325 for 40 min. longer. Cool before serving.

NORTHERN SLIGHTS

NORTHERN SLIGHTS

Summer Menu
(Avec Argent)
Red Caviar Appetizers
Cold Cherry Soup
Salmon Remoulade
Mushrooms and Beans
Celery Stuffed with Danish Blue Cheese
Swedish Rye Bread
Chocolate Almond Whipped Cream Torte

Summer Menu
(Sans Argent)
Open Face Sandwiches
Fresh Tomato Soup
Ham Mousse
Norse Macaroni Salad
Swedish Rye Bread
Applesauce Torte

Winter Menu
(Avec Argent)
Scandinavian Fish and Cheese Appetizers
Apple Soup
Game Birds with Cognac and Cream
Cauliflower • Pineapple Salad
Limpa Rye Muffins
Nesselrode Pudding

Winter Menu
(Sans Argent)
Fishballs with Dipping Sauce
Mushroom Soup
Seaman's Beef
Swedish Style Spinach
Cruditiés
Dill Dough Bread
Sandbakelsers • Coffee

Scandinavia is a land of sparse and yet soothing comforts for the human condition.

Outside of the cities, the people live in vast and silent isolation from each other, separated by frozen tundra and forest and fjord and those long dark impenetrable winters. For stimulation, they have to turn inside—to the pleasures of home and hearth and good clean Nordic sex.

They also eat a lot to pass the time.

Thus a Scandinavian theme is a natural for the host or hostess who wants to orchestrate a small and sensual dinner party. When wintertime comes around, and especially during the holidays—and especially if you have access to a hot tub or sauna—you should think Scandinavian. Get into the idea that, the harsher the weather is outside, the cozier your'e going to make it inside.

To get into the mood, let's go on a multiple-choice fantasy trip to the far northern latitudes:

Through a blind lottery conducted by the local meditation society you have won A WEEK OF BLISSFUL SOLITUDE at a retreat somewhere in Scandinavia. After careful deliberation, you end up spending the week (choose one of the following):

(a) at a farmhouse on a Norwegian fjord
(b) at a ski chalet in Sweden
(c) at an abandoned fishing village in Finland
(d) at a cheese-taster's hermitage in Denmark
(e) at a Lapp reunion East of the Sun and West of the Moon

Now it is Friday and the week is almost over. You have been a good meditator and learned many valuable things about yourself during the endless days of vacant rumination. But let's face it. You're bored. You're lonely...even horny. You want a little action. Your joints are stiff from not being used. You've always heard that the Scandinavians were an open and unembarrassed people in their sexual proclivities, and now you're dying to find out for yourself. As the week has gone by, you've found yourself spending more and more time gazing out the window, hoping someone will come to visit you. Your meditations have been increasingly interrupted by idle daydreams about who that unexpected visitor would be, and it has gotten to the point that, when you peek out the window, you are having hallucinations of beautiful blond strangers coming toward you from out of the interminable Arctic night.

Then, this Friday evening, on your last night in solitude, at seven (the day and hour of Venus) it happens. There is a knock on your door, and when you open it, a little cautiously, you see standing before you a beautiful stranger very similar to the one you have been imagining all along. That stranger is (choose from one column only):

(a) Bjorn Borg
(b) The crown prince of Denmark
(c) The Stockholm Boy's Glee Club
(d) Howard Cossell

(a) Miss Sweden of 1979
(b) The Nymph of the North Wind
(c) Greta Garbo
(d) The Stockholm Boy's Glee Club

You ask the stranger to come in out of the cold. The stranger, having walked a great distance, is grateful for your hospitality. The stranger has brought a bottle of aquavit and now pours two glasses full and, looking you in the eye, offers a heartfelt toast: "To Odin!" You look the stranger in the eye and murmur in return: "Skoal"

The stranger has also brought dinner, and now the two of you sit down to gorge yourselves on pickled herring, caviar, smoked salmon, cheese and flatbread, and strong dark beer. During the dinner your conversation turns increasingly, at the stranger's suggestion, toward the subject of:

(a) Grimm's Fairy Tales
(b) Kierkegaard's philosophy of transcendant individualism
(c) The Soviet Threat to Finland
(d) Sex

For dessert, you treat yourself to (any two choices):

(a) Danish pastries
(b) A cup of black coffee
(c) Nesselrode pudding
(d) Selected nibbles of the stranger's earlobe

After dinner, the two of you slip out of your clothes, quite effortlessly, and into a waiting hot tub. You float there shoulder to shoulder, tingling with the heat of the water and the anticipation of the moment, your thighs brushing together underwater, as you gaze up through the skylight at the Northern Lights dancing heel to toe. And then, finally, the two of you retire to the oversized featherbed to:

(a) patch the quilt
(b) drink "Between the Sheets" (see recipes)
(c) read an Ibsen play
(d) sleep like a couple of polar bears
(e) none of the above

If you don't have a sauna bath or hot tub in your own home, there are several possible alternatives. In certain enlightened cities nowadays, you can rent a mobile hot tub by the hour or the evening; for the right price, a rental company will back the tub up to your door and leave it there for your private enjoyment. If you don't mind leaving the house, you and your companion can go to a hot-tub emporium and soak there by the hour. Or think of a neighbor who has a hot tub or sauna and arrange to use it for an evening in return for, say, the leftovers from your smorgasboard. Or simply be brazen and pop into the Jacuzzi at the nearby apartment complex.

Be warned that the excessive use of alcohol and the withering heat of a hot tub can be a dangerous combination. That's only one of the reasons for soaking in pairs.

If you are in a position, so to speak, to luxuriate with a massage after taking a sauna or hot tub, you might want to use this formula for body oil that was given to me by a friend who's a sensuous Leo lady:

- ¼ C. olive oil
- ¾ C. vegetable oil
- ½ tsp. tincture of green soap
- 1 tsp. turpentine (the kind you buy at an art-supply store.)
- 2 drops scented oil such as lavendar, cinnamon, sandlewood, etc..

This is a stimulating emollient that can be left on the skin, but is best showered off to keep your sheets from becoming oily.

Skoal!

INVITATIONS:

The simplest and cheapest (and least imaginative) invitation would be a card or piece of note paper from a Scandinavian import shop. But let's try to be more creative.

If you want to slip an invitation to someone in your office, hide it inside a piece of Danish Pastry the next time you go out on a coffee run.

At holiday time send an invitation attached to a straw Christmas ornament, or to a drinking vessel into which you offer to pour your own homemade *glögg.*

Photocopy a map of Scandinavia and mark an X for the mythical destination of your rendezvous.

For a hot-tub party, scrawl the invitation across a scented towel.

SCENTS:

Although we tend to think of the smell of pine forests in conjuring up a Scandinavian reverie, I shy away from pine for one reason: It never fails to remind me of a turnpike restroom. I'm afraid pine has lost its romance for most of us, through oversaturation.

In Scandinavia itself, the fragrance of summer and winter are as different as day and night. In the summer, the Nordic dinner tables fairly overflow with the bounty of fresh flowers provided by the long hours of sunlight, so if you want to go native just select your scents from out of the flower garden. If you're eating outside amid nature itself, a citrus fragrance will add a tangy accent. In the winter, the aroma of a Scandinavian home is of wood smoke and soup from the kettle on the stove. I like to exaggerate these homey smells by putting a few drops of essential oil—cinnamon or clove—on a light bulb oil ring, or by using lamp oil or candles freighted with these scents.

TABLE SETTING:

Scandinavia has produced some of the world's most renowned designers of silver and tableware, including pottery, porcelain and stainless steel. Names that come to mind are Dansk, ittalia, Arabia and Orrefors. These companies have exported far and wide and are easy to find in retail stores, with copies of the originals even more abundant. The bold and brightly colored fabrics of Scandinavia, such as Marimekko, are also popular and can be purchased in tablecloth widths. If you like the pattern, you can stretch it over a wooden frame once the party is over and use it as a wall hanging. When you choose one of these striking designs for your tablecloth you'll want to use a plain white porcelain dinnerware with it. Many of these dinnerware sets come with serving plates that can be brought directly to the table from the radar range. (And, since I've brought the subject up, let me say that microwave cooking can be a boon for the single working person who can prepare lavish meals using conventional methods, when he or she has the inspiration, then freezing them for reheating later.)
then freezing them for reheating later.)

If instead of a bright tablecloth, you choose a coarsely woven one, then go with stoneware for a heavier wintry, positively Viking expression.

Should you be so supremely lucky as to have Royal Copenhagen china, then use fine linen cloth.

Scandinavian crystal is available in a wide variety of patterns and prices. One store in Chicago, the Crate and Barrel, specializes in crates of crystal at quite reasonable cost; so you don't have to go to Georg Jensen's for your tableware unless you want to brag that it set you back $750 a place setting.

For incidental decorating touches, you can hardly turn the corner these days without running into an import shop that sells Scandinavian candles and candle holders, napkin rings, paper goods and other useful and useless doodads.

If you are eating from snack trays, don't skimp on your decorations, just scale them down. If you can't afford certain touches, improvise! Cover a piece of styrofoam with foil, plunge small tapers into it and then secure the base to a tray with floral clay and bury it under fresh ivy. Fresh flowers can be added by sinking small pill bottles into the styrofoam and filling them with water. In summer or winter you can put out tiny pots of dill tied with ribbons.

For the Christmas season (which lasts until January 13th in some parts of the northland) just toboggan on down to the library and check-out some Time/Life Cookbooks. Look at a few pictures of Scandinavian holiday tables and let the warmth from them overwhelm you, then go home and approximate the feeling as best you can. In home decorating—as in Christmas itself, and love-making, too—it's the spirit that counts and not what you have to work with.

If you are serving the liquor known as aquavit, try this. Cut the top off of a half-gallon milk carton, set the aquavit bottle inside, fill the rest of the carton with water, and stick it in the freezer. Before serving, peel off the cardboard carton, and bring the aquavit to the table in it's own little palace of ice.

CLOTHING:

My tastes swing wildly back and forth between Garbo looks and the Shield Maiden Brynhild; my fantasies between Leif Erickson in jockey shorts and Sigurd in golden mail. In the winter, you can't go wrong by wearing snuggly after ski togs, or at least one of those luxuriant sweaters of Nordic design. A truly authentic costume might include cross-country skiing knickers and knee-length wool stockings, but in my humble estimation it takes a generous imagination to feel sexy in knickers.

MUSIC:

Experimentation is the name of the game.You might want an evening of classical Scandinavian music, or you might want to mix it in with some popular and middle-of-the-road stuff. Most modern libraries have media centers where you can check out albums of international songs in addition to classical recordings.

I'd suggest any of the old Nordic masters, especially the symphonies of Sibelius and Grieg. Sibelius's Second Symphony is a particular favorite of mine. If you're going to discuss Kierkegaard, try some string quartets by either of those composers.

If you want the mood to be lighter, then give a listen to a pop group called ABBA; the lyrics and harmonies are sweet, and at low volume it's just enough to brighten conversation. If you'd like some very pleasant jazz without lyrics, try Pat Metheny.

RED CAVIAR APPETIZERS

Serves 2

- 4 hard cooked eggs, peeled
- ⅓ C. lemon mayonnaise (See Page 137)
- 1 T. butter
- 1 small jar red caviar
- Sour cream
- 8 rye bread rounds, buttered
- Lemon wedges
- Parsley

Cut eggs in half, remove yolks and mash into a paste with butter, then blend in mayonnaise and beat until fluffy. Pile egg yolk mixture into whites, make a depression in the center and garnish with caviar. Put a dollop of sour cream on rye rounds then put caviar on top of sour cream. To serve, alternate eggs and rye rounds on a tray and garnish with lemon wedges and parsley.

COLD CHERRY SOUP

Serves 4-6

- 1½ C. fresh sour cherries pitted, or pitted, canned or frozen sour cherries
- ¾ C. red wine
- ¾ C. water
- ½ C. sugar or to taste (frozen cherries will probably be sweetened.)
- 1 T. flour
- ½ stick of cinnamon
- ½ C. sour cream

If using fresh cherries, simmer in the water with cinnamon stick until cherries are tender. Lift out cherries, then pit over pan to catch all juice. Return the pitted cherries to the pan, add the wine and sugar and bring to a boil. Reduce heat and simmer while stirring to dissolve sugar. If using canned cherries, omit step one. If using frozen cherries, do not add more sugar until tasting after they have cooked tender. Meanwhile, stir flour into sour cream with a whisk and let stand. When cherry mixture has cooked and the sugar is corrected, remove the cinnamon stick and put the cherry mixture into a blender in batches to purée. With the last batch add the sour cream and flour mixture. Return all to the pan and cook at a simmer until flour is cooked. Chill. To serve, thin if needed using half red wine and half water. Garnish each bowl with a dollop of sour cream or whipped cream.

MUSHROOMS AND GREEN BEANS

Serves 2-4

- ½ lb. fresh mushrooms, sliced
- 2 T. butter
- ¼ C. heavy cream
- Salt and Pepper
- ½ lb. slender fresh green beans, strings removed

Sauté mushrooms in butter. Add cream gradually. Cover pan and cook over low heat until tender. Remove from heat but keep warm. At the same time steam beans until tender. Remove from steamer and toss with sugar, salt and pepper. To serve, put beans in serving dish and cover with mushrooms.

SALMON WITH REMOULADE SAUCE

Serves 2

2 1" thick salmon steaks each weighing about 6 oz.
½ C. white wine
2 C. water
1 small bay leaf
1 T. white vinegar
1 small onion, peeled
1 small carrot, scraped
Sprig parsley or dill
Pinch thyme
2 peppercorns
Pinch salt

Simmer covered, about 25 minutes, all ingredients except salmon. Cool broth completely, strain and then pour over salmon in shallow pan. Bring to boil over high heat, cover tightly, then reduce heat and simmer 10 minutes. Let fish cool completely in pan without removing lid. Then refrigerate. To serve, remove from bouillon and drain on a paper towel. Put on serving platter and garnish with lemon and parsley.

REMOULADE SAUCE

1 C. mayonnaise
½ tsp. Dijon mustard
1 tsp. paprika
1 T. lemon juice
½ tsp. lemon rind, grated
2 T. catsup
1 T. celery, minced
1 T. capers, minced (optional)
1 T. parsely, minced
1 T. cucumber, seeded, minced
½ C. whipping cream
Salt and pepper
Dash Tabasco

Blend all except whipping cream, until well blended. Salt and pepper to taste. Let stand, covered in the refrigerator to blend flavors. To serve, whip the cream and fold in. Put in serving bowl. Leftover sauce will keep several days refrigerated, and is delicious with a shrimp salad.

BRUNHILDA'S BREW

6 oz. beer
6 oz. Clamato juice
1 slice lemon

Have ingredients icy cold. Stir together gently in tall glass or beer mug.

CELERY STUFFED WITH DANISH BLUE CHEESE

Serves 2-4

1 small wedge Danish Blue Cheese
Mayonnaise/sour cream
Celery for stuffing
Dill or parsley, minced
Cherry tomatoes, optional

Mash cheese and blend with sour cream and/or mayonnaise to make filling. Fill celery. Sprinkle with dill or parsley. Arrange on serving plate with tomatoes if desired.

CHOCOLATE ALMOND WHIPPED CREAM TORTE

1 small ready to serve Angel food cake
1 C. whipping cream
4 T. sugar
4-5 T. cocoa (unsweetened)
½ C. almonds, slivered and toasted
1 tsp. vanilla
Shaved chocolate curls
Extra toasted almonds

Cut cake in three layers. Cover to keep moist. Chill beater bowl, with cream and blades before whipping. Mix sugar and cocoa together. Beat cream at high speed and as it thickens add sugar mixture bit by bit, but do not overbeat. Cream should peak. Add vanilla last. Spread bottom layer with whipped cream and sprinkle on almonds. Repeat for next layer. Put top layer on and frost cake completely. Garnish with chocolate curls and almonds. Chill. Cut with serrated knife.

FRESH TOMATO SOUP

Serves 2-4

1 large or 2 medium fresh tomatoes, peeled and chopped
2 medium to large green onions, minced
2 T. butter
1 small potato, peeled and shredded
1 C. chicken stock, condensed
1 C. water
1 T. flour
Pinch celery seed, ground
Pinch sugar
Salt and Pepper to taste
Sour cream
Dill weed, minced

Melt butter in large skillet and sauté onions and potatoes over low to medium heat. Let turn slightly golden but do not brown. Add tomatoes, stir in and let cook briefly before adding chicken stock and water. Add liquids, cover and cook until potato is tender. Make flour paste by blending flour in about ¼ C. water. Put a cupful of hot soup in blender, add flour paste and blend until smooth. Pour into container and reserve while blending rest of soup. Put all the soup back into pan and cook at simmer until flour is cooked and soup is thickened. Season. Thin if necessary. Serve hot or cold, garnish with sour cream and dill.

HAM MOUSSE

Serves 2-4

- 1 C. ground ham, fully cooked
- 1 envelope Knox gelatin softened in ¼ C. water
- 1 C. chicken bouillon
- 2 tsp. salad mustard
- Dash Worcestershire
- 1 T. finely minced onion
- ¼ C. dill pickle chopped
- ½ C. mayonnaise
- 1 T. catsup

Bring the bouillon to a boil in a small saucepan, add the softened gelatin and dissolve completely. Remove from heat and stir in the mustard and Worcestershire sauce. Put mixture in refrigerator to set partially. Meanwhile blend the catsup into the mayonnaise for color. When gelatin mixture is almost set, blend in the mayonnaise, then the ham and vegatables. Pour into buttered mold, cover and chill until set and ready to use. Unmold and garnish.

APPLESAUCE TORTE

Serves 6

- 1½ C. thick applesauce
- ¾ C. almonds, ground
- ½ C. powdered sugar
- 2 eggs, separated
- Whipped cream
- 1 8 inch round sponge cake or lady fingers

Butter a deep baking dish big enough to hold cake (or lay in lady fingers). Cover the cake with the applesauce. Mix almonds, sugar and egg yolks together, adding the yolks one at a time, beating well after each addition. Beat egg whites stiff but not dry. Fold the whites into the yolk mixture. Cover applesauce with this mixture. A pastry tube can be used to pipe it on. Set dish in shallow pan of hot water and bake in 350 degree oven for 15 minutes or until the almond paste is nicely browned. To serve, take warm to table and spoon out. Pass whipped cream in separate dish.

NORSE MACARONI SALAD

Serves 2

- ½ C. raw macaroni
- ⅓ C. sour cream
- 1 heaping tsp. cream style horseradish
- 1 tsp. Lawry's "Pinch of Herbs"
- Dill weed, salt and pepper to taste

Cook macaroni in boiling water with the Pinch of Herbs and dash of salt. When tender, drain and blend in the remaining ingredients. Chill. To serve, garnish with summer vegatables such as tomato wedges, green onions and green peppers.

SCANDINAVIAN FISH AND CHEESE APPETIZERS

There are many locations in the United States where you can buy locally smoked fish. These are usually superior to those that are prepared for export because they are fresher, and generally no preservatives are used. If you have a local source of smoked fish, trade-off authenticity for a fresher product. In addition to smoked fish, try some of the herring packed in sour cream or just pickled. You may also want to try fish steaks in a variety of sauces. Any of the tinned fish from Scandinavian countries are worth trying.

To accompany the fish, providing a complimentary taste, put out a sampler of cheese. Your cheese shop will let you sample the cheese before you buy, I'm sure, and some of the ones to try are: Havarti and Cream Havarti, Danish Blue, Crema Dania and Tybo. There are Danish "Bries", "Camemberts" and "Port Du Saluts" too, but first try those more indigenous to Denmark.

Serve with a variety of flat breads and crackers from these Norse lands.

APPLE SOUP

Serves 2-4

4 tart apples
1 pint water
½ stick cinnamon
2 strips lemon peel about 2" long
1 T. cornstarch
White wine
Sugar

Wash and core apples but do not peel them. Cook the fruit in the water with cinnamon stick and lemon peel until very soft. Rub through a sieve. Mix the cornstarch with a little water and put both the purée and the cornstarch mixture back in the saucepan. Over low heat, stirring constantly, allow the mixture to come to a boil and add wine and sugar to taste, and more water to bring to proper consistency. Let cook until cornstarch mixture has become clear and all flavors are well blended. To serve garnish with sour cream which has been sweetened lightly or whipped cream. Can be served hot or cold...with simple cookies.

CAULIFLOWER AND PARMESAN

Serves 2-4

2 C. cooked cauliflower
1 T. flour
2 T. butter
¾ C. milk
1 egg yolk, slightly beaten
Salt, pepper and sugar
2 T. Parmesan cheese, grated
1 zwieback or other crumbs

Put cooked cauliflower in buttered baking dish. Melt butter in small saucepan and blend in smoothly the flour, then the milk and beaten egg yolk. Stir constantly. Add a pinch of sugar, salt and pepper to taste, and last the cheese. Pour over the cauliflower and top with crumbs. Brown in 350-375 degree oven.

GAME BIRDS WITH COGNAC AND CREAM

Serves 2

2 Cornish game hens
Salt and pepper
1 medium onion, cut in half and stuck with 1 clove each
½ C. butter
3 green onions minced
½ C. dry white wine
1 C. beef bouillon
½ tsp. dry sage leaf, crumbled
1 C. heavy cream
2 T. Cognac
1 jar apple rings
1 jar cooked prunes, pitted
Parsley or watercress

Wipe birds inside and out. Season cavity with salt and pepper and insert onion half in each. Melt 4 T. butter in pan suitable to hold the two birds, which can be used for browning, and which can be covered and put in oven. Brown the birds on the breast side, then on the sides, then turn birds on their backs to finish browning. Lift birds from pan. Pour in wine and beef broth. Stir with wooden spoon, getting all bits of browned butter incorporated. Rub birds with sage, salt and pepper, return to casserole and cover. Put in 400 degree oven and roast 30 minutes, basting frequently. Uncover and roast 10-15 minutes. When birds are done, put on hot platter, surround with apple rings centered with pitted prunes, and garnish with parsley. Meanwhile add cream to casserole and stir over low heat on top of burner. Simmer 2 to 3 minutes and correct seasoning. Remove from heat and stir in Cognac. Strain sauce into serving dish.

LIMPA RYE MUFFINS

About 20 2" muffins

1 C. rye flour
¾ C. white flour
4 tsp. baking powder
½ tsp. salt
¼ C. brown sugar
1 tsp. caraway seeds
1 tsp. anise seeds
1 egg, slightly beaten
½ C. milk
¼ C. orange juice
1 tsp. orange rind, grated
¼ C. oil
¼ C. molasses

Using a mortar and pestle, grind the caraway and anise seed just slightly. Mix them in a bowl with the rest of the dry ingredients. Make a well in the center of dry ingredients and in one addition put in all the liquid ingredients which have been mixed together. Keep stirring to an absolute minimum. Batter should be lumpy. Stir only long enough to moisten...not over 20 seconds. Line muffin tins with paper liners. Fill about ⅔'s full. Bake in 400 degree oven for 20 to 25 minutes. Serve hot or cold. Freeze surplus muffins.

NESSELRODE PUDDING

Serves 4-6

- **1 C. heavy cream**
- **⅓ C. plus 1 T. sugar**
- **2 egg yolks**
- **1 pkg. Knox gelatin softened in ¼ C. water**
- **⅓ C. sherry**
- **1 scant T. rum**
- **⅓ C. almonds, blanched and ground**
- **⅓ C. citron, finely cut or mixed fruit as for fruitcake**
- **Whipped cream**
- **Candied Cherries**

Beat cream, sugar and egg yolks together in heavy saucepan over low heat. Add gelatin, continuing to beat until gelatin mixture comes to boil. Remove from heat and stir until cool. (Can be put in mixer bowl at low speed). Add the sherry, rum, nuts and fruit. Butter a small mold and pour pudding in. Chill until firm. To serve, unmold and garnish with whipped cream and candied cherries.

"DILL DOUGH" BREAD

1 large loaf

This is a fabulous bread for more reasons than lending itself to a pun. It makes a large loaf, and when I have time, I am going to experiment with making it into rolls; so I can freeze some. Meanwhile:

- **1 C. cottage cheese**
- **1 pkg. dry yeast, softened in ¼ C. warm water and dissolved**
- **1 egg lightly beaten**
- **2 T. sugar**
- **1 T. dill**
- **1 T. instant onions**
- **1 T. salad oil**
- **1 tsp. salt**
- **¼ tsp. baking soda**
- **2¼ - 2½ C. flour**

Heat cottage cheese over low heat stirring constantly until JUST LUKEWARM. DO NOT OVERHEAT. Stir in dissolved yeast, sugar, egg, dill, onion, oil, salt and soda. Blend thoroughly, then add 2 cups flour. Blend well. Turn out on board sprinkled with ¼ C. flour and knead a couple of minutes...add more flour if necessary. Put in oiled bowl, turning ball of dough to oil on all sides. Cover and let rise in warm (70-80 degree) place until double in bulk. (About 1 hour) The dough is ready when two fingers plunged in center leave the impression. Punch down dough with fist and turn out on floured board and knead again briefly. Make into a ball and put in a greased 2 qt. casserole. Let rise covered another ½ hour or until again double in bulk. Bake at 350 degrees 40-50 min. Bread is done when it sounds hollow when tapped on the bottom. Cool, out of pan, on wire rack. Smear crust with butter while still warm. (This is great toasted!)

FISHBALLS WITH DIPPING SAUCE* — Serves 2

Salted water to cover ½
lb. raw shrimp
1 fillet of sole
1 bay leaf
¼ C. breadcrumbs
1 egg
1 T. parsley minced
Pinch thyme
Salt and Pepper
Dash Tabasco
Egg and crumbs for coating
Oil for frying

Simmer shrimp and sole after dropping in boiling salted water with bay leaf. About 7 minutes. Drain. Shred fish with two forks. Shell shrimp and de-vein, then chop. Add remaining ingredients except the coating ingredients, and form into small balls, pressing together firmly. Dip balls into slightly beaten egg then roll in crumbs. Place on waxed paper until all are ready to fry. You can do these ahead to this point and hold in refrigerator, covered. To fry, heat oil to 375 degrees and lower balls into hot oil a few at a time. Fry until golden brown. Serve with picks and dipping sauce.

DIPPING SAUCE

½ C. sour cream
2 T. mayonnaise
1 T. catsup
Pinch or more dill weed
1 tsp. horseradish or to taste
¼ tsp. cayenne
Dash Worcestershire
Salt and pepper

Blend all together ahead of time so flavors will blend. Refrigerate until ready to use.

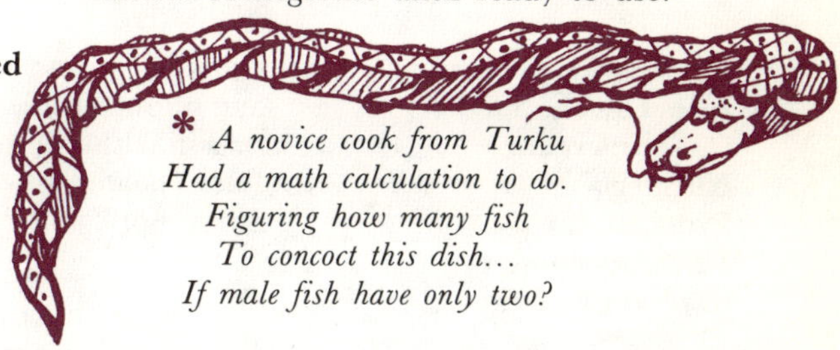

* *A novice cook from Turku*
Had a math calculation to do.
Figuring how many fish
To concoct this dish...
If male fish have only two?

SEAMAN'S BEEF — Serves 2-4

4 beef medallions cut from round or similar cut, put through meat tenderizing machine
¼ C. flour seasoned with salt and pepper
Butter
3 medium potatoes, peeled and sliced ¼" thick
1 medium onion, peeled and sliced ¼" thick
Bouillon to cover

Shake potatoes and onion in bag with flour. Melt butter and brown meat quickly on both sides. Lift out. Arrange casserole in same pan or rinse out pan juices with bouillon. Reserve. Put a layer of potatoes and onions on bottom of pan, and then beef next, then rest of potatoes and onions. Cover with bouillon. Cover pan and bake at 300 degrees for 1½-2 hours or until meat is tender. Serve from casserole.

SANDBAKELSER

Makes 30-36

⅓ C. blanched almonds, ground
¾ C. butter or half margerine
¾ C. sugar
1 egg white beaten lightly
1 ¾ C. flour

Combine butter, sugar and almonds until creamy. Beat in egg white with a fork or whisk. Blend in flour thoroughly. Chill dough. Preheat oven to 350 degrees. Using a ball of dough about ¾ " in diameter, press into a sandbakelse mold (tiny fluted tin) so inside of mold is covered by a thin coating of dough. Place molds on a cookie sheet and bake 12-15 minutes, until cookies are golden brown. To unmold, have a wax paper on counter, invert tin and tap gently. Cooky should slip out, but if molds are old and a bit pitted as mine are, a quick spray of Pam helps. Cool cookies and store in air tight tin.

Serve these plain or fold slightly frozen raspberries or strawberries into whipped cream, and spoon into the hollow side of the sandbakelser.

SWEDISH STYLE SPINACH

Serves 2-4

1 10 oz. pkg. frozen spinach, chopped
½ C. sour cream
Nutmeg
Pinch sugar
Salt and pepper
1 hard cooked egg

Cook according to directions on pkg. Add sugar and nutmeg while cooking. Remove from heat and season with salt and pepper. Fold in sour cream. Put in heated bowl and garnish with chopped egg. Serve hot.

BETWEEN THE SHEETS - or - UNDER THE COMFORTER

Shake together over ice:
1 oz. Southern Comfort
1 oz. applejack
½ oz. apricot brandy
Twist of lemon

ODIN'S OBSESSION

1 cube butter
1 C. brown sugar
1 tsp. cinnamon
½ tsp. vanilla
Pinch cardamon
Rum
Apricot brandy

Cream together all ingredients except rum and brandy. Put one or more tablespoons butter mixture in cup. Add boiling water and when butter is melted, add 1½ oz. rum and ½ oz. apricot brandy. Serve hot.

GREEK ORGIA

GREEK ORGIA

Summer Menu
(Avec Argent)
Greek Mushrooms
Ripe Olive Soup
Shrimp and Feta Cheese Casserole
Artichokes with Lemon Butter
Greek Salad
Kourabiedes • Coffee

Summer Menu
(Sans Argent)
Eggplant Appetizer
Cream of Spinach Soup
Greek Marinated Fish
Zucchini Pancakes
Sliced Tomato Salad • Pita
Kamposta Lampsa • Coffee

Winter Menu
(Avec Argent)
Greek Meatballs • Mayiritsa
Leg of Lamb
Spinach with Rice
Greek Salad • Crusty Bread
Baklava • Coffee

Winter Menu
(Sans Argent)
Taramosalata • Lentil Soup
Moussaka • Greek Salad
Italian Bread • Figs Venus
Coffee

The Greeks had a word for it—an entire vocabulary, in fact—the original script to THE JOY OF SEX.

The term "orgy," for example, comes to us from the Greek orgia (which, interestingly enough, was almost always used in the plural). The word "erotic" is descended from Eros, the Greek God of love. "Aphrodisiac" comes from the goddess Aphrodite who, according to legend, "strikes fond love into the hearts of all and makes them in hot desire to renew the stock of their races." Even the harmless term "symposium" is a marriage of the Greek words for "drinking together". And of course the phrase, "Would you like to come up to my apartment?" is thought to have been first uttered during a Saturday-night-live session of the Socratic Dialogues.

So if you are casting around for a classical theme for a romantic dinner date, go back to the source and make it a Grecian affair. The Greeks more or less invented decadent dining. They ate while reclining on couches. They went at the food with their bare hands, wiped their greasy fingers on pieces of bread, then threw the bread to the dogs. The Romans later refined this technique by bringing napkins to the dinner table and sometimes using them to carry home uneaten food, thus creating the first doggie bags. But it is the Greeks that we want to emulate, the heroic followers of Epicurus, the philosopher king of all hedonists.

So close your eyes now...and transport yourself to an island in the middle Aegean...to a couch for two among the olive trees...or to a table at a small whitewashed cafe on the clifftop.

For dramatic inspiration, merely turn to the hot-and-heavy pages of Greek mythology. The ancient myths were so often concerned with passion and pursuit that your only problem might be in deciding which one of them you and your guest will want to recreate, in the interests of authenticity and a romping good time. Following are a few of the myths that have erotic possibilities:

* Imagine (if you are a lady) that you are the maiden Danae, and you have been locked in a bronze underground chamber in your father's palace to prevent you from ever having children. Your only window on the world is a small portal in the ceiling, and you are very, very lonely. But then one day your presence is discovered, and not by any mere mortal, but by Zeus himself, the god of all gods (and a real skirt-chaser, they say).

Zeus is so charmed by what he can see of you through that little portal that he transforms himself into a shower of pure golden light—and unbeknownst to your stodgy father upstairs—comes beaming down through the skylight, crashing through the ceiling, and gloriously impregnates you with his redemptive divinity, his luminous swaggering godhead, his seed-of-all-seeds.

* Re-enact the myth of Pygmalion and the ivory statue. Pygmalion is a dreamy lad who, weary of the second-rate dames he's been hanging out with, carves himself a statue of the perfect woman—a snow-white fairy princess—and then proceeds to fall in love with it. Poor Pygmalion: Day after day he caresses the statue and kisses it, as if it were real flesh and blood, and at night he lies it down in bed next to his own fevered bod. On the feast day of Aphrodite, Pygmalion dares to pray that his ivory beauty might come to life. And that night, as Ovid described it 2000 years ago, this is what happens to our hero: "Pygmalion grasped the image of his girl and lay beside her on the bed and showered her with kisses. She seemed to be warm. He touched her with his lips again and felt her breasts with his hands. At his touch the ivory grew soft, and it's rigidity gave way to the pressure of his fingers; it yielded just as Hymettan wax, when melted in the sun, is fashioned into many shapes by the working of the hands and made pliable."

* Imagine that you are a Homeric siren of the sea and that your date, like Odysseus, has to lash himself to the mast of his ship to keep from surrendering to your temptations. Don't be afraid to give the old myth a new ending. Imagine, for example, that the mast is dry and brittle, and doesn't do the job.

* If you are the kind of woman who is aroused by jealousy, then have your lover whisper his indiscretions in your ear, even as the lusty Zeus whispered to Hera upon their conjugal bed. "Never has such desire, for goddess or woman, flooded and overwhelmed my heart," vowed Zeus. "Not even when I loved Ixion's wife! Or Danae of the slim ankles! Or the far-famed daughter of Phoenix! Or Semele! Or Alcmene of Thebes! Or Demeter Queen of the Lovely Locks! Or the incomparable Leto! Or when I fell in love with you yourself! 'Never' have I felt such love, such sweet desire, as fills me now for you!"

* Imagine that the two of you are Pyramus and Thisbe—he the most handsome man and she the most beautiful woman in all of the eastern world. You live next door to each other and fall madly in love, but your parents forbid you to marry, so you spend your evenings whispering sweet nothings to each other through a chink in the wall between your rooms, and when it is time to say good night you each kiss your own side of that cold, cold wall. But then, one fair evening, you arrange a rendezvous in the woods...

* If you are a fellow who finds himself alone on a Saturday evening, you can always recreate the myth about Narcissus and that little nymph, Echo. Narcissus is such a hunk that, one day while leaning over a pool of water to get a drink, he falls in love with his own reflection, Echo's problem, on the other hand, is a bizarre speech impediment: She is unable to begin a conversation of her own, and yet helplessly repeats everything she hears. She wants to tell Narcissus how much she loves him, but can

only babble after him in silly repetition. In time, Echo wastes away, a shadow of her former self, until only her idiot voice remains, while Narcissus just lies there at poolside with no one to play with except himself.

* Finally, there is the raunchy myth in which Pasiphae, the ravishing wife of King Minos, gets the hots for a large white bull, and together they conceive the minotaur.

It is uncomfortably common in Greek mythology for the heroines to end up suffering some brutal demise while their men go on to become gods. But we should feel free to revise the myths and create our own post-Greco-suburban fantasies. Staunch feminists can always take heart in the legend of Sappho, the poetess from Lesbos who supposedly formed the first gay-ladies' alliance.

In any case, the Romans eventually conquered Greece and everything changed. Zeus became Jupiter, Eros became Cupid, Aphrodite became Venus, and the Greeks and Romans became decadent together. Much later, the Onassises conquered Greece and it got even more decadent. The aspiring young Odysseus, in his 80-foot yacht, now couldn't set sail without a captain, a nanny, a bodyguard, and a bartender.

If you have a yacht of your own, you can close the book right here and let your steward attend to the details. Otherwise, read on and we'll try to cook up an evening of Olympian pleasure, fit for the greedy gods within us.

INVITATIONS:

It has probably been about 30 years since you did a connect-the-dots picture, right? Well, here's your chance— probably your last chance—to play the game.

Create a dot-to-dot picture that would make an intriguing invitation to begin a Grecian romance.

If that's not quite your style, and you live near a city with a large Greek population, you could pick up a copy of the Greek-language newspaper and paste your invitation inside, as if it were an ad.

A gourmet shop might be able to supply you with a small assortment of Greek glazed fruit to accompany your invitation. Or, to be more to the point, send a packet of the herb thyme, labeling it with its Greek name, (thymus vulgaris), and adding your own explanation.

SCENTS:

Lemon and herbs are predominant scents in the Hellenic kitchen, so stick to these earthy fragrances. Ann Tucker Fettner's book "Potpourri" has the recipes for several potpourri mixtures using herbs indigenous to Greece. For any potpourri, use a jar that can be opened to allow the fragrance to permeate the room, or closed to capture it.

Another familiar scent would be the bay leaf, which gets us back to Greek mythology. Daphne supposedly was saved by being changed into a bay tree while she was being pursued by Apollo, and from this story comes the superstition that any one carrying a bay leaf is protected from evil. Which, in turn, inspires me to write:

A saucy young maiden from Thrace
Liked her edible thing with mace,
But bay would protect her
From that lecherous sector
Which liked edible things in lace.

TABLE SETTINGS:

Would that I could bless each one of you with a hanging garden overlooking the Aegean. Your glass topped table would be set with fine china, crystal and silver, and sheltered from the brilliant late-afternoon sun by trellises draped with grape vines. A hammered copper tray filled with native fruits and appetizers would grace the center of your table and the butler would be—even at this moment—pouring out two glasses of ouzo.

Well, this same scene can be created in your own garden or greenhouse, except perhaps for the butler.

In Greece, one can look down any busy waterfront and distinguish the upretentious outdoor cafes from the finer restaurants by the absence or presence of white tablecloths. However, all eating establishments share a preference for simple furniture—plain square wooden tables and ladderback chairs. A bottle of ouzo or wine is usually on the table, along with plates of mezes (appetizers or sweetmeats). Since the Greeks aren't much for clockwatching, it is often difficult to tell whether it's coffee-and-sweets time or ouzo-and-mezes time, but one way or another the table setting remains simple with food as the primary embellishment.

Wild anemones and daisies grow in profusion in Greece, and these flowers can probably be purchased from your florist for use in a centerpiece. Another idea is an arrangement of perfectly shaped lemons, oranges and limes in a basket of leaves. Greek and Italian import stores sell those wrought-iron wine cradles that let you fill your glass with a tip of the bottle. For dishes, use earthenware or plain china.

If the weather is good, set your table up on the patio or in the garden, Mediterranean style. At night, set out votive candles in windproof glasses or tapers in glass flues.

You might want to do as the ancients did and eat with your fingers while reclining on couches. Just don't try to send me the reupholsterer's bill.

Greeks traditionally eat dinner late—at 9 or 10 o'clock. If you decide to make this your fashion, too, then be sure to serve plenty of high-protein mezes with the before-dinner ouzo to give you and your guest endurance.

Speaking of ouzo, don't be surprised if, after a few glasses, your companion leaps up and starts jumping around to the bouzouki music like Zorba himself. And be forewarned of the Greek custom of throwing flowers and dinner plates at the feet of enraptured dancers. In fact, if your guest happens to be of Greek ancestry, paper plates might be advisable.

Another custom that I found charmingly peculiar to Greece was that small bakeries often served as extensions of their neighborhoods' kitchens. These shops first baked their daily assortment of breads, *tyropita* and sweets for their customers, and then, as the ovens were cooling, allowed the women of the neighborhood to pop in their own eggplant casseroles, spitted meat and other specialties. The women who frequented each shop seemed to form a tight little clan. Their dishes were on view to the whole group, and it was obvious how much pride and competition went into the production.

CLOTHING:

Since Jackie O's tenure as queen of Peloponnesus, the traditional fashions have been fairly well obliterated, so you can dress (or undress) according to your whim, as if you were a goddess, too. Which you are! Unless, of course, you are a god.

Ladies might well find a Grecian-style gown on a lingerie rack. Recently, for example, Halston came out with a gown with one shoulder strap that, to me at least, is decisively Athenian. Although it is shown in loungewear sections, it is very elegant and can be worn comfortably outside of the bedroom.

A gentleman might want to outfit himself like the movie version of Zorba. This would leave him a bit baggy in the trousers, perhaps, but you know what they say about a young man needing room to grow.

MUSIC:

Greek music is well traveled. It has served historically as the roots for many other people's folk-song traditions—such as the Arabs, Indians, Turks and Persians—and that's why Greek music today often sounds like music from the Near East. Listening to Mikis Theodorakis's score from "Zorba the Greek," I close my eyes and find myself at a bazaar in Baghdad.

The bouzouki is the instrument most characteristic of Greek music. A mellow introduction to its sound is provided by a pair of albums, "The Bouzouki Sound," Volumes 1 & 2, that back up the bouzouki with full orchestra. It might not be authentic, but it does make nice background music.

GREEK MUSHROOMS

Serves 2-4

½ lb, button mushrooms or slices of larger mushrooms, or canned
1 clove garlic, peeled crushed
1 small onion, minced
¼ C. white wine
2 T. white wine vinegar
2 T. parsley minced
½ C. olive oil or other oil
1 T. lemon juice
1 bay leaf
1 tsp. oregano
Salt and freshly ground pepper

Clean fresh mushrooms with damp paper towel. Trim stems close to cap. Place all ingredients in stainless steel or enamel pan and bring to a boil. Stir gently and lower heat. Simmer 3 or 4 minutes, less for canned mushrooms or slices. Remove from heat and chill. To serve, let stand at room temperature about ½ hour, drain mushrooms and serve with picks. Accompany with crackers.

RIPE OLIVE SOUP

Serves 2-4

1 4 oz. can chopped ripe olives
1 egg yolk, beaten
1 T. butter
1 T. flour
1½ C. chicken bouillon
1 C. cream or equal parts evaporated milk and water
2 T. green onions chopped
Salt and pepper
Sour cream
Chives

Wilt the green onions in butter in a small heavy saucepan. Add drained olives and sprinkle on the flour. Blend in then add the bouillon stirring constantly over low heat. Do not boil. Meanwhile, blend the egg yolk with the cream. Stirring constantly, add the egg mixture slowly to the soup. Heat to serving temperature but do not boil. If too thick add a bit more cream. Season to taste. Ladle into bowls and garnish with sour cream and chives.

ARTICHOKES WITH LEMON BUTTER

Serves 2

Trim the stem end off two small artichokes, then with kitchen scissors clip off the thorny ends of the petals. Lower artichokes into boiling salted water to which you have added a wedge of lemon (or squeeze juice from half a lemon, save the juice and add the squeezed out half.) Simmer about 30-35 min. or until a petal from the base pulls away easily. A pressure cooker works well for artichokes, check your pressure cookbook for directions...mine cooks them in 12 min.

Melt butter and add lemon juice to taste for dipping. Serve butter in a small bowl and artichokes on plates with room for discarded petals.

SHRIMP AND FETA CHEESE CASSEROLE

Serves 2

- **2 large, firm tomatoes peeled, seeded and chopped**
- **1 medium onion, chopped**
- **1 clove garlic, peeled and minced**
- **20 small shrimp (not cocktail size) shelled and deveined**
- **⅓ C. white wine**
- **¼ C. parsley, chopped**
- **½ C. butter**
- **½ C. Feta cheese, crumbled**
- **Salt and freshly ground pepper**

In stainless steel or enamel skillet over moderate heat, cook the butter and onions until soft but not brown. Add tomatoes, white wine, parsley, garlic, salt and pepper to taste. Cook mixture at a simmer, partially covered for 35-40 min. stirring occasionally. Mixture should not be watery...cook a little longer if it is. Remove from heat. Cool. Stir in shrimp. Spoon into buttered casserole or individual au gratin dishes. Sprinkle with cheese. Bake in hot oven, 450 degrees near top of oven until cheese is melted and casserole bubbly. If browning too fast move to lower shelf. Serve hot in casserole.

GREEK SALAD

The Greeks, as the Europeans, shop for their fruits and vegetables at the market daily. They choose the freshest looking, seasonal ingredients for composing their salad, and then combine them according to personal preferences.

A simple dressing is made from the freshest olive oil and white wine vinegar or lemon juice. The commonest proportion being 3 parts oil to 1 part vinegar. Salt and freshly ground pepper are added along with fresh or dried herbs. Oregano is almost always added. Garlic is a matter of choice, but is frequently added to the dressing, whole, then removed. A simple way to peel and bruise garlic is to put it on a chopping block, then give it a whack with the broad side of a heavy knife or cleaver.

Use any of the following ingredients in your choice of combinations. Compose the salad as opposed to tossing it. Then just before serving prepare the dressing by shaking it in a jar. Pour over salad immediately.

Greens of all sorts
Diced celery
Tomato wedges
Cucumber slices
Feta cheese
Anchovies
Strips of peppers
Radishes
Artichoke hearts
Olives
Chick peas
Cauliflower
Broccoli
Onions
Cooked potatoes
Avocados
Various beans
Cooked sausage

KOURABIEDES (Greek Butter Cookies - My Way)

1 C. butter
1 C. margerine
1 C. confectioner's sugar
1 egg yolk
1½ tsp. vanilla
1 T. orange liqueur
½ C. nuts, finely chopped
4 C. flour
Confectioner's sugar

Put butter and margerine in bowl of electric beater and let it soften to room temperature. Add sugar and beat at med. to high until the mixture is light and fluffy like a butter cream frosting. At this point add the egg yolk, vanilla and orange liqueur and beat again until fluffy. Now start adding flour and nuts, being sure that you are reaching the bottom of the bowl when mixing. As the dough gets heavier you may want to finish mixing by hand so you don't burn out your mixer motor. The dough should be light and easy to handle. If it seems sticky, chill.

Roll dough in 1" balls in the palms of your hands, and place each on ungreased cooky sheet. Bake at 350 degrees for about 15 min., until golden brown. Have a flat pan ready with a sifting of confectioner's sugar on it; so the cookies can be removed from baking sheet while warm and set in sugar. Sift more sugar over the tops of cookies while warm. These cookies are very fragile, but keep well in an air tight tin.

Serve with glacéed fruits and coffee.

The secret of all tender, melt-in-the-mouth cookies, is a thorough creaming of the shortening and sugar. Do use an electric beater if possible, and don't skimp on this process. I use a Kitchen-Aid with a "whip" type beater blade, and cream the sugar and shortening for about 12 min. for this recipe.

GREEK MARINATED FISH

Serves 2

1 lb. red snapper, sole or halibut fillets
Seasoned flour for dredging
½ tsp. ground rosemary
½ tsp. oregano
¼ C. lemon juice
⅓ C. salad oil
2 cloves garlic, peeled and mashed

Dredge fish in seasoned flour and fry fish in large frying pan with the oil. Brown each side 4-5 min. Test for doneness (will flake easily). Remove to hot platter when done. Remove excess oil from pan and add the garlic, rosemary, vinegar and lemon juice. Let simmer a few minutes then remove garlic. Pour hot marinade over fish. To serve, garnish with lemon wedges

EGGPLANT APPETIZER

Serves 4-6

1	small eggplant
¼	C. sesame seed,toasted
1	small onion
2	T. vegatable oil
½	tsp. ground cumin
¼	C. parsley
3	T. lemon juice
	Dash Tabasco
¼	C. vegetable oil
	Salt to taste
	Freshly ground pepper

Peel eggplant and cut into cubes ½" square. In a saucepan of boiling, salted water, scald the dice and cook until tender. Drain and squeeze between 2 layers of paper towels. In a dry skillet, toast sesame seed over low heat, shaking skillet from time to time. Remove from heat. In a heavy skillet, sauté onion in 2 T. oil until softened but not brown. Cook 5 min. Transfer to blender. Add eggplant, garlic, cumin and salt. Cook 5 minutes. Transfer to blender and purée. With blender running, add the oil in a slow stream as for mayonnaise. Transfer purée to bowl. Stir in sesame seed, parsley, lemon juice, Tabasco, salt and pepper to taste. Let chill, covered overnight. Serve with crackers or pita bread.

CREAM OF SPINACH SOUP

Serves 2-4

1	pkg. frozen spinach, chopped
1	T. salad oil
1	C. chicken bouillon
3	green onions, minced
1	tsp. lemon juice
	Sour cream or buttermilk

Wilt chopped onion in a small skillet in the oil, but do not brown. Add to spinach, bouillon, salt and pepper in a small saucepan and bring all to a boil. Reduce heat and simmer gently about 6 to 8 minutes. Remove from heat, add lemon juice, put in a blender in batches and purée. On low, blend in sour cream or buttermilk to proper consistency. Chill. To serve correct consistency and seasoning. Ladle in bowls and garnish as desired

For those of you who think of buttermilk in negative terms, be advised that buttermilk, these days, is cultured much the same as sour cream. You can use it in soups, adding fewer calories, and the taste is very similar.

SLICED TOMATO SALAD

Serves 2

- 2 medium, firm tomatoes sliced
- ¼ C. olive oil
- 1 T. lemon juice
- 1 clove garlic, mashed and peeled
- ½ tsp. salt and pepper
- 1 tsp. dried basil or 2 tsp. fresh basil minced
- Dash Tabasco

Slice tomatoes in ½" thick, crosswise slices. Arrange on serving plate. Cover with marinade until serving time. Do not leave out over two hours this way. To serve, sprinkle with parsley.

KAMPOSTA LAMPSA ATHENA (Orange Compote)

Serves 2

- 2 Navel oranges
- 2 T. Grand Marnier, Cointreau, or Triple Sec
- ½ C. White corn syrup
- Sour cream
- Candied ginger
- Flaked coconut

Remove only the orange part of skin from oranges with peeler, and place with water to barely cover in small saucepan over moderate heat. Simmer until zest is tender. Drain off all but ⅓ C. liquid. Add the syrup and bring to boil, stirring constantly. Reduce heat and simmer about 2 minutes. Remove from heat and add Grand Marnier. Blend and let the mixture cool. Meanwhile, peel oranges, removing as much outer white membrane as possible. Cut in cross-wise slices about ½" thick. Arrange in serving compote and cover with cooled syrup. To serve, garnish with sour cream (slightly sweetened if desired), finely minced candied ginger and flaked coconut.

ZUCCHINI PANCAKES

- 1 medium zucchini (8" length) shredded
- 1 tsp. salt
- 1 egg, beaten
- 1 T. flour
- Butter
- ⅓ C. feta cheese, crumbled
- ½ tsp. fresh mint, minced or ¼ tsp. dried mint, or ½ tsp. basil
- Freshly ground pepper

Mix zucchini with salt and let stand 1 hour. Squeeze moisture from zucchini with hand, then paper towel. Sprinkle flour over zucchini and toss to coat. Add seasonings, then fold in crumbled cheese and egg. Fry in butter, making patties from 2 T. batter. Do no more than two at a time watching carefully not to burn. Turn when golden brown. Serve hot.

KEFTETHES (Greek Meatballs)

Serves 2-4

- ½ lb. ground chuck
- 1 small onion minced
- 1 small clove garlic, squeezed through garlic press
- 1 egg
- 1 slice dry bread soaked in water and squeezed dry
- 1 pinch ground cumin
- ½ tsp. oregano
- 1 tsp. parsley
- Salt and pepper
- Oil for frying

Blend everything well with fork or hands. Chill covered several hours or overnight if desired. To serve, form into 1" balls, pressing firmly so they will hold their shape. Brown in skillet in about 3 T. oil. Turn to brown on all sides and cook completely. These can be served with a tomato sauce if you like.

* An unusual but delicious sauce for these can be made from ½ C. chili sauce, 1 T. grape jelly and 1 tsp. lemon juice. Heat all these ingredients in saucepan and pour over meatballs. Serve with picks.

MAYIRITSA (Greek Easter Soup)

Serves 2-4

This is traditionally served at Easter, but as long as you are going to have a boneless lamb roast prepared for this menu, you might as well use the bones. Ask your butcher to save them for soup, but discard excess fat.

- Lamb bones and lean meat
- 2 stalks celery with leaves
- Water to cover
- 1 small onion
- Salt and pepper

Simmer about 2 hours and then strain into bowl for refrigeration. Chill to solidfy fat. Remove fat. (This soup can be made with chicken stock.)

- ¼ C. rice, washed
- 1 egg well beaten
- 2 C. broth (above)
- 2 T. lemon juice
- 1 T. fresh dill or ½ tsp. dried dill weed
- Salt and pepper

Reduce broth above to make 2 C., or add water to make two cups. Bring broth to boil and add rice. Cover to cook rice over lowest heat until tender. Remove from heat. Ladle ¾ C. hot broth slowly into egg beating as you do. Return egg mixture to soup in kettle. Return to heat but do not boil. Add lemon juice and dill. Correct seasoning and serve immediately.

GREEK SALAD

See Greek Orgia—Summer Menu __ (Avec Argent)

*LEG OF LAMB **

Ask your butcher to bone and roll the leg of lamb, and leave it as one large roast or have it cut up into two smaller ones, depending on the number of guests you are going to serve. Have the butcher save the bones for soup. (See recipe this chapter.) Use a meat thermometer to achieve the desired degree of doneness. I like lamb just a bit on the pink side; so at an internal temperature of 160-165. For well done, figure about 30 min. per pound, or a temp. of 175 to 180 degrees.

Pierce the roast in several places and insert slivers of peeled garlic. Rub the surface of the roast with salt, ground rosemary, freshly ground pepper and lemon juice. Put on a rack in an open baking pan and put into a pre-heated 450 degree oven. Immediately reduce the heat to 350 degrees. When proper temperature is reached on meat thermometer, remove roast from oven and let rest 10 minutes before carving. Serve pan juices after adding boiling water, if desired.

SPINACH AND RICE

Serves 4

- **⅓ C. rice, washed**
- **2 T. olive oil**
- **1 small onion**
- **1 tsp. lemon juice**
- **1 10 oz. pkg. frozen spinach, chopped**
- **½ tsp. salt**
- **½ C. sour cream**
- **Parmesan cheese**

Sauté the rice and onion in oil over low to medium heat, about 10 min. until onion is wilted, but not brown. Add boiling water to cover and simmer until rice is tender. Add thawed, drained spinach. Blend. Hold over heat until spinach is hot through and all is well blended. Add lemon and correct seasoning. Remove from heat and fold in sour cream. Garnish with Parmesan cheese.

* *A lusty Adonis from Crete*
Achieved a remarkable feat.
For a lady Aquarian,
An avowed vegetarian.
Agreed to partake of his meat.

TARAMOSALATA

Serves 2-4

- **2** slices white bread, crusts removed
- **2** oz. tarama (carp roe) or red caviar
- **1** egg yolk
- **¼** C. lemon juice
- **1** generous tsp. onion, chopped
- **1** C. olive oil or salad oil
- Dash Tabasco

Dip bread in water and squeeze out in paper towel. (If caviar is used do not soak bread, but break into chunks.) Put bread, roe, onion, lemon juice and egg yolk into blender and blend until smooth. Scrape down sides of blender, add oil in steady stream with blender on low as for mayonnaise. Transfer mixture to a bowl and chill.

This makes a beautiful coral pink mixture, and when chilled can be piped through a pastry tube to make an attractive serving. Garnish with parsley and black olives, and serve with crackers or dark bread. Wedges of lime are also a nice addition. (If you like anchovies, caviar and other salty fish, you will probably like this...try leftovers on baked potatoes, too.)

Baklava

As a pioneer in the field of decadent dining, let me tell you it isn't fun if it gets to be too much work! This is one place where I would cheat from ground zero. Making baklava is a real labor of love, and if that quality isn't already in evidence in your relationship...buy the baklava.

MOUSSAKA

Serves 4

- **2** medium size potatoes, peeled and cut into ¼" slices
- **1** medium onion chopped
- **2** T. vegetable oil
- **1** clove garlic minced
- **1** lb. lean ground beef or lamb
- **¼** tsp. mace
- **⅓** C. Kefaloteri or Parmesan cheese, grated
- **½** tsp. cinnamon
- **2** eggs
- **1** C. milk
- Salt and pepper
- Fat for frying

Deep fry the potato slices until golden brown, drain and reserve. To assemble, sauté chopped onion in the 2 T. oil until wilted. Lift out the onions and reserve. In the oil remaining in the skillet, brown the ground meat, and just before removing from the heat, add the minced garlic, and stir to wilt garlic. Remove from heat and blend in the tomato sauce and spices.

In a 1½ qt. baking dish, place a layer of half the potatoes. Add the meat mixture, then cover with remaining potatoes. Beat the eggs and milk together and pour over the meat mixture. Top with grated cheese and bake at 350 degrees about 45 min. or until lightly browned and bubbly. Serve in casserole.

Note: Eggplant or zucchini can be substituted for potatoes, in which case, pan fry to brown these vegetables.

LENTIL SOUP

Serves 2-4

1 pint beef or chicken broth
¼ to ½ C. lentils
1 small onion, chopped
1 stalk celery, sliced
1 carrot, chopped
1 small clove garlic, minced
2 T. vegetable oil
⅓ C. tomato sauce
1 T. vinegar
Salt and pepper

Simmer lentils in broth with salt and pepper according to directions on lentils. When almost tender add rest of vegatables and cook until tender add rest of vegetables and cook until tender. Stir in tomato sauce, vinegar, salt and pep-Ladle into bowls and garnish with parsley, chives or lemon slice.

FIGS VENUS

Serves 2-4

1 No. 303 jar figs, drained and halved
1 T. confectioner's sugar
1 T. flaked coconut or toasted almonds
½ C. sour cream
1 T. or more, strawberry liqueur

Blend sugar and liqueur into the sour cream. Let stand about ½ hour to let flavors mingle. Add coconut or almonds. Put drained figs into a dessert dish and spoon sour cream mixture over. Garnish with fresh srawberry or nuts or coconut or all. (You may chop figs and mix with the sour cream mixture and serve all over ice cream.

Here's a do-it-yourself limerick: An armless young lovely named Venus.......

MARGINALLY MEXICAN

MARGINALLY MEXICAN

Summer Menu
(Avec Argent)
Shrimp Cocktail Guanajuato
Avocado Soup
Barbecued Pork Chops San Miguel
Carrots with Brown Butter
Mexican Slaw • Hard Rolls
Pineapple Pudding

Summer Menu
(Sans Argent)
Tortilla Chips with Picante Sauce
Black Bean Soup
Barbecued Chicken
Grilled Green Onions
Green Bean Salad • Hard Rolls
Fresh Pineapple and Melon

Winter Menu
(Avec Argent)
Picante Dip and Chips
Chicken Soup with Almonds
Pork with Pineapple and Rice
Corn Salad • Hard Rolls
Camote y Piña

Winter Menu
(Sans Argent)
Chili Cheese Dip and Chips
Tortilla Soup
Red Snapper Vera Cruz
Banana Nut Salad
Hard Rolls
Buñuelos Sundaes

Reality is whatever we want it to be, a fantasy that confirms itself, a game of pick-and-choose.

Take Mexico, for example. Some people might try to tell you that the *real* Mexico is hot and dusty, poor and squalid, and specializes in exporting heartburn and diarrhea. Yet, to an orthodontist from Ypsilanti whose only experience has been a week at the Club Med in Acupulco, the real Mexico might just as easily be meeting two young ladies from Antwerp and learning how to do the Belgian Waffle Maneuver in a crowded bathtub. To an illegal alien living in San Antonio, Mexico is a place to escape. To an archeologist, it is a shard. To an anthropologist, it is an old Indian shaman.

We have become a nation of dilettantes and eclectics—gluttons for borrowed atmosphere. We are cross-cultural snobs, adopting as our own those customs that tickle our fancy, and conveniently forgetting the rest.

Well, why not? As far as I'm concerned there is no reason to look back. Whatever our tastes might be, we should feel free to invent a Mexico to match them. If you get the idea that you'd like to have a south-of-the-border dinner party, you can fashion your own private Mexico out of the random illusions of your imagination.

What do you picture? Palm trees? Pitchers of margaritas? Strolling mariachi bands?

Aztec sacrifices?

Emilio Zapata in pink leotards?

Make it happen.

Just remember that, no matter how eccentric your notion of foreign intrigue might be, it takes only one other person to share them in order to make a consensus—that is to say, a fiesta.

My own images of Mexico come from the time that I lived there in the mid-1970s, in the small mountain town of San Miguel de Allende. The life style in San Miguel was very casual, the population an ambient mixture of natives and foreign expatriates. After I'd been there for a few weeks, I couldn't help noticing that, although I wasn't getting many party invitations in my mailbox, I was doing one hell of a lot of partying.

In San Miguel the most festive gatherings seemed to just manifest themselves out of thin air. A late-afternoon coffee at one of the little cafes around the plaza, or a happy-hour drink at La Cucaracha, often led willy-nilly to a full-scale dinner party.

This informal approach to home entertainment is as Mexican, to me, as tortillas and beans. However, when I try to duplicate it back in the States I find that, paradoxically, it helps to be prepared. The following couple of suggestions, then, are designed to make an impromptu Mexican dinner party a casual affair, not only for the guests, but for the cook as well:

1. Keep a few cans of appropriate soups in stock. With the amazing variety of prepared soups available under such labels as Pepperidge Farms, it's easier than ever these days to go international. In the summer, cans of gazpacho, madrilene, jellied consommé or fruit soup should be kept refrigerated, ready to open and serve. In the winter, store some cans of black bean or lentil soup or chowder that can be heated without much ado while you're putting together the middle of the meal. Invite your guests into the kitchen for the cocktail hour, or even for the soup course, so that you don't get left out of the conversation.

2. Always keep a fresh carton of vanilla ice cream on hand, along with pitted, black sweet cherries, bananas or peach slices, and either rum or brandy. This will allow you to pull off some fabulous flaming desserts— cherries jubilee, bananas Foster, peach flambé—in an instant. (See Birthday Bashes Recipes for cherry and peach recipes. End of this chapter for bananas Foster.)

Now that you've taken care of the practical details, it's time for fun.

If you and your guest(s) drink several tequila sunrises and find yourselves in a hilarious mood, you might consider celebrating the Mexican water festival. As it was practiced in San Miguel de Allende, the celebrants dropped bags of water off of balconies and onto each other's heads. I can't quite recall knowing the significance of this, but I'd suggest that for an intimate party you and your companion could observe this holiday more amiably by taking a long shower together.

While you're at it, make the shower truly an esthetic occasion by painting each other with body paints in Mayan or Aztec or Toltec designs. Try body cosmetics marketed in primary colors, and for guidance in painting Mexican designs you might want to pick up the Dover Press coloring book on the subject that is sold in some museums. The idea is to paint each other before stepping into the shower, because the cosmetics turn into soap bubbles under water. After this rite (or wrong), you can massage each other with body liqueurs that come in such soothing and aromatic flavors and tastes as creme de cocoa, creme de coconut, and creme de menthe. I find these indulgences considerably more appealing than some of the cleansing rites that called for sacrifices of young maidens to the gods. Which prompts me to offer another bit of advice: "Don't be a virgin when they're looking for a sacrifice!"

On another annual occasion, the Mexicans of San Miguel took raw eggs, blew the eggs out of the shells, filled the shells with confetti, then covered the pricked ends with decorated tissue paper. When the spirit moved them, they cracked the eggs over each other's heads and showered one another with confetti. Again, the particular meaning escapes me, but it seems like a unique way to get any fiesta off to a rollicking start.

INVITATIONS:

Suppose you want to make a party happen instead of leaving it to cruel chance. Why not write the invitation in felt-tipped marker across the face of a flour tortilla? Some specialty food stores in the Southwest sell tortillas a foot and a half or two feet in diameter, large enough for the most long-winded overtures. A variation would be to make your own version of a Mexican fortune cooky by folding a paper invitation inside of a taco shell and mailing it in a crush-proof box.

Mexican note paper and greeting cards can be found in import shops everywhere, and even in some grocery stores in the Mexican-American neighborhoods. You can also enclose your invitation with a small bark painting or yarn painting or some other simple gift from south of the border.

If you are sending out only one or two invitations and want to put some time into the project, you can have a lot of fun by creating a painting-on-velvet. Buy a remnant of black velvet and stretch it on an embroidery hoop, then decorate it to your heart's delight with day-glo acrylic paints. Or if you don't trust your artistic abilities, affix a suitable day-glo decal to the velvet and then paint on the lettered invitation. As a final touch, you can glue on or sew some ball-fringe around the edge. The post office, by the way, sells padded envelopes that are perfect for elaborate invitations such as these.

Your invitation will certainly find its way to the invitee in better fashion than some of my mail in San Miguel. The local mail truck was an ancient station wagon with a couple of the rear windows missing, and one day I happened to be following it to the town of Celaya and couldn't help but notice, to my alarm, that all of San Miguel's posted letters were going the air-mail route—fluttering out of the mail truck's windows like so many doves. I caught up to the truck and made some wild exasperated gestures at the driver, but he only made wilder gestures in return, and kept on driving.

SCENTS:

Few of the fragrances that American tourists associate with Mexico would lend themselves to a romantic evening. I'm talking about that sickly sweet odor that so often rises up from tropical cities, a commingling of auto exhaust, human sweat, dust, and decaying fruit. If this is the real Mexico, then I'll take chemistry.

Vanilla is a Mexican essence that makes for a nice natural fragrance in scented candles. Another idea is to put a few drops of vanilla into a kettle of boiling water; this will mellow out the strong odors of some Mexican cooking. The same technique can be used with essential oils such as cinnamon and clove.

TABLE SETTINGS:

I have seen Mexican pottery and glassware in such unlikely places as the Salvation Army Store in Oskaloosa, Iowa. If you live in the Southwest, you can outfit yourself colorfully and inexpensively by snooping around flea markets and garage sales. Otherwise, try the omnipresent gift and import shops. A few authentic pieces of Mexican dinnerware can be mixed in with your own pottery to give the entire table a Latin flavor.

Mexican pieces can be blended in subtly with tableware from other countries. Hand-painted doves from Tonola, or a tree-of-life candelabra would go very nicely, for example, with the brown stoneware soup bowls that are made by Arabia of Finland.

A coarsely woven cotton tablecloth will look smart for any occasion, from casual to formal. Try creating your own rough weave by taking a remnant of monk's cloth or huck or some other coarse woven fabric and pulling some of the threads along the edge to create a design. These materials might be available only in white or natural, but with a box of Rit you can transform them into the most festive of Mexican colors. If you have the time and patience, you can also fringe the edges after dying the cloth.

To make your table look like the tables of countless thousands of cantinas all over Mexico, just pick up a piece of oilcloth or vinyl (from an upholstery-fabric outlet) and scallop the edges. Years after your Mexican affair has faded into history, you'll still be able to use this simple tablecloth for dinning outdoors or on the porch.

I'd suggest that you fold your napkins in a fan pattern. (Ask your book dealer or librarian for books on napkin folding such as "Olga's Frumpy Folds," or even on origami.)

A Mexican dinner might be the one time that you'll want to use paper flowers, because they're so evident in every mercado throughout Mexico and they add such riotous splashes of color to the traditionally white-on-white gringo abode. You can buy these flowers ready made or you can get energetic and make your own flowers, using tissue paper and a book of directions from a hobby shop. Unpainted pottery candle holders are very Mexican, as are pottery birds and other figures that can be added to the centerpiece.

Mexican import shops have loads of stuff that will help you to decorate an entire room in a Spanish accent, such as bullfight posters, tinware, wrought iron and glazed papier-mache.

Buy a piñata and break it open at the high point of the evening, whether it is Christmastime or not. Better yet, make your own piñata and fill it with whatever suggestive favors come into your fertile mind.

CLOTHING:

Somewhere in the back of your closet you probably have an embroidered Mexican shirt or dress. If not, it's time you got one. Mexican fashions tend to be loose and breezy and brightly colored—just the thing for lounging around with a playmate.

A senorita who wants to look elegant might be able to find a gauzy slipover floor-length Mexican gown or facsimile in the loungewear section of her favorite department store.

MUSIC:

Some people can't stand mariachi music. They say that it's too loud and it all sounds the same; they can't tell the good from the bad.

Precisely! If you have any skill at all at playing the guitar and singing, you can probably pull off a one-man mariachi concert that won't embarrass you. Wouldn't that delight any guest, to be serenaded, no matter how ineptly? The key for the amateur musician is to obscure your talents with exaggerated sentimentality, to mock yourself before your guest has a chance to, and to slip in some suggestive lyrics.

If your tastes run more toward Mexican elevator music, you might pick up one of the "Manuel" albums, which provide orchestral productions of Mexican songs intended for "easy listening."

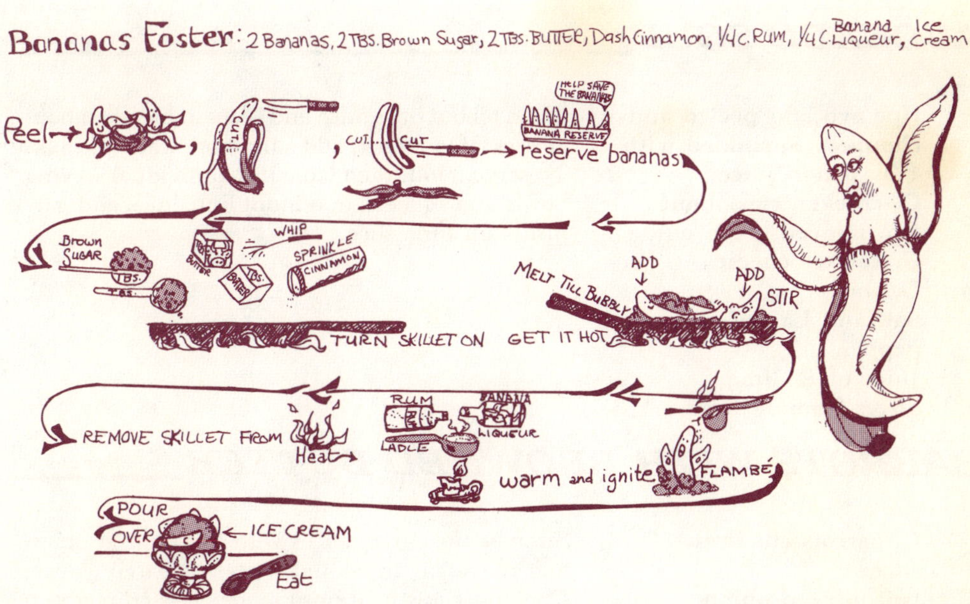

SHRIMP COCKTAIL GUANAJUATO — Serves 2

In the market at Guanajuato, where I first ate this dish, the cilantro, onions, tomatoes and peppers were put in the bottom of a drinking glass of dubious cleanliness. The shrimp were layered on top, then another sprinkling of vegetables and the dressing. Bottles of Tabasco-like pepper sauce were available to spice it up more if desired. One called "Esta Si Pica" translates as "this really stings", and it does!

20 medium, cooked shrimp peeled and deveined
2 T. fresh cilantro (flat leaf parsley, or substitute celery leaves, chopped)
1 small onion minced
1 medium tomato, peeled and cubed
1 pepper, chopped (any variety from bell to jalapeño as desired)
Vegetable oil
Lemon or lime juice
Salt and pepper

Put the ingredients in a bowl, using the oil and lemon juice in the proportions of 1 part juice to 3 parts oil. Toss all gently to mix, then serve in a small individual serving bowl or sherbet. Serve with your choice of crackers.

AVOCADO SOUP — Serves 2-4

1 ripe avocado peeled and chopped. Sprinkled with 1 T. lemon juice
1 C. chicken consommé
1 tsp. minced green onion
¼ C. cottage cheese
¼ C. water
Salt and Lawry's seasoned pepper
Juice of ½ lime
Slices from ½ lime

Blend all but lime juice and slices in blender about 30 secs. If too thick, add a bit more water or milk. To serve, chill, then ladle into individual serving bowls and squeeze in a bit of lime juice and garnish with lime slice.

CARROTS WITH BROWNED BUTTER — Serves 2

1½ C. carrots cut into ⅛" slices
1 tsp. minced onion
1 tsp. sugar
2 T. butter (must be butter)
Salt to taste

Simmer the carrot slices with the minced onion and the sugar in enough water to barely cover. Cook over low heat until tender. When ready to serve, melt the butter in a small heavy saucepan until it turns just golden brown. Drain the carrots and toss in the butter. Salt to taste.

BARBECUED PORK CHOPS SAN MIGUEL

Serves 2

- 4 small to medium, lean pork chops
- ½ C. orange juice
- ½ C. brown sugar
- ½ C. catsup
- 1 tsp. chili powder
- 1 pinch ground allspice
- Salt and pepper

Cook pork chops over hot coals or in oven broiler until nicely browned on both sides. Meanwhile blend remaining ingredients into a smooth paste, About 10 minutes before chops are done, brush one side then the other and let the sauce cook, but do not burn. Any barbecue sauce with sugar will char quickly and become bitter if you are not careful.

MEXICAN SLAW

Serves 2-4

- 2 C. cabbage shredded
- ½ C. pineapple tidbits
- 1 C. apple chopped
- 2 T. mayonnaise (Best Foods)
- 2 T. sour cream
- 1 T. cider vinegar
- 1-2 T. sugar
- ½ tsp. Gebhardt's Chili Powder
- ½ tsp. salt
- ¼ tsp. celery seed

Toss cabbage and fruit together. Then mix together the ingredients for the dressing. Combine and chill, covered until ready to serve. Serve on lettuce leaves or in small salad bowls.

PINEAPPLE PUDDING

Serves 6

- 12 ladyfingers
- Apricot jam
- 2 C. fresh pineapple tidbits
- ½ C. almonds, blanched and ground
- 4 egg yolks beaten
- 1 C. sugar
- ½ C. Sherry
- Pinch cinnamon
- 1 tsp. vanilla
- 1 C. sour cream
- Toasted, slivered almonds for garnish

Split the ladyfingers. Spread with thin layer of jam. Combine the pineapple, ground almonds, egg yolks, one half of the sherry, and the cinnamon in a saucepan. Cook, stirring constantly, over low heat, until thickened. Combine vanilla, rest of sugar and sour cream. Mix and let stand. When pineapple mixture is cool, spread half over half of ladyfingers, which have been arranged in the bottom of serving dish. Add a second layer of ladyfingers, then another layer of pineapple. Sprinkle rest of sherry over all, then stir the sour cream mixture again, and spread over pineapple. Garnish with toasted almonds. Chill several hours, covered.

BLACK BEAN SOUP

Serves 2-4

2 slices bacon, fried out until crisp, then crumbled
2 green onions minced
1 medium tomato peeled, seeded and chopped
1 can black bean soup
Pinch oregano
Dash Tabasco
⅓ C. sherry
Warm water
Salt and Lawry's seasoned pepper

Using the bacon grease left from frying the bacon, wilt the green onion. Add the tomato, cover and simmer about 10 min. Add condensed black bean soup, the oregano, salt and pepper to taste and the Tabasco. Heat, then blend in the sherry and enough water to bring to proper consistency. Serve hot with grated cheese, or ice cold with lemon or lime wedges. Garnish with crumbled bacon.

BARBECUED CHICKEN

Serves 2

1 small frying chicken, split in two halves, rinsed and dried
1 T. chili powder
¼ tsp. ground cloves
¼ tsp. ground sage
Lemon juice
Salt and pepper
Butter or margerine

Using hands, rub the chicken with lemon juice, then sprinkle the spices on, and rub in well. Broil the chicken over a charcoal fire which has acquired some white ash. Turn chicken frequently to brown and cook evenly during the first half hour. Baste with melted butter during the last part of cooking— from 15 min. to 30 min. depending on size, and heat. You can add commercial barbecue sauce or your own during final minutes of cooking.

CHICHARONES OR TORTILLA CHIPS WITH PICANTE SAUCE

Serves 4-6

Both chicharones (fried pork rind) and tortilla chips are available packaged, and this is the way to go in the summer, although in winter, I sometimes make my own tortilla chips from slightly stale tortillas. In San Miguel, I used to buy my chicharones from the chicharones vendor, who came by my apartment every afternoon about 4 o'clock. The pork rinds he sold were sprinkled with chili powder, and they were great with a poor man's marguarita (beer with lime and salt).

For your fiesta, I'd suggest serving either snack with picante sauce. (In Spanish, caliente means hot in terms of temperature, and picante means hot with spice—a fine distinction.)

In the southwest there are many fine locally made picante sauces, but nationally, it is harder to find good ones. Two such are: Pace's Picante Sauces and Old El Paso Taco Sauce. Gebhardt's sauce is available only locally, but their chili powder is available nationally, and I recommend it.

GRILLED GREEN ONIONS WITH LIME

Serves 2

6 small green onions per person
Fresh lime wedges
Salt and pepper
Oil for grilling

Cut away all but about 2" of the green stalk of the onions. Cut off the root end, and clean off any wilted leaves. Select a skillet or better a griddle which will allow the onions to lie flat. Coat the frying surface with oil. Heat until quite hot. Place onions side by side and weight down as you would a grilled cheese sandwich. Be careful not to burn, and roll onions to brown lightly on all sides. To serve, sprinkle with salt and put a wedge of lime on the side to squeeze on just before eating. Butter may be added too. Serve hot.

GREEN BEAN SALAD

Serves 2-4

1 10 oz. pkg. French style, frozen green beans
1 2 oz. jar pimientoes
1 T. green onion minced
1 T. vinegar
2 T. salad oil
Salt and Lawry's seasoned pepper

Steam green beans until just barely tender. Cool. Toss in the pimientoes and onions. Dress with the oil and vinegar, salt and pepper to taste. Cover and refrigerate. To serve, spoon onto lettuce leaves and garnish with tomatoes if desired.

FRESH PINEAPPLE AND/OR MELON

Serves 2-4

½ fresh pineapple, and/or ½ fresh melon such as honeydew or cantelope
½ C. white wine
¼ C. raspberry or strawberry liqueur

Prepare pineapple and melon in usual way and make bite size chunks. Put chunks in glass bowl and add wine and liqueur. Or substitute strawberry soda. Cover and chill until ready to serve. Serve in sherbet dishes.

PICANTE DIP WITH TORTILLA CHIPS

Serves 2-4

1 4 oz. carton sour cream
1 T. Old El Paso Jalapeño Relish, or more as desired
Pinch Lawry's seasoned salt and pepper

Blend all and let stand overnight for flavors to blend. To serve, heap in bowl and surround with tortilla chips.

DO MAKE IT FROM SCRATCH

SUGGESTED DO'S AND DON'TS FOR YOUR MEXICAN FIESTA

DO DRESS FOR THE OCCASION

DO SUPPORT LOCAL MUSICIANS

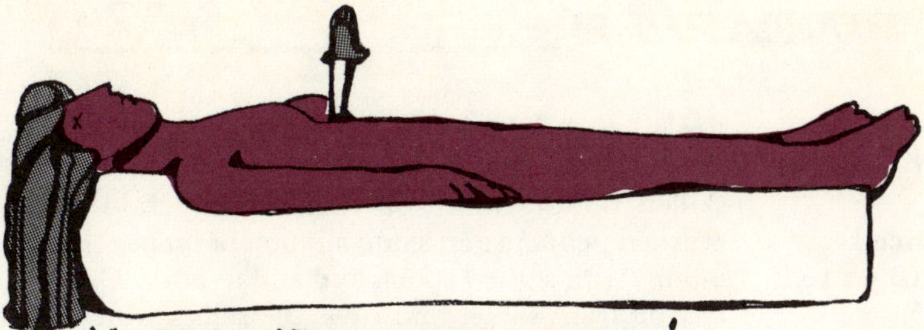

DON'T BE A VIRGIN WHEN THEY'RE LOOKING FOR A SACRIFICE!

DON'T TIE THE KNOT IF YOU AREN'T SERIOUS

DON'T BE PIGGY

PORK WITH PINEAPPLE Serves 2-4

1½ lbs. boneless pork tenderloin cut in 1" cubes
1 T. salad oil
1 medium onion sliced
½ tsp. Durkee's crushed red pepper
⅛ C. sherry
1½ C. pineapple chunks in 1" pieces..fresh if possible
1 2 oz.can pimientoes
½ tsp. mint, chopped or dry flakes
Salt and pepper
Bouillon to cover

Brown pork cubes in salad oil. Drain and put in heavy saucepan. Brown onion lightly in same skillet, adding more oil if necessary. Add the crushed peppers and sauté a moment longer. Lift onions with slotted spoon and add to pork. Drain any oil from skillet and rinse the skillet with the sherry. Scrape down all the brown bits, and pour over pork and onions. Add rest of ingredients. Cover and simmer about 1½ hours or until pork is tender. To serve put in a nest of rice cooked according to your favorite method.

TORTILLA SOUP Serves 2-4

2 Stale 6" corn tortillas (fresh can be used)
2 T. bacon grease or butter
2 C. beef or chicken stock
2 green onions minced
1 T. tomato paste or ¼ C. puree
1 tsp. fresh cilantro, or substitute fresh celery leaves, minced
Grated cheese

Cut tortillas into ¼" strips. Fry in bacon grease until crisp. Fold in paper towel and keep warm. Wilt onions in same skillet then add tomato paste. Blend in and add stock. Simmer about 8 min. Add cilantro and simmer a few minutes more. Season. In each bowl put some tortilla strips and ladle hot soup over them. Serve with grated cheese and tortilla chips.

BANANA NUT SALAD Serves 2

2 medium bananas
1 T. lemon juice
1 T. cream cheese
2 T. mayonnaise
1 tsp. sugar
½ C. nuts, chopped, may be peanuts
Lettuce leaves

Peel bananas and cut in two lengthwise, then in two crosswise. Rub each piece with lemon juice. Cream the cheese and sugar together. Blend in mayonnaise. Spread each banana with the mixture, then roll in nuts. To serve, arrange on lettuce leaf.

RED SNAPPER VERACRUZ STYLE* Serves 2

2 large red snapper fillets
Seasoned flour
Oil for frying
4 green onions minced
1 small clove garlic
1 C. tomato purée or 2 C. fresh tomatoes diced
Pinch cinnamon
Pinch ground cloves
1 Fresh jalapeño, seeded and minced (canned peppers may be used.)
2 T. lemon juice
Pinch sugar
6 small new potatoes, cooked and peeled
1 medium bell pepper, sliced
Pimiento stuffed olives
Avocado slices
Lemon or lime wedges

Dust the snapper with seasoned flour. Heat oil in a heavy skillet and sauté the fish on both sides until golden brown and easily flaked with a fork. (About 7 min.) Reserve and keep warm. In the same skillet sauté the onion and garlic without browning. Add more oil if necessary. Add tomato, cinnamon, cloves and bell pepper to tomato. Simmer about 5 min., then add the lemon juice, jalapeño, sugar, salt and pepper to taste. Bring to a boil and add the potatoes and fish just to heat through, but do not cook longer. To serve remove fish and potatoes to a hot platter. Spoon sauce over fish and garnish with olives, avocado slices and lemon or lime wedges.

* *A picante senorita named Brenda*
Really cooked in her own hacienda
A gentleman dapper
Asked for her snapper
But fish wasn't on the agenda.

CORN SALAD Serves 4-6

This is incredibly good, and because it is good at room temperature is great for potlucks or picnics.

1 12 oz. can corn niblets
½ C. celery cut in ½ " dice
1 2 oz. jar pimiento, cut
3 green onions minced, including part of green
½ small green pepper diced
½ small cucumber diced
Worcestershire sauce
Dash Tabasco
1 T. cider vinegar
2 T. salad oil
Pinch of sugar
Salt and pepper

Combine all the vegetables in a bowl. Mix dressing using all the rest of the ingredients. Blend all together and chill covered until ready to serve. It is best when it stands several hours or overnight. Serve in bowl or on lettuce leaves. This keeps well as a relish.

SWEET POTATO AND PINEAPPLE PUDDING (Camote y Piña)

Serves 4-6

If you ever yearned to eat just the bottom part of a pineapple upside-down cake, this pudding should be in your repetoire, as that is just what it tastes like. The inventive Mexican peasants utilized some of their most plentiful ingredients to create this simple but deliciously rich dessert.

1 C. cooked sweet potatoes or yams, puréed (can be canned ones)
¾ C. brown sugar
Scant ½ C. water
1 C. fresh pineapple grated or well drained, canned crushed pineapple
½ tsp. cinnamon, or to taste
½ C. toasted pecans or almonds, if desired
Nuts for garnish
½ C. sour cream
1 T. sugar
1 tsp. vanilla

Put sugar and water in heavy saucepan and cook until it spins a thread. (When a drop from the spoon held above the pan drops slowly and creates a fine hair-like thread in the air, it is ready.) At this time add the puréed potatoes to the syrup and blend, then simmer for about 10 minutes over low heat. Add the pineapple and cinnamon and simmer for 3 to 4 more minutes. Stir in the nuts if desired. Cool at room temperature. Meanwhile make topping from sour cream, sugar and vanilla making sure that sugar is dissolved. When pudding is cool put in serving dish/dishes and top with sour cream and garnish. Chill.

Author's note: One of my favorite refreshments while shopping each day at the mercado, was a liquado. A liquado is a blend of fruit juices and fruit and sometimes with egg and sugar added. One could select ingredients from locally ripened fruits, which certainly added to the delicious flavor, but a reasonable facsimile can be made in your own blender.

The procedure at my favorite liquado stand was to ask first for an orange juice base (about 1 C.) then I would choose varying amounts from such ingredients as papayas, bananas, pineapple, peaches, strawberries, mangoes, coconut milk, eggs and sugar. Everything was put in a blender and blended at high speed. It was the consistency of a milk shake, and was a great picker-upper.

PAGAN PICNICS

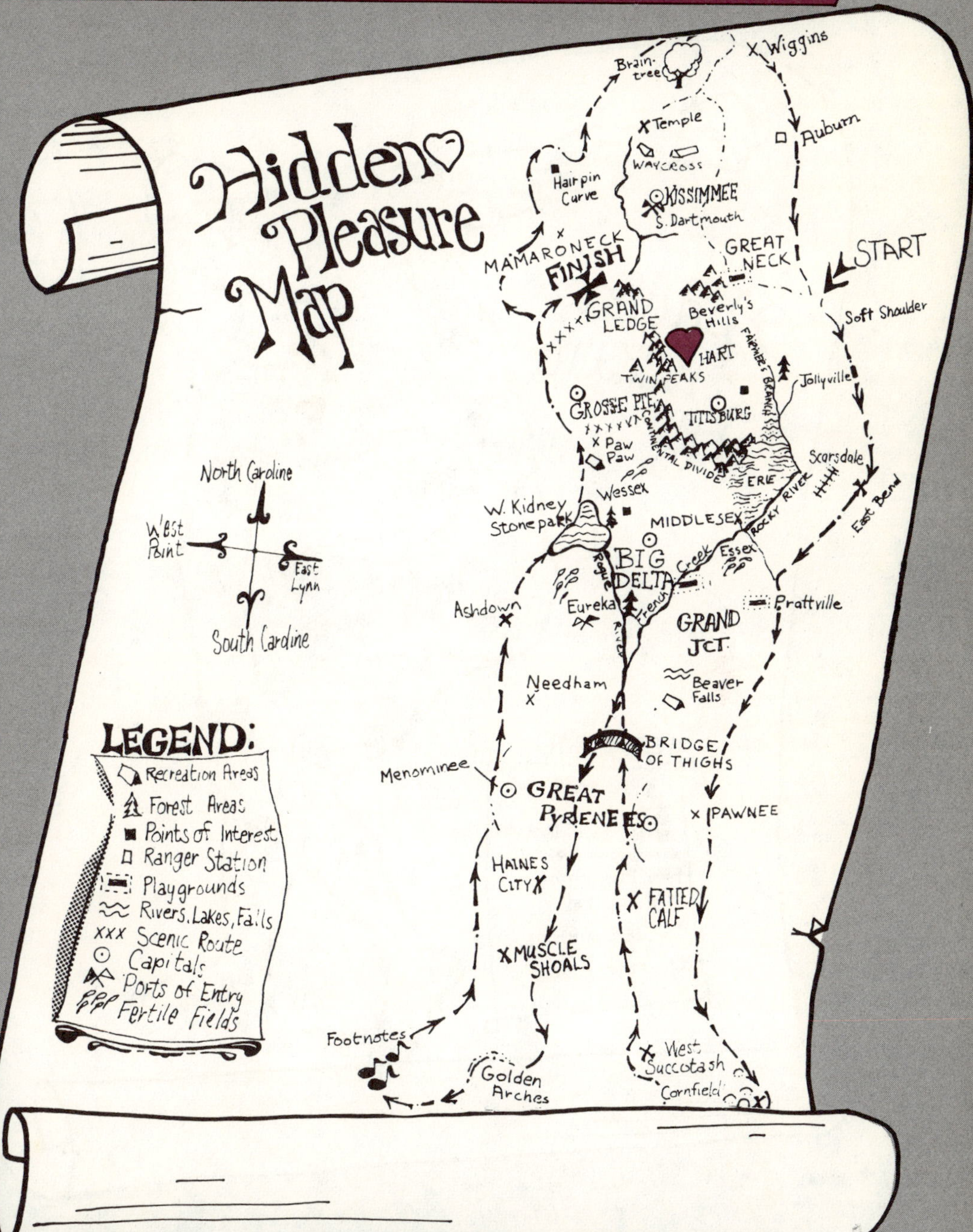

Hidden Pleasure Map
START
Nuckols (KY.)
Arma (KAN.)
South Arma (ME.)
Meddy Bemps (ME.)
Pittsfield (MASS.)
UGH Lake (ME.)
Titie Creek (FLA.)
Nipple Mt. (CO.)
Cowlick (AZ.)
Smuteye (ALA.)
Nose Rock (CA.)
Tuweep (AZ.)
Blue Eye (ARK.)
Oral (S.D.)
Big Neck (ILL.)
Shoulder Mt. (ME.)
Hartland
Sideview (KY.)
Upper Tract (W. VA.)
Bellyache Mesa (N.M.)
Alligator (MISS.)
Gungy Wamps (CONN.)
Gas City (IND.)
Tickle Naked Pond (VT.)
IDA OK
Kill Pecker Cr. (WYO.)
Isle of Mann
French Lick (IND.)
Ding Dong (TX.)
Dille's Bottom (OH.)
Blue Balls (PA.)
Rash (ALA.)
Julesburg (CO.)
Skinned Ass Canyon (NM.)
Capps (ARK.)
Palm Springs (CA.)
Ishi Pishi Falls (CA.)
Neely (ARK.)
Finger Lakes (N.Y.)
Slackland (ALA.)
Clay (NE.)
Healy (AK.)
Clay (OH.)
Steptoe (WA.)
Barstow (TX.)
Blackfoot (S.D.)
LEGEND:
Recreation Area
Forest
Points of Interest
xxx Scenic Route
Playground
Capital
Port of Entry
Lakes & Ponds

The American picnic is suffering from a good reputation.

We tend to think of picnics as family rituals—Daddums hunched over the barbeque grill brandishing a can of charcoal lighter; Mummsy in her Hawaiian-print muu muu off picking wildflowers; Dick and Jane romping through the poison oak; the faithful sheepdog in the back of the station wagon wolfing down the marshmallows.

Now that's all very nice, and I've got nothing against families, and in fact I have one of them myself. But I happen to prefer picnics with a little more flair—some romance, let's say, some decadence. Once in a while, you mothers ought to leave Dick and Jane at home and take Daddums out into the woods for a romp of your own.

If there isn't a Daddums in your life and you'd like to move in that direction—nature is the perfect setting for two people to realize they are one. Say, for example, you'd like to get on better terms with that new art director at the office...that you want to project an initial image of wholesome innocence, and yet you're dying to stretch out on a blanket with this beguiling acquaintance.

Engineer a picnic.

It might surprise him to be asked under the circumstances, but as a woman, let me say that life's little mysteries aren't always as mysterious as they seem, having engineered a few in my day.

This scenario should go something like this: Pack a lunch for two in the morning, and then at about 10:45 assume a woebegone expression and say to the art director: "Gee, do you suppose you could help me out? I was supposed to have lunch with Bob Redford, but I decided to cancel it, and now I've got two lunches on my hands. Would you like to go to the park and eat a little something by the statue of Robert E. Lee? If we leave early, we can get a spot at the front end of the horse."

Choose a simple menu, and be sure you have a place to keep the lunch cool until noontime. You want to be remembered for something other than food poisoning. Also figure out a graceful way to carry the lunch—in an oversized handbag or a day pack.

For a more ambitious adventure, think of an enticing picnic spot that can be reached by a short hike. Then consider having a co-conspirator spread out your lunch so that it's waiting when you arrive on the scene. Imagine the look on your fellow hiker's face when he lays eyes on that feast, complete with champagne on ice. This is a very workable plan, because you can arrange to pay your co-conspirator back in kind.

I'll declare right here that I'm too old myself for a strenuous hike through the woods, and, although stretching out on a blanket on the ground sounds exciting, it's a case of the spirit's willing but the flesh is weak. Fortunately, there's an alternative for us seasoned hedonists—the recreation vehicle, or bedroom on wheels. If you don't have one, or can't borrow one, you can rent one. Park it at some secluded location—overlooking the aspens in autumn, or gazing out at the sailboats on Lake Erie—and have the table set for luncheon. You can drive the RV or reach it on foot, and again you might want to keep it a secret from your companion. When the two of you walk into the clearing and see that Winnebago sitting there, act surprised to find the keys in your pocket, or else hide them in advance in the branch of a tree. Alternatively, have your guest meet you at the appointed location. (See "Invitations".)

Another way to go is the tailgate picnic. Pretend you're at Ascot for the races or at Henley for the regatta, or go to a football game and join the tailgaters in the parking lot before kickoff time.

In the middle of a long winter night , a picnic on the floor in front of the fireplace can be a delightful change of seasons. Put a sound-effects album on the turntable—birds singing, crickets chirping, frogs doing whatever they do. (Pet stores have birdsong records that are used to entertain canaries.) Put on a sun dress, dark glasses and Coppertone. Who knows?—if you stoke up the fireplace you might even get a tan.

If you don't have a fireplace—or even if you do—try scouting around for a mountain cabin, a hunting lodge or a beach house that, for a consideration, can be yours for a few hours or, better yet, for a whole weekend's worth of winter-summer picnics.

INVITATIONS:

Why not send your guest a treasure map, with X marking the site of the picnic?

Don't give away too much with the map, but rather keep the reader guessing. Ask the guest to join you at the beginning of the treasure hunt, or challenge him to follow the map by himself and meet you at the spot marked X. Either way, if he gets lost, don't worry. Who needs someone who can't find his way to the table.

If you like the idea of renting a camper, you can send your guest the keys, along with either a full explanation or a map with a set of clues. There's an advantage to being at the RV to recieve your guest: The drinks are cold and the food is hot, your hair is combed, and the music is playing.

Another idea: Write the invitation on a red-and white-checkered napkin.

For a winter picnic, inscribe your initials on a travel brochure from some fetching southern clime, or cut out the tropical pictures and design your own brochure. Use pictures of you and your guest under a palm.

SCENTS:

In summer, Mother Earth will take care of these arrangements. If you rent an RV, check it out beforehand to make sure the air isn't stale. Be cautious with deodorizing sprays in such a small space. Instead, you might want to boil some water with a few drops of vanilla, cinnamon, or clove oil added.

In winter, try to find some pinon wood to burn in your fireplace and you'll have the sweetest-smelling living room this side of Santa Fe.

TABLE SETTINGS:

Many stores are showing plastic picnicware in a bewildering variety of colors. These dishes look mighty chic on the display shelf, and they're practical too, but please take time to consider how a steak would look sitting on a purple plate, or a sliced tomato on a shocking pink one.

If you're leaving home for a picnic, you might make a list of the equipment you'll need and then think of ways to consolidate and lighten the load. A hike through the woods to a surprise luncheon will require even more advance planning. If your co-conspirator is able to drive to the site, you might even have him set up a table and chairs and put out fine china and crystal, which take on an extraordinay luster in a natural setting. Wouldn't that be stunning?

The camper picnic presents fewer problems: You can stock it before you drive to your destination, and then when you get there you can even bring a few ants inside for authenticity.

As for tailgate picnics, I've seen some pretty elaborate spreads in my time. Years ago my husband and I had season tickets for the Universty of Michigan football games, and for the first game of the season Jerre tried to persuade me to bring along a chafing dish full of meatballs. I felt that it would be too ostentatious, but how could I have known that the parking place next to ours would be reserved by some of the Ford family? Their chauffeur stepped out of the limousine and set up a table arrayed with silver serving dishes that would put Cartier's Christmas display to shame.

Since that time, I've concluded that a chafing dish full of meatballs isn't the least bit ostentatious.

If you're having a winter-summer picnic—making believe, perhaps, that you're on the beach at Melaque just south of Puerto Vallarta—I wouldn't advise bringing a yard of sand into your house, but why not rent some potted palm trees from your local florist?

MUSIC:

Some natural settings speak for themselves. The wind and wildlife provide a music far more harmonious than anything we could import. But let's face it—most of us live in the cities and our choices are more limited. When we go on a picnic it's sometimes nice to have a few tunes along to drown out the wildlife of the city—the singing of air brakes, the chatter of little jackhammers, the mating call of the Harley-Davidsons.

A battery powered cassette player will let you be your own disc jockey. One of the most advanced models available, the Intimate Stereo by Infinity, will play both FM radio and cassettes in stereo, has room for two sets of earphones, and is still small enough to be carried with ease. Some machines replay the tape automatically so that you don't have to fumble with them when you're trying to fumble with something else more important. For the same reason, bring along 90 minute tapes instead of the shorter 45 or 60 minute cassettes.

You can make your own tapes in advance if you want to take the time, choosing the selections and the order in which they're presented, and even adding your own comments in between— commercials for yourself, more or less. You might get a real kick out of composing your own mood music, and two 90 minute cassettes will give you six hours of listening without hearing the same song more than twice. Of course, these tapes can be played for at-home dining as well.

PAGAN PICNICS

Winter Menu
(Avec Argent)

Shrimp with Dipping Sauce
Hot Tomato Juice My Way
Meat Pasties in Cheese Crust
Desert Sands • Irish Coffee

Winter Menu
(Sans Argent)

Hot Tomato Bouillon
Bacon and Braunschweiger Sandwiches
Sauerkraut Relish
Peach Crumble

PAGAN PICNICS

Summer Menu
(Avec Argent)

Stuffed Celery
Iced Tomato Juice with Beer
Pita Sandwiches
Picnic Potato Salad
Melon

Summer Menu
(Sans Argent)

Stuffed Eggs
Cream of Gazpacho Miller
Roast Beef and Turkey with Sauce Alexis
French Bread
Melon and Fruit Cassis

STUFFED EGGS

Serves 4-6

6 eggs
1 T. softened butter
¼ tsp. salt
½ tsp. Worcestershire
1 tsp. cider vinegar
1 T. prepared mustard
2 T. mayonnaise

Have eggs at room temperature. Cover with cool water in a small saucepan and simmer just below boiling for 15 min. Turn eggs occasionally at first to center the yolks. At end of cooking period, drain, cover with cold water, then peel starting at big end. Cut eggs in half and remove yolks to small bowl. Mash to a paste and add the rest of ingredients. Put the yolk mixture into the egg whites, and put the two halves together for easier packing on a picnic. A wide mouth thermos will hold eggs after chilling, until serving time.

CREAM OF GAZPACHO MILLER

Serves 2-4

1 small green pepper
3 green onions
1 medium cucumber
3 stalks celery
3 tomatoes, peeled and seeded
1 C. tomato juice
½ C. mayonnaise
Dash Worcestershire
2 drops Tabasco
1 tsp. lemon juice
1 tsp. cream-style horseradish
Salt and pepper to taste
Croutons

Dice all the vegetables (DO NOT USE BLENDER). Set aside. In a blender or with a wire whisk, blend the rest of the ingredients. Combine vegetables and juice mixture. Add more tomato juice if need be. To serve, ladle into bowls and top with croutons just before serving. For a picnic, carry soup in thermos and croutons in separate container.

COLD ROAST BEEF AND TURKEY WITH SAUCE ALEXIS

Serves 2

2 ¼" slices roast beef
2 ¼" slices turkey, cooked
½ C. mayonnaise
1 tsp. red caviar
1 tsp. green onion, finely minced

Beef and turkey can be purchased at a good deli. The slices are usually quite large; so cut into strips and roll up like a jelly roll, securing with a toothpick. Blend the caviar with the mayonnaise and onion, taking care not to bruise the caviar. To eat, dip the meat into the sauce. Keep sauce chilled until just before eating.

*Variation: Cream cheese softened with sour cream instead of mayonnaise. Great dip!

MELON BALL AND FRUIT CASSIS

Serves 2

⅓ C. watermelon balls
⅓ C. honeydew balls
⅓ C. cantelope balls
Grapes, blueberries, cherries, pineapple, etc..
White wine or champagne
Creme de Cassis

Combine fruit after it has been prepared as necessary. Cover with about 1 C. white wine to which 1 T. creme de cassis has been added. Refrigerate, covered until ready to serve or pack. Serve as cold as possible.

STUFFED CELERY

Serves 2-4

1 3 oz. pkg. cream cheese
1 T. blue cheese
1 T. butter
Salt to taste
Dill weed
Celery

Mash the cheese and butter together and blend into a light filling. Salt to taste. Cut the cleaned celery into handy size pieces for packing. Fill celery and sprinkle a bit of dill weed on top. Refrigerate until ready to transport. Keep cool. (Keep the celery cool, too.)

ICED TOMATO JUICE AND BEER

6 small cans Snappy-Tom, ice cold
6 cans beer, ice cold

Mix one for one. Stir gently to retain carbonation of beer. If you prefer a less spicy drink, use plain tomato juice. Mix one at a time.

PITA SANDWICHES Serves 2

2 whole pita
½ lb. ground beef
½ C. avocado chopped
½ C. tomato chopped
½ C. feta cheese, crumbled
Shredded lettuce
Alfalfa sprouts
Green onion, optional
Oil and vinegar
Salt and pepper
Oregano, crumbled

Brown beef and season. Cut each pita round in half. Carefully separate cut edge creating a pocket. Layer ingredients starting with lettuce and ending with cheese and sprouts. Sprinkle with oregano. If packing for later, do not add salt or dressing. Carry separately. The plastic bottles from trial size shampoo is great for carrying oil and vinegar. Keep food cool until serving time.

AUTHOR'S NOTE:

Prior to your picnic, you might want to familiarize yourself with some of the common plants you could encounter. A handy one to recognize is poison ivy. Poison oak and sumac should be next. Your local library will have books to help you identify either of these in case you threw out your old Girl/Boy Scout Manual.

When it comes to wild mushrooms, my theory is: a little knowledge is a dangerous thing. A lot of knowledge would enable you to find some choice edible mushrooms, but I for one, don't know enough about them to take a chance. However, some friends from Italy, while visiting here, found basketsful of lovely mushrooms in a mountain meadow near Boulder.

Giovanna had been raised in a family which spent Sundays in the lower Alps hunting for mushrooms; so I trusted her judgement. She told me the variety, which she found here, would sell for $10 an ounce in Bologna. She proceeded to create the "Steaks Bologna".

You may not be interested in looking for wild, edible things, but contemplate using those foods traditionally said to be aphrodisiacs: basil, dill, fennel, coriander seeds (drop a few in coffee), lettuce, celery, carrots, onions, and chicory.

PICNIC POTATO SALAD

Serves 4-6

I call this "Picnic Potato Salad" because it does not have any mayonnaise in it. This does not mean it can stand at very hot temperatures for many hours, but I just feel more comfortable with it. A small UNOPENED jar of mayonnaise may be taken along, and some added just before eating for those who prefer it. This recipe makes a great hot dish, and if you desire to serve it hot, do add ½ C. mayonnaise before heating in a casserole for 25 to 30 minutes at 350 degrees.

1 qt. hot cooked potatoes, diced
¼ C. white wine (Vermouth is great)
3 T. salad oil
1 T. white vinegar
Salt and pepper
2 T. onion, minced
½ tsp. dill weed, dried or 2 tsp. fresh dill, minced
½ C. sour cream
1 tsp. prepared mustard
1 C. diced ham, bologna, or corned beef optional. Do use if serving hot

Combine the cooked potatoes with wine, oil and vinegar while hot. Season to taste and let stand an hour or longer, turning occasionally. Blend sour cream with mustard, onions and dill weed, and then fold into potatoes. Refrigerate. Just before serving or packing, add meat if desired. Keep cold until serving time.

MELON

Serves 2

1 small melon such as honeydew or cantelope
Grapes, cherries, strawberries, etc..if desired

Select the best seasonal melon. Cut in two and remove seeds. Put melon back together filled with other fruits and wine or a liqueur or flavoring if desired. Don't use bananas or peaches unless you sprinkle them with lemon juice.

SHRIMP WITH DIPPING SAUCE — Serves 2

1 C. cooked shrimp or crabmeat
½ C. sour cream
¼ C. plain yogurt
1 clove garlic, crushed in press or minced
1 T. chives, minced
1 T. lemon juice
1 tsp. dill weed
1 tsp. parsley
Salt and pepper
Dash Tabasco
Catsup to color

Blend all ingredients except shrimp or crabmeat and refrigerate. To serve, dip shrimp in dipping sauce. Or blend sauce with crab and serve with crackers.

HOT TOMATO JUICE MY WAY — Serves 4-6

1 qt. tomato juice
1 small onion
1 small green pepper
1 stalk celery with leaves
Salt and pepper
Dash Tabasco if desired

Chop all the vegetables coarsely and add to the tomato juice. Simmer in small stainless steel or enamel saucepan about 15 min. Strain. Season to taste. Heat to boiling and serve in bouillon cups or mugs. This can also be served cold, and further, it makes great aspic with Knox gelatin. (See directions on gelatin package.)

MEAT PASTIES IN CHEESE CRUST — Serves 2

½ lb. coarsely ground round steak
1 medium potato, diced in ½" dice
¼ C. onion, finely chopped
¼ C. carrot, turnip, or parsnip, finely chopped
Salt and pepper
Parsley
Beaten egg
Cream
Crust

Mix the meat and vegetables together, and season lightly with salt and pepper. Roll crust out into 5" circles and put about 3 T. filling in center of crust. Fold crust over. Moisten between folded edges, and crimp edges with tines of fork. Brush tops with beaten egg, prick tops, then bake in 325 degree oven about 1 hour. About 15 minutes before the pasties are done, make a small slit in the top and insert funnel and pour 2 T. cream into each pasty. These can be served hot or cold. The Welsh miners ate them cold, but I prefer mine hot.

CHEESE CRUST

½ C. butter
½ C. lard
¾ C. cheddar cheese, finely grated
3½ C. flour
1 egg
1 tsp. white vinegar
1½ tsp. salt
Milk

With a pastry blender, cut the shortening into the flour until the size of peas. With fingers, lightly toss in the cheese. Now make a well in the center of the dough. In a measuring cup, beat the egg with a fork and add enough milk to make ¾ cup liquid. Stir in the salt and vinegar until salt is dissolved. Dump the liquid all at once in the flour. Stir until dough balls up. Correct consistency either with a bit more flour or liquid. Chill before using.

DESERT SANDS

This is, without reservation, my favorite cooky recipe. As an accompaniment to Irish Coffee, it becomes a great dessert...for a winter picnic or anytime. As with all my recipes, I've tested them one way or another for taste, convenience, suitability, etc...This one had the acid test as a "warmer-upper" at the waterfront stadium in Cleveland during the Brown's games.

½ C.butter, must be butter
½ C. sugar
Pinch salt
1 tsp. vanilla
1½ C. sifted flour

Melt the butter over low heat in a heavy saucepan, letting it brown just until it foams and takes on a very light color. Remove from heat immediately and start beating and beat until cool. I put the melted butter in my mixer bowl and set the speed on low and let it go. The butter will be syrupy when cool. Add the sugar and vanilla to butter and cream together at medium speed. Mix the salt with flour and add to creamed mixture... Blend in well. This mixture will be crumbly but will hold its shape when squeezed. To form cookies, take a heaping teaspoonful, using a spoon from your table silver. With your free hand, squeeze the dough so it will hold the "spoon" shape. Slip gently onto cooky sheet. If it falls apart, put back into bowl and try again. Chill the batch briefly on the cooky sheet, then bake at 350 degrees for 10 to 12 minutes or until golden. These are quite fragile, but keep well in an airtight container.

IRISH COFFEE

Make from your favorite recipe, or add 1½ oz. good whiskey to each cup of coffee plus 1 to 2 tsps. sugar per cup. Top with whipped cream which has been sweetened slightly and flavored with vanilla. For Brown's games, I had the coffee ready in a thermos, and a can of pressurized whipped cream. Take care when adding pressurized cream. Do it at an angle so you don't shoot the coffee out of the cup.

HOT TOMATO BOUILLON

Serves 2

1 individual serving size Snappy-Tom or V-8 juice
1 can beef bouillon

Put beef bouillon into a small saucepan and add juice. This will make a concentrated bouillon, so if you like it less heavy, add water to taste. Bring to boil and serve or put in heated thermos.

BACON AND BRAUNSCHWEIGER SANDWICHES

Serves 2

6 slices rye or pumpernickel bread
3 thin slices sweet onion
6 slices bacon, cooked crisp
Braunschweiger
Mustard/mayonnaise optional

Spread bread with mustard and or mayonnaise (or butter) if desired. Use slices of the spreading variety of braunschweiger. Add onion slice and two slices bacon to each sandwich. Wrap sandwiches well and keep cool until ready to serve.

I loved him and he loved me:
So we carved our initials on a tree.

Thus emblazoned to remain forever
At our special place beside the river.

Today I don't know whether to cry or laugh.
They cut down the tree for a jogger's path!

SAUERKRAUT RELISH

Don't pass this recipe by, thinking you don't like sauerkraut. It is a delightful, crunchy relish and is a good accompaniment for sandwiches. In my continuing effort to make this book practical and helpful, may I suggest packing some breath mints or after dinner mints with this lunch?

2 C. sauerkraut, chopped well and drained
1 medium onion, chopped
1 medium green pepper, chopped
¾ C. sugar
½ C. salad oil
⅔ C. vinegar
½ C. water

Mix vegetables together. Mix dressing ingredients together and pour over the vegetables. Marinate at least overnight before serving. Will keep at least 2 weeks in the refrigerator, if it lasts that long. Serve cold or room temperature.

PEACH CRUMBLE

Serves 6

3 C. peaches, sliced
½ C. butter or margarine
1 C. brown sugar
¾ C. flour
½ tsp. salt
¼ tsp. nutmeg
1 tsp. cinnamon
½ C. sour cream
2 T. sugar
½ tsp. vanilla

Arrange peaches in well-greased 8" x 8" baking dish. Cream the flour, butter, brown sugar, salt, nutmeg, and cinnamon until crumbly. Sprinkle over peaches. Bake uncovered in a 350 degree oven for 45 min. or until juice is bubbling through and crust is nicely browned. Meanwhile, blend 2 T. sugar and vanilla into sour cream. Let sour cream stand, then stir again to dissolve sugar completely. Serve dessert hot or cold with sour cream topping. To pack for a picnic, I use lidded plastic containers, and carry the sour cream separately.

INDECENTLY ITALIAN

A chaste pastry clerk
    from Turin
Kept her bakery as
    neat as a pin
Till the butcher next door
Knocked her
    buns on the floor
And dropped his salami therein.

INDECENTLY ITALIAN

Summer Menu
(Avec Argent)

Prosciutto with Melon/Figs
Zuppa di Funghi con Pollo
Bistecca alla Florentina
Insalata di Fagioli con Caviale
Italian Bread • Amore Galore

Summer Menu
(Sans Argent)

Cheese Stuffed Celery
Viva Italia Zuppa
Chicken Breasts Tuscany
Spinach Parmesan
Rice Salad Italienne • Italian Bread
Coffee Amaretto Ice Cream
Parfaits

Winter Menu
(Avec Argent)

Marinated Mushrooms
Tomato Bouillon
Steaks Bologna
Broccoli Romano
Green Salad • Italian Bread
Cassata Siciliana

Winter Menu
(Sans Argent)

Mozzarella in Carrozza
Mama's Pavese
Pasta alla Carbonara
Green Salad • Bread Sticks
Gelato di Vaniglia Con
Salsa di Pesche

If you are looking for an excuse to have a saucy Italian dinner party, I can't think of a better way than to fall back on the long list of Italian holidays that give a somewhat religious sanction to *la dolce vita.* There is St. Giuseppe's Day on March 19th, Liberation Day on April 25th, Midsummer Night on June 24th, St. Peter and St. Paul's Day on June 29th. Or you can invite a guest to celebrate a holiday of your own creation. How about a feast for St. Joseph, the patron saint of aspirin and big-city hospitals? Or, in moral opposition to All Saints' Day during which anything goes?

I've been getting indecently Italian myself for a good long time. I remember one day in particular, in 1953, when I decided to pull myself out of a funk. I was tired of cooking dinner every night with a baby on each hip, and I figured it would be fun to bed the tykes down early and deck myself out in lush brocade and dine with my husband Jerre in Renaissance splendor. We would converse about the fall of the Roman Empire while contemplating the prospects for a tumble of our own.

So inspired, I embarked on my first serious attempt at Italian cooking. I made spinach noodles from scratch and stretched the greenish dough out to dry across the backs of the kitchen chairs. It made a curious sight, and when my husband came home from work he put it into perspective. He took one quick glance into the kitchen and then, with a puzzled look on his face, asked me: "How come you washed all my old GI underwear?"

Since then, I've learned to finish my basic food preparation before my guest arrives, in order to preserve the illusion of romantic adventure, (and to leave myself free to enjoy the evening).

To me, part of the romance of creating an international ambience is in knowing something about the background of a country's cooking, and since Italian cuisine is acknowledged to be the mother cuisine of all the Latin European countries maybe we should dwell on it for a moment. Italian cooking has been evolving for thousands of years. Roman chefs originally drew upon the ancient Greeks' cooking techniques and refined them over the centuries until, by the time of the Renaissance in the 16th century, Italy was considered to have the most refined cuisine in Europe. Many people think that the French always held that honor, but in fact they had to learn from the Italians a lot of the finesse. The story goes that in 1533, when Italy's Catherine de'Medici traveled from Florence to Paris to marry future French King Henri II, she took teams of chefs with her and regaled the locals with the finest of Florentine cooking. The French chefs, wisely, took it all in.

The very word *recipe* comes from the Latin word for "procure" and relates to the time-honored custom of procuring from the markets the very best produce available each day. Selecting quality ingredients is essential to Italian cooking, because the individual tastes are so distinct and robust—almost naked. Whereas, traditionally, the French relied on delicate sauces and ambiguous meanings, the Italians honor the dignity of each flavor.

The saying goes, "You are what you eat," and so it goes for the French and the Italians, especially the men. French men are wily and garnished with subtlety. Italian men are hearty and robust and distinctively zesty (and sometimes mighty fragrant, as well).

When we talk about Italian cooking, we shouldn't think only of the cheese-and-tomatoey concoctions of Southern Italy, but also of the many regional cuisines of Northern Italy.

Let's look at a map of Italy. While it is often described as a "boot-shaped nation," the most casual inspection reveals that it is actually shaped like a stalk of broccoli wearing high heels. The northern regions make up the head of this dancing broccoli, and each region has its own flavor. In Venice, which was once sea merchant to the world, the cooking is still brought alive by the spices that Marco Polo brought back from the Far East. In Genoa, another seafaring city, it is the herbs and vegetables brought back from other lands that have stayed to accent local dishes. In Florence, the capital of continental cuisine during the Renaissance, the food remains the simplest and least Italianized, with a minimum of seasonings and pretense. And so it is: The Milanese cook their food slowly...the best hams come from Parma and the original bread sticks from Turin...truffles come from the Piedmont mountains and Chianti from Tuscany. The northern regions cook with butter, the southern regions with less expensive olive oil. The northerners like their noodles flat, the southerners curly. And the capital city of Rome, situated in the middle of the broccoli stalk, is where these different tastes all come together, in magnificent chaos.

This is why it's fair to say that the menus offered in this section constitute a gastronomical Roman orgy. We have Pork Chops Modena and Chicken Breasts Tuscany. We have Spinach Parma Style and Cassata Siciliana. We have Amaretto from San Marino and prosciutto from Bologna. Yes, we have no bananas, or pizza, or spaghetti, or lasagna, but instead the best of northern Italian regional cooking.

It is partly out of sheer orneriness that I have skimped on pasta dishes. Too many Americans think of pasta as a main course rather than as a first or a soup course, as the Italians do. So I decided to even the score by more or less leaving the noodles on the shelf.

As a theme for an Italian evening, I've always favored the Renaissance because of its connotations of rebirth and renewal. If you're looking for an idea for celebrating a 50th birthday, the Renaissance could be your ticket for snapping out of the doldrums of the Middle Ages.

In a more contemporary vein, you can pick up your guest with a motor scooter and ride home astraddle the same quivering seat. You can announce the evening as a Fellini film festival and then, once the house lights dim, explain that your videocassette recorder has been repossessed.

You can conjugate the verb *amor* with emphasis on the conjugal aspects. You can read together from Dante, about Beatrice the goddess of divine love. Between the main course and dessert, you can engage in that venerable Italian custom by which the gentleman pinches his companion in the hindparts.

In general, any activity that favors indulgence over prudence might be deemed fair sport for an evening of dinner, Italian style. In case of overindulgence, you might take a cue from...

The tenor who sang in Trieste
Who denied a recent request,
For the note in his throat
Sounding very remote
Was lasagna that didn't digest.

You might, like the tenor, keep a bottle of Brioschi on hand—that old Italian equivalent of Alka Seltzer. It could serve against an attack of Mediterranean flatulence at an inopportune moment in the evening.

INVITATIONS:

Reprints of famous Italian paintings can be found in most bookstores, museum shops and art-supply stores. Some are even in the form of postcards, ready for mailing. Pick out a suitable reproduction and write your invitation on the back. You might choose Boticelli's "Birth of Venus" or Titian's "Venus and the Lute Player" or, more bashfully, Angelico's "The Madonna of Humility." Michelangelo's "David" would also make a stirring invitation. A bit of research should turn up an appropriate visualization for almost any mood. If you want to ham it up, paste a photo of your own face over the face in the picture.

If, in preparing for an Italian evening, you decide to make it a "Family" affair, you could wrap a frozen fish in a newspaper, with the invitation attached. Presumably, you'd deliver this yourself with the knowledge that your invitee would find it just after it had thawed (becoming then a "dead" fish), but before it started to ripen. If I lived in the Chicago area, I wouldn't pursue this line of thought for a Valentine's Day party.

If you plan ahead, you can grow a pot of typical Italian herbs such as basil, fennel, coriander or parsley, and then deliver it with an invitation card enclosed. If you don't plan ahead, your florist might be able to accomodate you with these herbs on short notice.

If you really want to make it a labor of love, you can glue alphabet pasta on a card to spell out your intentions.

SCENTS:

Psychologists have found that fragrances are the most powerful triggers for recalling past events and associations. Bearing that in mind, you have the choice of whether you want to be remembered for the scent of your best perfume or the smell of broccoli cooking.

Actually, there are many alternatives.

If you choose one of the Italian menus that use broccoli, I'd suggest cooking the broccoli the day before and then just heating it up on the night of the dinner. If odors still linger—and with Italian cooking they most assuredly will—don't try to mask them with other heavy odors. Instead, set candles out on the dinner table or on occasional tables around the room. Candles are wonderful. They soften the harsh light of reality and put a twinkle in your eyes. They eat up odors and tobacco smoke with their flames. And if they are scented candles they will add a gentle fragrance of their own. For this hearty group of dinners I would use candles with earthy scents such as sandlewood, bayberry, cinnamon or citrus.

If you light with electricity instead of candlepower, you can scent the room with one of those clever little rings that can be set upon the top of a light bulb like a crown and soaked with a few drops of perfumed oil in various scents. Don't drop oil directly onto a hot light bulb—unless you want to explode some life into the party or make the room smell so awful that your guest has to be evacuated. If you want to experiment, start with a cold bulb of low wattage and put on a drop at a time, letting it warm awhile.

TABLE SETTINGS:

The wide variety in the climate, topography and people of Italy is reflected not only in cooking styles but also in craftwork, clothing, architecture and art. Venetian glass and lace have long been recognized as standards of formal elegance, while neighboring regions produce some of the finest ceramics in the world. Look, for example, at the designs of Richard Ginori (for Di Docca of Florence), such as the "Blanco" china pattern that sells at a respectable $60, for a five-piece place setting. (A finer china from the same designer is "Perugia", at $175 a setting.)

In a simpler mode, you can recreate the atmosphere of a typical Italian tavern by setting your table with the sort of plain heavy platters that you can find at Woolworth's, or at a restaurant supply outlet. Authenticity, however, is nothing but a state of mind in creating these dinners, so take stock of the dinnerware and tablecloths that you have on hand, and if anything strikes you as Italian, then it is! Especially if you're on a limited budget, buy only what you can use for other occasions so you don't feel cheated if this particular dinner date turns out to be a dud.

Most cities have fabric-outlet stores that sell seconds, discontinued patterns and remnants. At one such store I recently bought, for a grand total of $16, enough material for ten tablecloths plus the fringe to border them. All it takes is some pinking shears and perhaps a needle and thread (but even a stapler or duct tape will do), and you can fashion a tablecloth that will hold up through the most decadent of feasts. If you live in a small apartment and eat off of snack trays, don't let that discourage your creativity. A red-and-white checkered place mat and a wicker-covered wine bottle on each tray is a start at setting an informal table the way they're set from Cortina to Naples.

For summer dinner parties I lean toward a fresh-feeling pastel tablecloth or mat—in a solid color if flowered plates are used, or in a pastel floral if you're using plain china. Mixing patterns is an art and unless you have a flair for it, stay with a simple formula. This is surely the time to arrange a centerpiece of fruit and vegetables. If you are serving on individual trays, you can make arrangements of grapes in tiny wicker baskets for each place.

Winter is the time for weightier or more formal settings. A wooden cutting board with arrangement of fruit or cheese can be set out on a checkered or woven cloth for an informal table. A remnant of brocade, either as a full cloth or a runner, can be used under crystal, gilt and prisms to set a more luxurious table. Second-hand stores or antique shops might yield up some Venetian-style glass goblets or vases that would hold floating candles. If you don't find old crystal, Cristallo de Censo is a reasonably priced Italian crystal found in many department stores.

Another choice in table settings might be occasioned by a Sicilian-style "family" dinner. This could be the Early Speakeasy style—mismatched china and silver with drinks served in tea cups and perhaps assorted bullet holes in the wall.

For any Italian dinner, the ambience can be enhanced by having an automatic slide projector casting images of Italian art against a wall while you're dining. For heaven's sake, don't sit there working the projector yourself or boring your guest with slides from your first marriage. All I'm suggesting is a little subliminal advertising. Another idea is to have a print of one of the old masters matted and placed on an easel in the background and then given to the guest as a parting gift.

CLOTHING:

Once again, Italy offers many choices, from peasant to Pucci and Gucci. Almost any lady, I think, would welcome the excuse to dress up for an evening like Sophia Loren playing the wronged peasant girl, her blouse off the shoulder, her skirt all but bearing the instructions, "Rip Along Dotted Line." For a fancier look of seduction, you can emulate Rome's most exclusive ladies of the night, who park their Bugattis in front of the Excelsior and Ambasciatori hotels and can often be seen in those suggestive crocheted tops with nothing underneath.

For the speakeasy or "family" scene, any of the flapper styles would be great for women, while men can dress in the obligatory double-breasted pin-striped suits that seem to collect dust in the back of many closets.

MUSIC:

You can turn this night into one of musical splendor by playing any of the concertos or symphonies of Albinoni or Boccherini, or the concertos of Vivaldi, especially the "Six Concerti a Cinque".

If you are brave and you've seen the movie "A Clockwork Orange", you might try re-enacting the scene that goes along with Rossini's "William Tell Overture."

Last but not forgotten, there's Louie Prima.

RANDOM THOUGHTS ABOUT SPICES AND HERBS

A small mortar and pestle is a MUST for serious cooks, and should be in everyone's kitchen as a money saver. The way it saves money is this:

Whole spices and herbs are cheaper than ground. (A lot of money goes into grinding and packaging.) Further, whole spices and herbs have a longer shelf life as they retain their flavor within their pods. Using a mortar and pestle to grind them just before using them, releases their pungency at the moment you want it; so you can also use less.

Many cities have health food stores and other specialty shops where you can buy bulk spices in the amount you need. For example, as of this writing, in Boulder, whole cloves are 85 cents an ounce at a local health food store. Ground cloves at the super market are $2.49 for 1.25 oz. It takes a little determination to grind whole cloves into a fine powder, but it can be done.

"Freshly ground pepper", as called for in many recipes, can be had by grinding peppercorns in a mortar and pestle rather than a peppermill. You can grind from very coarse to very fine depending on your taste.

Seeds such as anise, fennel, rosemary, etc...are best ground...not only for releasing flavor, but rosemary, in its whole form, is rather like eating pine needles.

In Indian cooking, a *chaunk* is prepared for making curries and other dishes. A *chaunk* is a collection of various herbs and spices put together in a small saucer so that "all at once" the collection can be added to hot fat to "pop" almost like popcorn, thus releasing and enhancing the flavors. Such things as black mustard seed, cumin seed, sesame seed, chili pequins and cashews are included in *chaunks.* If you want to do something "different" with a vegetable, try putting a pinch of each of those seeds and nuts mentioned above on a saucer. Then heat some butter or oil in a small saucepan. As soon as the butter is hot, add the seasonings and nuts all at once and stir the ingredients for about 30 seconds, then pour this hot mixture over cooked vegetables. (Turmeric can be added for color, and/or a pinch of curry powder.)

Flat leaf parsley is coriander, or in Spanish, *cilantro.* It is also called Chinese parsley. I have used leaves from the hearts of celery, minced finely, when I couldn't find coriander leaves. The flavor is not quite the same, but good nonetheless.

PROSCIUTTO WITH MELON/FIGS — Serves 2

This appetizer depends on the availability of melon and figs at your market. Also, the availability of prosciutto. Prosciutto is an Italian style ham; so if you live in an area where you can't find prosciutto, substitute thin slices of a good ham.

Choose a melon and/or fresh figs from the seasonal supply. Cut melons, remove seeds, slice in thin slices and peel off rind. Arrange 3 or 4 thin slices per person on a serving plate, and lay ham over them. Figs can be cut in two and put to one side, or if serving figs alone, serve two by cutting in wedges and placing ham over them.

ZUPPA DI FUNGHI CON POLLO — Serves 2-4

1 can cream of chicken soup
½ C. fresh mushrooms
2 green onions, minced
Butter
Light cream
Dry sherry, to taste
Salt and pepper

Wipe mushrooms clean with damp towel. Trim and chop. Melt butter in a small skillet, add mushrooms and onions and sauté over low heat until mushrooms are tender. Add the condensed soup and blend. Add enough light cream to bring to proper consistency. Correct seasonings. Heat to serving temperature, remove from heat, add sherry and serve immediately.

BISTECCA ALLA FLORENTINA — Serves 2

1 Porterhouse or T-Bone steak per person
⅔ C. olive oil
3 T. lemon juice
1 T. wine vinegar
Salt and pepper
Ground rosemary
Clove of garlic, cut

Wipe steaks with paper towel. Rub steaks each side with garlic and rosemary. Mix oil, lemon juice and vinegar. Put steaks in flat glass dish. Sprinkle with salt and pepper. Pour on marinade. Let stand about 2 hours, turning from side to side. To cook: lift from marinade and drain. Put over hot coals. Brown one side then the other to desired doneness. Serve on hot platter.

INSALATA DI FAGIOLI CON CAVIALE Serves 4-6

- 2 C. white beans cooked, (canned northern beans are fine for this.)
- ½ C. celery, thinly sliced
- ¼ C. red onion, minced
- 1 T. fresh parsley, minced
- 2 T. pimiento, canned, chopped
- 1 T. red caviar
- 1 T. lemon juice or wine vinegar
- 1 T. salad oil if using canned beans, otherwise 2 T.
- Salt and pepper
- Lettuce leaves

If you are using canned beans, drain away part of the liquid in the can. If you cook your own beans, drain thoroughly. Mix all the vegetables together, then dress with dressing made from lemon juice, and oil. Salt and pepper to taste. Arrange in bowl lined with lettuce leaves and sprinkle the caviar on as garnish. (This keeps well refrigerated.) Serve chilled.

AMORE GALORE Serves 2 or more

For each person:

- ½ oz. Galliano
- ½ oz. peach brandy
- 1 scoop vanilla ice cream
- ½ fresh peach, peeled, very ripe

Put all in blender and blend completely. Pour into large wine glass. Garnish with whipped cream and crystallized violet if desired. (This can be made ahead and kept in freezing compartment. To serve: remove from freezer about 15 min. prior to serving, then garnish.)

CHICKEN BREASTS TUSCANY

Serves 2 or more

1 medium chicken breast per person
3 T. vegetable oil
4 T. lemon juice
1 T. onion, minced
1 egg, beaten lightly
½ C. flour
Salt and pepper
Oil for frying
Black olives

These ingredients will suffice for 4 breasts...for more increase ingredients proportionately. Make a marinade of the oil, lemon juice, onions, salt and pepper. Cut each breast into two pieces and put into the marinade, turning to coat all sides. Let stand for about 2 hours in glass container. To cook: remove the chicken from marinade and pat dry. Shake chicken in bag with flour, salt and pepper, then dip in beaten egg, and let excess drip off. Fry in hot oil ½" deep in skillet. 15 to 20 minutes should be sufficient to brown and cook on both sides. To serve: arrange on hot platter and garnish with olives.

VIVA ITALIA ZUPPA

Take this recipe on faith...it is delicious! The name comes from the fact that this tricolor soup represents the Italian flag.

1 can cream of pea soup
1 can tomato soup
Buttermilk
Sour cream
Minced chives
Salt and pepper
Dill weed

Determine the number of people you are going to serve, and adjust this recipe accordingly. Mix pea soup and tomato soup separately with equal portions of buttermilk. i.e. ½ C. pea soup to ½ C. buttermilk. Reserve in separate bowls. Meanwhile blend enough sour cream with buttermilk to equal volume and consistency of soup mixtures. Add dill weed to taste to sour cream mixture, and season with salt and pepper. You are going to "swirl" these three mixtures in a marbleized pattern so don't have the mixtures too thin. To assemble: Use a flat soup bowl and put a band of each across the bowl. With a rubber spatula, using only the tip, create a swirl of three colors. Garnish with chives. Serve chilled.

The Tuscan chef was a prude,
And thought it exceedingly crude
to print "breasts" on the menu
knowing that when you..
Eat them, they have to be chewed.

CHEESE STUFFED CELERY

Serves 2 or more

4 oz. cream cheese
4 oz. Kaukauna sharp cheddar cheese
2 oz. canned pimientoes, chopped
Dash Tabasco
Celery

Soften cheeses to room temperature. Put all but celery in mixing bowl and blend thoroughly. You can use an electric mixer. When cheese mixture is blended, chill. Prepare celery in bite size pieces. Fill the celery with the cheese mixture. Prepare only the amount of celery you need and if you have cheese left, use for sandwiches.

SPINACH PARMESAN

Serves 2-4

1 pkg. frozen spinach, chopped
¼ C. butter, must be butter
Parmesan cheese, grated
Salt and pepper

Cook spinach according to directions on package. Meanwhile, over low heat brown the butter LIGHTLY. Drain spinach completely and pour butter over it. Toss with fork to coat. Season to taste and sprinkle generously with grated cheese. Serve immediately.

RICE SALAD ITALIENNE

Serves 2-4

1 C. cooked rice
¼ C. green pepper slivers
1 T. red onion, minced
2 T. black olives, chopped
1 T. white wine vinegar
3 T. salad oil
Pinch paprika
Pinch dry mustard
Pinch basil, crumbled
Salt and pepper
Lettuce leaves

While rice is still hot, put the dressing on and toss rice to coat. Cool mixture and add the peppers, olives and onions. Correct seasoning. Chill. To serve: Mound on lettuce leaves and garnish with tomato wedges if desired.

COFFEE AMARETTO ICE CREAM PARFAITS

For each person:
1 large scoop coffee ice cream
1 oz. Amaretto
Whipped cream
Chocolate sprinkles or nuts

Soften ice cream and swirl in the Amaretto in each serving. Spoon into parfait glasses (or wine glasses) and cover with plastic. Set in freezer compartment. To serve: Remove from freezer about 10-15 minutes prior to serving. Garnish with whipped cream and sprinkles or nuts or both.

FUNGHI MARINATI (Marinated Mushrooms)

Serves 2

- **1 lb. button mushrooms**
- **⅔ C. olive oil or salad oil**
- **½ C. water**
- **Juice of 1 lemon**
- **2 T. wine vinegar**
- **1 bay leaf**
- **1 tsp. oregano**
- **Salt and pepper**
- **Worcestershire sauce**
- **1 clove garlic, mashed**

Clean mushrooms with damp paper towel and remove stems. Combine all other ingredients and bring to boil. Drop the mushrooms in, reduce heat and simmer, stirring gently about 5 min. Remove from heat, let cool in marinade. Chill before serving, but if oil congeals, bring to room temperature before serving. Serve with crackers and cubes of cheese, if desired.

TOMATO BOUILLON

This is a substantial dinner; so I would start with a light soup. A good brand of tomato or V-8 juice mixed with equal parts beef bouillon, then heated, would be just right. Serve in cups or mugs with crackers.

STEAKS BOLOGNA

Serves 2

- **2 filets of beef, ½ x 3 x 4", with pockets for filling**
- **2 slices mozzarella cheese, ⅛" thick**
- **2 thin slices prosciutto (optional)**
- **2 T. sautéed mushrooms**
- **1 beaten egg**
- **Flour for dredging**
- **Salt and pepper**
- **Bread crumbs**
- **Oil for frying**

Have your butcher cut a pocket in the steak and flatten it to proper size, or do it yourself. In each steak pocket, put a slice of cheese, prosciutto and mushrooms. Season flour with salt and pepper and dredge each steak. Dip each in egg, then in crumbs. Press steaks between palms so they will hold together while cooking. Have cooking oil about 375 degrees. Brown on each side about 5 min. for rare meat. The cheese should melt and the mushrooms be hot through. Serve on heated plates with garnish as desired.

BROCCOLI ROMANO

Serves 2-4

- 2 C. broccoli flowerlets
- 1 T. oil
- 1 T. butter
- ⅛ tsp. garlic powder
- ½ C. dry white wine
- Salt and pepper
- Parmesan cheese, grated or Romano if desired

Heat oil and butter in saucepan until haze forms. Remove from heat and stir in the broccoli until all is coated with oil. Sprinkle with garlic powder, salt and pepper. Return to moderate heat and add white wine. Simmer uncovered, stirring, about 5 min. Cover, reduce heat and simmer about 15 min. more. To serve: lift from pan with slotted spoon. Arrange in heated serving dish, and sprinkle generously with cheese. (Cook the broccoli a day ahead, reheat and add cheese before serving to prevent odor.)

CASSATA SICILIANA (With apologies to the Sicilians)

Serves 2

Since many of you will be cooking for only two, it seems a waste to give you a recipe that will serve 12. I have improvised a recipe from a traditional Cassata Siciliana, and I urge you to do the same with other unwieldly recipes.

The original recipe calls for 1 lb. of ricotto cheese, sieved, then blended with cream. What this ends up being is cream cheese; so I just started with cream cheese, only in a lesser amount. The cake called for is a type of sponge cake, and when sponge cake is called for in a recipe, it usually means it is meant to soak up some flavorful liquid. At your market or bakery, you can find pound cakes, individual sponge cakes of the variety sold for shortcakes, and lady fingers. Any of these will do. Now that you have the idea, let's proceed for two:

- 4 pound cake slices or 8 lady fingers or 2 round shortcakes
- 3 oz. cream cheese
- 1 T. heavy cream or evaporated milk
- 2 T. sugar
- 1 T. apricot, peach, orange liqueur or other
- ½ C. candied fruit and nuts mixed-chopped
- 1 T. chocolate chips or jimmies
- Chocolate frosting

Soften the cream cheese then blend in ingredients in order given. Spread between 2 layers of cake. Press layers together firmly. Using your choice of chocolate frosting, add a touch of liqueur to it and frost top and sides of cake or individual cakes. Wrap loosely in plastic wrap and let ripen at least 24 hours in refrigerator. To serve: remove from refrigerator to take a bit of the chill off.

MOZZARELLA IN CARROZZA

Serves 2-4

8 slices Italian bread, cut ½" thick
4 slices Mozzarella cheese, ⅛" thick
1 egg, beaten
⅔ C. milk
Salt and pepper
Flour for dredging
Garlic salt if desired
Oil for frying

Trim the crust off bread in such a way as to make uniform slices. Cut cheese to fit and make 4 sandwiches. Cut each sandwich in two and dip each side in milk, then dredge with flour each side. Rest on paper towel until all are dredged in flour. Then dip all in egg seasoned with salt and pepper. Place on wax paper until ready to fry. Put ½" oil in skillet and heat to 375-400 degrees. Fry sandwiches on each side until golden. Drain on paper towel. Serve hot.

A dipping sauce is nice with these, and I had one on Cortina, Italy that reminded me of cocktail sauce. It was very good; so I made one that tasted much like it. ⅔ C. catsup, ⅓ C. chili sauce, 1 tsp. cream style horseradish, 1 tsp. Worcestershire sauce, and a dash of Tabasco.

MAMA'S PAVESE (And she isn't even Italian!)

Serves 2-4

For Two:
2 C. rich chicken broth
1 T. tomato paste
1 egg
2 T. Parmesan cheese, grated
½ tsp. oregano, crumbled
½ tsp. parsley, minced
Salt and pepper

With a wire whisk, blend the tomato paste into the chicken broth and season broth with salt, pepper, parsley and oregano. Bring the broth to a boil. Meanwhile beat the cheese and egg together until well blended. When the broth boils, pour the egg cheese mixture in SLOWLY, beating constantly with whisk. Turn off heat while this stirring action takes place and remove immediately from heat when all is blended. Serve immediately.

GREEN SALAD

The green salads from France, Greece and Italy are like cousins; so don't be afraid to borrow from each of these cultures to suit your own taste. A green salad from Northern Italy would be apt to have onions instead of garlic for piquancy; so you even have choices within the country itself. I would select an assortment of greens, including some escarole and romaine in addition to Bibb and/or icebeg lettuce. Prepare the greens by washing and drying them. (Dried greens hold the dressing.) A few slices of mushrooms and some slices of red onion added to the greens will make a more interesting salad. The dressing is almost inevitably 3 parts oil to one part vinegar with such additions as mustard, oregano, basil and other herbs. I usually use a dash of Worcestershire although it really isn't Italian. Shake the dressing in a jar before pouring on salad. Add the dressing and salt and pepper just before serving. Garnish with tomato wedges, olives, etc...if desired.

PASTA ALLA CARBONARA

Serves 2-4

This would be a "soup" course in Italy, but it is hearty enough for a main course, and reasonable enough to qualify for this menu.

- **¼ lb. fresh mushrooms, sliced**
- **6 slices bacon, cut in 1" pieces**
- **2 T. butter**
- **½ C. white wine**
- **3 eggs lightly beaten**
- **½ C. Parmesan cheese, freshly grated**
- **Salt and pepper**
- **1 lb. hot, cooked spaghetti**

Sauté the mushrooms and bacon pieces in the butter until the mushrooms are tender and the bacon cooked through. Stir frequently. Add wine and cook until wine evaporates. In a small bowl combine the eggs and cheese. Meanwhile cook the spaghetti, drain it and season it with salt and pepper. In a heated bowl, combine the cooked spaghetti with the mushrooms and bacon, then add the egg cheese mixture and stir with a tossing motion to combine all and cook the egg with the hot mixture. Serve at once in heated flat bowls or on plates. Additional cheese and melted butter may be served.

GELATO DI VANIGLIA CON SALSA DE PESCHE

Serves 2

- **2 medium, ripe peaches**
- **2 scoops vanilla ice cream**
- **1 T. confectioners sugar**
- **1 T. banana liqueur**
- **2 T. peach brandy, rum or Cognac**
- **1 T. brown sugar**
- **1 T. butter**

Wash and pit peaches, peel one but not the other. Cut unpeeled peach in chunks. Put in blender with confectioners sugar and banana liqueur. Blend and reserve. Slice other peach. Melt butter in skillet and dissolve brown sugar in it. Put the peach slices in skillet and sauté slices over low heat until tender. Add blended fruit mixture and simmer with slices until blended. Heat the 2 T. brandy and flame over the sauce. While warm ladle over vanilla ice cream in serving dishes.

HAND-ME-DOWN HAREM

HAND-ME-DOWN HAREM

Summer Menu
(Avec Argent)

Cheese Pastries
Cucumber and Yogurt Soup
Broiled Skewered Swordfish
Zucchini with Sesame
Spinach Salad • Turkish Delight
Coffee

Summer Menu
(Sans Argent)

Eggs Izmir • Cherbah
Cold Shredded Chicken with Walnut Sauce
Cucumber Salad with Yogurt
Wheat Bread • Ladies' Navels
Coffee

Winter Menu
(Avec Argent)

Lady Meatballs
Yogurt Barley Soup
Lamb Kabobs with Pilav
Green Salad • Pita
Sweet Rice • Coffee

Winter Menu
(Sans Argent)

Hummus • Cinnamon Wine Soup
Chicken with Pilav
Salad Bosporus • Pita
Poached Apples with Whipped Cream
Turkish Coffee

Imagine that you have won an all-expenses-paid weekend for two in Istanbul, and you choose as your traveling companion that one person you've always dreamed of being alone with.

Imagine that you've been whisked there on a magic carpet—a champagne flight—and now the two of you are standing on your hotel balcony gazing out over the minarets of old Constantinople. Off in the distance you see the Blue Mosque and, beyond that, the waters of the Golden Horn. The sights and sounds of the city lure you out of your hotel. You stroll arm-in-arm along the Bosporus. You wander through the bazaars, sampling sweets and pinching dates.

When the cobblestones have your feet crying for mercy, you hail a cab. A driver for the Crescent City Cab Company pulls up to curb with his brace of camels, and after a few false starts you go lurching off through the streets to the Topkapi Palace.

At the palace, a tour guide leads you through rooms filigreed in ivory and gold and mother-of-pearl, and regales you with stories about how the sultans once reigned in outrageous splendor here during the Ottoman Empire. The diamonds and emeralds and rubies that once adorned the royal court are now spread out before your eyes in glass display cases, under heavy guard. In days of yore within these palace walls, the guide recounts, thousands of guests were entertained every night while the sultan reclined in private audience with his courtiers and wives and concubines. After a while, you and your companion wander away from the tour, off by yourselves, to see what you can see. You pass under vaulted archways and into harem quarters. There, in a corner of one cubicle, you see some ancient graffiti, and a crude limerick that must have been scratched into the wall by some concubine hundreds of years ago. It says:

The sultan of Topkapi is a jerk
With his most unusual dirk
It is said in his harem
He uses it to scare 'em,
That Turk with his dirk and a smirk.

The two of you wander farther and deeper into the recesses of the palace until you reach what appears to be the sultan's own private bed chamber. The walls are hung with brocade draperies embroidered with spun silver, and diamonds glitter down from the domed ceiling like all the stars in heaven.

You spot a particularly cozy corner of the bedroom where colorfully woven pillows are piled high around a copper table. You look at each other mischievously, as if to say, "Why not?" You glance around to be sure no one is looking and then you snuggle into this luxurious cocoon—just for a moment or two—to try it out for size.

And then...BANG!...without warning, the door to the chamber slams shut.

You call out in alarm, but no one answers.

You run to the door and test it, but it has been bolted firmly.

You realize what has happened: The palace has been closed for the night, and you have mistakenly been locked inside.

Just the two of you.

No sooner have you settled back into the bed of pillows to appraise the possibilities of a night in old Byzantium, than a time-warp genie in a turban appears from out of nowhere, and inquires:

"Would you like to see our wine list, sahib?"

Now I'll have to admit that nothing even remotely like this has ever happened to me, and in fact I've never set foot in Turkey. But in spirit I am drawn compulsively toward a country that perpetuates belly dancing as an art form and that serves desserts with names like Lady's Navel and Maidens' Lips.

I, for one, am ready for a hand-me-down harem experience with some sultry sultan.

Actually, the word "harem," in Arabic, means literally "the forbidden," and refers to that secluded part of a palace reserved exclusively for women. Under Islamic law, sultans and caliphs were allowed to have as many as nine wives apiece in their harems, while lesser men were only allowed four. However, this was purely academic, since there was not a limit on the number of mistresses that a healthy and active Muslim stud could keep under one roof. Each legal harem wife had her own apartment and staff of servants (while presumably the consorts had to fight over who got to use the hair dryer next). It probably wasn't a bad life for the sort of women who didn't mind being a captive object.

The harem system fell out of fashion in Turkey in the early 1900s with the end of the sultan's reign and the encroachments of Western morality. The concubines, liberated from the harems, cast off their veils and kept everything else cinched tightly around their waists, for once.

It's sometimes fun, though, to bring back a disgraced epoch.

If you are a woman who enjoys getting carefree for an evening, and if you can see yourself swishing around in a harem costume with a ruby in your navel, then ask yourself this question: Whom would you choose to be your sultan for the night?

If you are a man, which friendly female acquaintance of yours can you see lounging across those pillows in the royal bed chamber waiting to dull the sultan's knife?

Do it like the Turks. Get down on the floor. Smoke a water pipe. Eat dates.

INVITATIONS:

It's hard to come by genuine magic carpets these days, but almost any shop that deals in miniatures (or doll house accessories) should have a scaled-down version of a Persian or Oriental rug. You can attach an invitation to the back of one, with a remark such as: "This is your transportation to an evening of high adventure..."

If you're going to be dressing as a belly dancer and wearing a jewel in your navel, attach it to the invitation and suggest that at the appointed time and place you will show it off to it's maximum advantage. And if you actually know how to belly dance or can take a few classes, all the better.

If these ideas don't interest you, an easy way out is to buy a blank card with a Middle Eastern print on the front and write your invitation inside. Such cards can be found at museum shops, art-supply stores and stationers.

SCENTS:

What aroma could be more instantly appealing than that of Turkish coffee brewing?

Many shops sell imported coffees ground to order, and if they know what they're doing they'll grind the Turkish beans to a fine powder. The Turks introduced coffee to the rest of the world, and from what I hear they drink it at the drop of a fez. It might be too strong or too sweet for your taste, but the aroma is terrific. The story is that coffee was discovered when some shepherds saw their goats eat some small dark beans and then watched in amazement as the animals "remained awake, jumped and gamboled the whole night." Similarly, one good strong cup of Turkish coffee might serve you better than an aphrodisiac as a romantic evening lengthens.

An excellent book by Ann Tucker Fettner entitled "Potpourri" contains lots of information about how to make your own perfumed sachets, pomander balls and incense, including Arabian incense powder. The scents of jasmine, frankincense, myrrh and patchouly blend nicely with the pungent aromas of Turkish cooking. Joss sticks, incense cones and powders, scented oils and scented candles can also be bought in most of these fragrances.

TABLE SETTINGS:

In the days of the sultans, literally thousands of guests chowed down at the royal palace every night. There were so many cooks that each course had to be prepared in a separate kitchen. Sultan Ahmed III, it is said, was fond of dining on his balcony under a full moon while, below him, dervishes whirled, pretty girls played catch with golden balls, and regiments of turtles paraded around the courtyard with candles on their backs.

It is difficult to duplicate this atmosphere, admittedly, in your average two-bedroom condo in Tucson. Even so, it's easy to transport yourself to Byzantium more modestly — by partaking of refreshments and dinner while sitting on cushions on the floor in the traditional Middle Eastern manner.

If you're fortunate enough to own a Persian or Oriental rug, it can be placed beneath the cushions. If you're not so fortunate, you might invest in a low priced imitation from a place like Woolco or Penney's. These small "domestic Orientals" will make excellent foyer or hearth rugs after the party is over. Because of the popularity of Middle Eastern designs, you can also find suitable floor cushions at discount and department stores.

Now that you're on the floor (a good position for any circumstances that might arise), you'll need a table. Before sawing off the legs from your Duncan Phyfe, you might consider simply placing a folded card table on top of a few bricks and covering it with a woven fabric from the Near East or India. Straw place mats would go nicely with a solid colored cloth beneath.

Turkish food is customarily served in small bowls arranged on a copper or brass tray for each guest. Rattan trays would also be appropriate, and less expensive. The bowls themselves are porcelain; any small ceramic or porcelain bowls, such as the lotus bowls carried by Oriental stores, will do excellently for a Turkish dinner.

If you're amuling through antique shops, keep your eye out for old brass or copper trays, pitchers, bowls and other serving pieces. In the past the Turks silvered their copperware so that they wouldn't have to eat directly from copper, and occasionally you can still find trays with some traces of silver remaining. If you latch onto one of these old pieces, it should have the place of honor as the centerpiece. A few blossoms, some leaves and a few pieces of fruit would put it in the proper context.

Whatever props you have to work with, keep the setting simple but rich in contrast of color and texture. The Time-Life series of cookbooks, "Foods of the World", has great photographs of native table settings from all over, and in this instance you might want to check out the Middle Eastern book at the library.

CLOTHING:

This is the time to wear a belly dancer's costume if you ever longed for the excuse, and if you're able to bring it off with grace.

It might be hard to find all the pieces to this costume in any one place, but you can start by looking at dance stores, garage sales, specialty clothing shops and costume stores. Don't worry about matching colors; part of the fun is to look unusual. You might consult a magazine called "Arabesque" for illustrations of belly dancing attire.

Starting from the ground up, the costume might consist of:

* Bare feet
* Billowing harem pants slung well below the navel
* A filmy circle skirt that will stand out when you twirl
* A sash around your hips
* A belt made of large golden or silver coins
* A coin bra
* A loose translucent blouse that leaves your belly exposed
* A bolero-type vest
* A head scarf, and a veil that can be lifted suggestively
* A generous and jangly assortment of necklaces, bracelets, rings, sequins, spangles, bangles, baubles, and beads.

If you'd rather not be so daring (or if there's a cold wind blowing off Lake Michigan), you can find Middle Eastern-style apparel made out of batik, madras print and embroidered cotton in many shops. These clothes are usually loose fitting and comfortable for sitting on the floor.

A gentleman might wear loose black pants with a white tunic and a dark vest. He can try fashioning a turban out of a white towel or some other fabric, or he can drape a pillow case over his head and secure it with a black sash for the oil-sheik look. A burnoose with a hood, or its cousin the djelaba will also serve well for this occasion.

Or, spirit a fez away from your uncle in the El Jebel Shrine.

MUSIC:

Middle Eastern music features such alien instruments as the *tabla* the *dorbakeh* and the *oud,* as well as more common instruments such as the flute and the oboe. Since Turkey sits astride the border of Europe and Asia, the foreign influences are strong and come from both East and West. A belly dancer friend of mine tells me, for instance, that she gyrates to rhythms from Saudi Arabia, Jordan, Tunisia, Morocco, Greece, and Afghanistan—almost anywhere, apparently, from Gibraltar to Djakarta. So you have wide latitude in your choice of records or tapes. The dreamy music from Scheherezade, while written by a Russian composer, will still come across with a Turkish flavor.

If you don't want to spend the money on an album that you might be using for just one night, see if your library has what you want. You can often find foreign music in the social-studies corner of the children's section.

You might want to buy a couple of pairs of finger cymbals to click along to the music. Small bells pinned to your clothing will emit a ring of authenticity when you're dancing, and if you help each other put the bells on it will bring you even closer to making music together.

CHEESE PASTRIES

Serves 2-4

- ¼ lb. feta cheese
- ½ C. cottage cheese
- 3 oz. cream cheese
- 1 egg
- 1 T. flat leaf parsley (cilantro) or 1 tsp. dried parsley
- 2 12" x 16" sheets of filo dough
- ¼ C. melted butter
- Pepper

Blend cheeses together, and add egg beating until smooth. Mix in the parsley and pepper. You will not need salt. Lay out the filo dough, one sheet at a time, keeping the other covered with a damp towel. Spread the entire sheet with melted butter. Then cut across the width of the dough so you have a 2" wide strip 12" long. You will be able to cut 8 strips. Put a heaping tsp. of the cheese mixture at one end of the pastry strip so you can fold one corner over making a small triangular shape. Continue folding that first triangle over from side to side making a multi-layered triangular pastry. Complete process to make 16 pastries. Place them on a buttered baking sheet and bake at 375 degrees for 12 min. or until golden brown. Serve hot.

CUCUMBER AND YOGURT SOUP

Serves 2-4

- 1 medium cucumber
- 2 tsp. lemon juice or white wine vinegar
- 2 C. plain yogurt
- 1 tsp. fresh mint, minced or ½ tsp, dried mint
- 1 tsp. salt
- Dash pepper
- 1 tsp. olive oil
- 1 tsp. green onion, minced
- ½ tsp. dried dill weed

Peel cucumber and split in two lengthwise. Scoop out most of seeds. Grate cucumber coarsely. Using a whisk, beat the yogurt until smooth and add the cucumber, lemon juice, oil, herbs, and blend. Chill. To serve: correct the seasoning and spoon into individual bowls. (Chilling the bowls is a nice touch.) Garnish with a few snips of fresh dill or a sprig of mint.

PILAV

- ½ C. long grain white rice, washed well
- 1½ C. chicken bouillon
- 2 T. butter, MUST BE BUTTER
- 2 T. melted butter
- Salt and freshly ground pepper

Melt the 2 T. butter in heavy saucepan letting it brown just slightly. Remove from heat and add rice, turning to coat each grain. Add bouillon and bring to boil, stirring. Then cover pan and reduce heat as low as possible. Let rice stand until tender, about 20 min. Season and pour on melted butter. Toss to coat.

KILIC SIS (Broiled Skewered Swordfish)

Serves 2

1 lb. swordfish fillets cut in 1" cubes
½ tsp. salt and dash pepper
1 medium onion, sliced and separated into rings
¼ C. fresh lemon juice
¼ C. olive oil
Bay leaves to alternate on skewers with fish cubes

In a glass bowl marinate the fish cubes in the lemon juice, olive oil, salt, pepper, and onion rings. Let sit at room temperature for 2 hours or in refrigerator for 4 or more. Turn cubes occasionally. Put bay leaves in a bowl and cover with boiling water to soften and release flavor. Soak at least an hour. To cook, skewer fish and bay leaves alternately, pressing close together. Broil over charcoal which has some white ash on it, or in a broiler, 3" below heat. Suspend the skewers over a pan in oven broiler so fish doesn't touch bottom of pan. Either way, baste with marinade and rotate to cook all sides evenly. Fish cooks quickly; so 8 to 10 minutes total should be sufficient. To serve: nest on pilav, on warm platter.

SESAME ZUCCHINI

Serves 2-4

1 medium zucchini, cubed
2 T. sesame seeds
2 T. vegetable oil
1 tsp. lemon juice
¼ tsp. dried mint
Salt and pepper

Brown sesame seeds in oil, shaking skillet so they brown lightly. Add zucchini, salt, mint and stir-fry until zucchini is tender, but crisp. Add lemon juice and pepper. To serve: garnish with parsley. Serve hot.

TURKISH SPINACH SALAD

Serves 2-4

½ lb. fresh spinach, washed and well dried
1 tomato cut in wedges
3 green onions, minced
1 small clove garlic, minced
Pinch thyme
3 T. yogurt
1 T. olive oil
1 T. lemon juice
Salt and pepper

Break prepared spinach into a salad bowl. Mix the remaining ingredients except tomato, and let stand for flavors to mingle. If letting stand over 1 hour refrigerate covered. Just before serving toss the spinach with the dressing. To serve: Put in salad bowls or on salad plates and garnish with tomato wedges.

TURKISH DELIGHT

This confection can be made at home, but it is available in tins, and in some specialty markets, fresh. I would not go to the trouble of making it for two people, but here is a recipe so you can make up your own mind.

3 envelopes unflavored gelatin
⅓ C. lemon juice
¾ C. cornstarch
5 tsp. rose water
½ C. coarsely chopped pistachios or walnuts
Confectioner's sugar

Sugar Syrup:
2 C. sugar
¼ C. white corn syrup
1 C. water
Drop food coloring if desired
Boil to 240 degrees on candy thermometer. Remove from heat.

Soften the gelatin in the lemon juice. Mix the cornstarch with ½ C. cold water and add to hot syrup, stirring constantly, then when blended cook until thick. Remove from heat and add gelatin mixture and stir until gelatin is completely dissolved. Add the rose water and the nuts. In an 8" square pan, put a layer of confectioner's sugar and pour candy on top. Let stand for several hours. Sprinkle top with more sugar and cut into squares. Roll edges of squares in sugar. Put in mini cupcake paper liners, if desired. Store air tight. These will keep several weeks. Refrigerate but bring to room temperature to serve.

TURKISH DELIGHT

1½ oz. Wild Turkey Liqueur
3 drops Rose water mixed with 1 T. heavy cream

Float cream on top of liqueur in liqueur glass.

EGGS IZMIR

Serves 2

A scrambled egg concoction from the shores of the Aegean which can be adapted as an almost instant hors d'oeuvre anytime. (This recipe can be doubled or tripled, but beyond that make separate batches.)

3 eggs room temperature
3 tsp. heavy cream
4 tsp. pistachios or pine nuts, chopped
½ tsp. green pepper, minced
Salt and pepper
Butter to fry

Beat eggs lightly with cream and add remaining ingredients. Scramble eggs in butter in "no stick" pan. Cool out and heap in decorative bowl. Garnish with a few chopped pistachios, or if using pine nuts add a bit of paprika. Serve with buttered rounds of dark bread.

COLD SHREDDED CHICKEN WITH WALNUT SAUCE

Serves 2-4

2 chicken breasts, split
1 small onion
1 carrot
2 stalks celery with leaves
Bouquet garni: bay leaf, sprig parsley, 5 peppercorns, 1 whole allspice
Salt and pepper
Water to cover

Poach chicken breasts with vegetables and bouquet garni until meat is tender, about 20-25 min. Remove skin and bones and cool meat. Reserve. Boil chicken stock rapidly to reduce to about 1 ½ C. Refrigerate chicken meat immediately.

Sauce

1½ C. English walnuts, blanched with skins rubbed off as well as possible*
½ C. onion, minced
Reduced chicken stock
3 slices firm white bread torn into chunks
½ tsp. Hungarian paprika
Dash pepper
Parsley, orange slices or preserved kumquats

Put the walnuts, the onions and about half of the chicken broth in a blender and blend 15 sec. at high. Then add the bread, paprika and pepper and blend, adding broth until sauce is consistency of mayonnaise. Chill. To serve, shred chicken and toss with about ¾s of the walnut sauce. Arrange on lettuce leaves if desired, garnish and serve with additional sauce.

*Wearing a veil in old Izmir
Made shopping a bit austere.
But, said lady shopper to vendor,
"Are your nuts very tender?"
He: "When scalded and rubbed, my dear!"

CUCUMBER AND YOGURT SALAD

Serves 2

1 C. plain yogurt
1 large cucumber, peeled and sliced thinly
1 T. onion, minced
3 sprigs fresh basil or ½ tsp. dried basil
1 T. lemon juice or white vinegar
Salt and pepper

If using fresh basil, mince the leaves and add to the yogurt along with the onion, lemon juice or vinegar, salt and pepper. When blended well, add the cucumbers and coat slices well with the yogurt mixture. This is best when chilled overnight.

CHERBAH (Soup)

1 medium onion, chopped finely
2 T. vegetable oil
1 sprig fresh mint, minced or ½ tsp. dry mint
2 medium fresh tomatoes, peeled, chopped
½ green pepper, seeded and chopped
1 small clove garlic, crushed
2 C. beef bouillon
1 egg yolk
½ lemon-juice only
Salt and pepper
Lemon slice garnish

Wilt the onions in oil over low heat so that onions do not color. Add mint and stir until wilted. Add tomatoes, peppers, garlic, salt and pepper. Cover and simmer over low heat about 20 min. or until pepper is tender. Add the beef broth, heat, remove from heat. At this time add the egg yolk which has been beaten with lemon juice, stirring rapidly so egg cooks uniformly in hot soup. Chill. When ready to serve, correct seasonings. Ladle into bowls and garnish with lemon slices and/or mint sprigs.

LADIES' NAVELS

Makes Many

2 C. water
2 C. sugar
1 tsp. rose water

Dough:
1½ C. water
3 T. butter
⅛ tsp. salt
2 C. flour
3 eggs
2 tsp. almond extract
Oil for deep frying
½ C. whipping cream
1 T. sugar
Crystallized rose petals

Combine all in heavy saucepan and bring to boil over moderate heat, stirring to dissolve sugar. Increase heat to high and cook until the syrup reaches a temperature of 220 degrees on a candy thermometer. Cool.

In a heavy 3 qt. saucepan, bring to boil the water, butter and salt. Stir. Pour flour in all at once. Beat with a wooden spoon vigorously until you have a solid dough. Quickly make a well in the center and add eggs one at a time, beating well so dough is smooth.

In deep-fat fryer, heat 4" oil to 360 degrees. Pinch off dough about size of walnut. Dip thumb in almond extract and make deep depression in center of each ball. Fry 5-6 at a time, for about 10-12 min. turning to brown all sides. With tongs remove and plunge each into glaze. Leave in glaze about 4 min. then lift on wire rack to cool. To serve, fill depression with whipped cream, and top with a rose petal.

LADY MEATBALLS*

Serves 2-4

- ½ lb. ground beef or lamb
- ¼ C. onion, chopped finely
- 1 medium size, boiled potato
- 1 egg
- 2 T. pine nuts coarsely chopped
- Salt and pepper
- Butter for sautéing onion

Sauté onion in butter. Mash potato well, then combine all ingredients and blend throughly. Shape into small balls, pressing together firmly. Fry in hot oil until browned on all sides. To serve, use picks. I found that Sharwood's Madras Curry Sauce is delicious with these.

* *A Turk buying spice in Rangoon*
Lured a maiden up to his room.
He took more than her lips
On this spice buying trip
And yearned to come again soon.

YOGURT BARLEY SOUP

Serves 2-4

- 1 T. butter
- 1 medium onion, chopped
- ¼ C. instant barley
- 2 C. rich chicken broth
- 1 C. yogurt
- ½ tsp. dried mint or 1 T. fresh mint
- 1 T. parsley, flat type preferably, chopped
- Salt and pepper

Prepare barley according to directions on package, using chicken broth. Sauté onion in butter. Just before barley is done, add rest of ingredients except yogurt. When barley is done remove from heat and stir in yogurt. Serve immediately sprinkled with a bit of paprika.

SIS KEBABI (Lamb Kabobs)

Serves 2

Marinade:

- ½ C. dry red wine
- 2 T. lemon juice
- 2 T. salad oil
- 1 tsp. oregano leaves, crumbled
- 1 medium onion, sliced
- Salt and pepper

Kabobs:

- 1 lb. lean, boneless lamb in 1½" cubes
- ½ lb. mushrooms
- 1 large green pepper
- 2 medium size, firm tomatoes cut in wedges
- 20 creaming onions parboiled or canned

Combine all the marinade ingredients in glass, stainless steel or plastic container. I find the leakproof, lidded plastic containers excellent for marinating as they can be turned upside down thus rotating the meat in the marinade. Marinate meat for 2 hours at room temperature. Longer in refrigerator.

To assemble: Make skewers of lamb with onions between lamb pieces. Make additional skewers of vegetables, alternating pieces. The vegetables cook faster than the lamb. Use a charcoal fire or your broiler. Suspend skewers over a baking pan so you can rotate them and also catch the drippings. Brush with more marinade while cooking. 8 minutes for pink lamb, 15 min. for well done. To serve, nest on Pilav, see Summer Menu (Avec Argent) this chapter.

SWEET TURKISH RICE

Serves 2-4

½ C. long grain rice, washed in cold water
2 C. water
1 tsp. cinnamon
Dash cloves
1 tsp. lemon rind, grated
½ C. dates, pitted and chopped
½ C. sour cream
½ tsp. vanilla
¼ C. plus 2 T. sugar
Chopped walnuts

Put the 2 T. sugar in the sour cream with the vanilla and set aside. Put the remaining sugar in the water with cinnamon, cloves and lemon rind. Bring to boil and add washed rice. Cover, reduce heat immediately and let barely simmer over lowest heat until rice is done. About 25 minutes. Remove from heat and stir in chopped dates. Let stand a few minutes if serving hot. If serving cold, refrigerate. To serve hot, top with generous dollop of sour cream mixture garnished with nuts. To serve cold, fold in sour cream lightly and top with nuts.

TURKISH COFFEE

Turkish coffee brewing instructions may best be obtained from the merchant where you buy your coffee. He knows best the grind he uses.

In passing, one custom in Turkey was, and may still be, that a potential bridegroom had to promise to keep his bride in coffee as long as she lived. Remember that some night when caffeine keeps you awake.

CINNAMON WINE SOUP

Serves 2-4

1 C. dry red wine
½ stick cinnamon
1 2" strip lemon peel
1 C. water
1 T. plus 1 tsp. cornstarch
2 T. sugar
1 egg yolk, beaten well
Sour cream

Simmer wine with cinnamon and lemon about 8 min. Keep heat low so you do not reduce liquid. Meanwhile using the 1 C. water, blend into the cornstarch. Add cornstarch mixture to the wine mixture stirring contantly, and continue stirring until the mixture thickens. Remove cinnamon and lemon peel, add sugar. Gradually pour about ½ C. of the hot soup into the egg yolk, beating constantly. Do not let the soup boil as you add the egg mixture back into the soup. Soup can be served hot or cold. To serve, garnish with sour cream dusted with nutmeg.

A THOUSAND AND ONE NIGHTS

1 oz. Wild Turkey Liqueur
1 oz. coffee liqueur
1 oz. cream
Blend with ice, sprinkle with nutmeg.

SALAD BOSPORUS

Serves 2

- ½ C. white pea beans (canned) rinsed, drained
- 1 tomato, peeled, seeded, chopped
- 1 small green pepper, seeded and chopped
- ½ C. black olives, chopped
- ½ small red onion, thinly sliced
- 1 T. flat leaf parsley, chopped
- Dressing recipe page 182
- Shredded lettuce

Combine all vegetables except parsley and shredded lettuce. Handle gently. Pour dressing over and fold in carefully. To serve, put a layer of shredded lettuce on serving plate and spoon on salad. Garnish with parsley, and whole olives if desired. Refrigerate if holding.

KAYMAKLI ELMA KOMPOSTOSU (Poached Apples with Whipped Cream)

Serves 4

- 1 C. sugar
- 1 C. water
- 10 Whole cloves
- ½ stick cinnamon
- 4 medium apples, peeled and cored
- Few drops red food coloring
- ½ C. whipping cream
- 2 T. sugar
- Or substitute softened vanilla ice cream

In a medium sized saucepan put the sugar, water, cloves and cinnamon stick. Bring to boil and stir until sugar dissolves. Add coloring if desired. Put apples in side by side. Spoon hot syrup over the tops of apples. Reduce heat and simmer covered about 15 min., basting apples occasionally. Cool in syrup. To serve, place apple in sherbet dish, top with whipped cream and garnish with crystallized rose petal or violet.

CHICKEN WITH PILAV

This is the perfect time to use one of those clay baking devices designed for chicken, if you have one. Otherwise, although the complexion of the dish will be different, use one of the baking bags available at your supermarket. Follow the directions on the package of the baking bag, but in addition put several slices of orange under the chicken inside the bag, or in the clay baker.

- 1 roasting chicken
- 1 orange cut in half and studded with cloves
- Salt and pepper

Rinse and wipe chicken inside and out with paper towel. Put orange halves in cavity. Rub with butter on outside and sprinkle lightly with salt and pepper. Roast according to directions with baking container. Meanwhile prepare pilav.

Elementary English

ELEMENTARY ENGLISH

Summer Menu
(Avec Argent)
Potted Shrimp • Cheese Soup
Leg of Lamb
Asparagus • Barley Casserole
Bibb Lettuce Salad

Summer Menu
(Sans Argent)
Tomato Cheese Croustades
Fish and Chips
Sweet and Sour Carrot,
Onion and Pepper Rings
Lemon Ice Weatherwax

Winter Menu
(Avec Argent)
Onion Cheese Tartlets
Cream of Celery Soup
Roast Beef with Yorkshire Pudding
Parsnips Beurre Noir
Brandied Peaches • Egg Nog Pie

Winter Menu
(Sans Argent)
English Cheese and Crackers
Pease Pottage • Baked Ham
Creamed Potatoes
Brussels Sprouts
Apricot Salad • Muffins
Deep Dish Apple Pie

The English are not renowned for either the extravagance of their passions or the exquisiteness of their cuisine. But first impressions can be misleading. After all, it was an English writer, Henry Fielding who served up that classic account of erotic gluttony—the beggar's banquet enjoyed by the young adventurer Tom Jones and the ravenous Mrs. Waters.

You might remember this scene best from the latter-day movie "Tom Jones", but I prefer the underdone flavor of Fielding's original telling, which leaves more to our imaginations. Let me recount it here, and suggest that the next time you're itching to get decadent—especially if you're an older woman who wants to get it on with a younger man, or you simply want to play out that same fantasy with your mate—then you could certainly do worse than to create your own version of this morsel of 18th century pornography.

Fielding's Tom Jones is an innocent and upstanding lad of 19— "one of the handsomest young fellows in the world"—who is making his way through the countryside toward London in search of his long-lost parents. One afternoon he happens to be standing on a hilltop when he hears the agonized screams of a woman in distress issuing from a woody thicket below, and he hurries to investigate.

He comes upon "a most shocking sight indeed, a woman stripped half naked, under the hands of a ruffian, who had put his garter around her neck and was endeavoring to draw her up to a tree." Tom leaps to the rescue and beats the villain senseless with his trusty walking stick. The woman falls to her knees in gratitude and gushes to her savior, "You look more like an angel than a man in my eye."

What is young Tom to make of this? He can see this woman before him is a woman of some seasoning, and yet when he looks at her now he isn't counting wrinkles—nor are his thoughts quite so angelic. Instead, his wondrous eyes are fixed upon the poor lady's savagely exposed breasts, which are generously formed and extremely white.

Presently, Tom agrees to escort the woman to the nearest town, so that no further disgrace can befall her. For some reason, she refuses Tom's offer to cover herself with his coat, and so they walk to town in single file, the honorable Tom in the lead, his eyes cast straight ahead in order not to be tempted, and the lady in the rear, occasionally stumbling and needing further attention, which Jones gallantly provides.

As soon as they arrive in the town of Upton, they find an inn where the woman can secure a room for the night. Tom hustles her up the stairs to an empty bed chamber, but the innkeeper espies them and protests, "Heyday, where is that beggar wench going?" Tom tries to explain that the woman is not a harlot but in fact the victim of a heinous assault. His story, though, is not convincing, and a rousing fist fight breaks out over the moral issues involved. Eventually, some soldiers come by and identify the woman in question as a Mrs. Waters, the wife of a captain in their regiment. The innkeeper apologizes to Tom Jones for the misunderstanding and supplies him with a gown so that Mrs. Waters can make herself decent.

However, the innkeeper was right in being suspicious. For the author concedes: "Mr. Jones and his ragged companion had certain purposes in their intention which, though tolerated in some Christian countries, connived at in others, and practiced in all, are however as expressly forbidden as murder or any other vice."

Tom can hardly be blamed for this, for he has fallen into the company of a careless woman. Captain Waters' wife, he learn, frequently goes off on these secret maneuvers of her own. A free-spirited soul, "she could feast heartily at the table of love without reflecting that some other already had been or hereafter might be, feasted with the same repast." And so, that evening, the two of them sit down to a banquet. Tom, who is hungry from the day's battles, plunges right in. But, Mrs. Waters has an appetite of another order;

"First, from two lovely blue eyes, whose bright orbs flashed lightning at their discharge, flew forth two pointed ogles; but, happily for our hero, hit only a vast piece of beef which he was then conveying into his plate, and harmless spent their force. The fair warrior perceived their miscarriage, and immediately from her fair bosom drew forth a deadly sigh. A sigh which none could have heard unmoved...so soft, so sweet, so tender, that the insinuating air must have found its subtle way to the heart of our hero, had it not unluckily been driven from his ears by the coarse bubbling of some bottled ale, which at that time he was pouring forth. Many other weapons did she assay; but the god of eating reserved his votary...for as love frequently preserves from the attacks of hunger, so may hunger possibly, in some cases, defend us against love."

The artless Jones goes on stuffing his face and ignoring the lady's enticements. But as soon as his belly is full, the author reports, "his attention to other matters revived," and for dessert "the fair conqueror enjoyed the usual fruits of her victory."

In such a way does the foundling boy, Tom Jones, learn about the happy conspiracy between wickedness and pleasure, and begin an education in the world.

INVITATIONS:

Whether you're renting an orphan to be your Tom Jones for the evening or giving a Shakespearean dinner party or recreating the London of Charles Dickens; whether you're going to dine in Victorian elegance or throw your bones over your shoulder like Henry VIII or simply scarf up fish-and-chips off paper plates; whether you're having the chimneysweep over for a breakfast of kippered herring and hot cross buns or the neighbor ladies over for crumpets and tea or Alistair Cooke over to get drunk on plum pudding and mead; whether you're going to take an after-dinner stroll on a nearby misty moor or stay home and read Chaucer and play darts—whatever your taste in things British, you can phrase your invitation in Old English script.

Pick up some plain antique-white note paper at a stationery shop and a sheet or two of Old English letters at an art or drafting supply store. For imitating an old broadside, The Formatt line of lettering has a typeface called Stonehenge that would suit the occasion perfectly. If your note paper is of good quality—part rag, that is—try crumbling it and dipping it in strong tea or coffee; the wrinkles will take the color more deeply and give an aged appearance to the invitation. Then burn the edges of the paper over a candle flame and flick off the charred pieces. Now, once you affix the lettering, your invitation will resemble a timeworn Publick Notice. Further authenticity can be lent by attaching a notary seal, with perhaps a couple snips of colored ribbon slipped under it, and by closing the envelope with sealing wax and an appropriate seal. These items can generally be found at stationery and office supply stores.

SCENTS:

I'd recommend buying several bars of Old English lavendar soap, and unwrapping them, then tucking them away under sofa cushions, behind the draperies, and behind the books on the bookshelf. This is an exceedingly practical way to keep the house smelling fresh, because you can leave the bars hidden long after the party and unearth them one by one as you need to use them.

Pomander balls and potpourri jars with high proportions of lavendar, which can be prepared at home, are also good sources of fragrance for an English dinner.

TABLE SETTINGS:

If you're a single person just starting to get things together for entertaining, it's wise to begin frequenting antique shops and second hand stores and looking for old china. It's possible today, what with the so-called matching services available, to purchase a set of china one piece at a time, as you can afford it. Such periodicals as THE ANTIQUE TRADER, SPINNING WHEEL, YANKEE and EARLY AMERICAN LIFE are founts of information about where you can buy, sell and trade old china and silver. Flea markets and auctions are always good places to snoop around, and if you don't find anything to buy it's still an interesting way to kill a slow week-end afternoon. The big antique shows can get pretty expensive, but the dealers are usually helpful and informative if they are aware that you're a beginning collector.

With so many possible sources these days, acquiring a china table service has become a mix-and-match affair, much like putting a wardrobe together. A good place to start looking is at British imports for England has been a prolific producer of tableware for centuries. Her factories produce everything from soft paste pottery through ironstone to bone china. Nowadays, some of the prestigious old potteries are merging. They are preserving identities, however, and for example, one can find Adams in the Wedgwood fold. Names to look for are: Aynsley, Royal Doulton, Royal Worcester, Wedgwood and Spode...to name but a few.

For a winter's evening, a small table set in front of a blazing fire would be a nice touch. If you want to do it the way the English do, turn off your central heating and discover alternate methods of keeping warm around the hearth. If you're limited to using snack trays for entertaining, then invest in some nice wooden ones and choose the mats as carefully as you choose other table linens.

As a nation of gardners, England appreciates tasteful floral arrangements. In the winter when fresh flowers are available only from the florists, it might be easier on your budget to fashion a centerpiece out of dried flowers or to use a combination of fresh greens, baby's breath and silk violets—anything except plastic flowers, God forbid. Of course, the larger the table the larger the arrangement should be. For a small and simple table, two roses floating in a rose bowl would be chummy. For snack tables, try a single rose with some fern in a tiny vase on each tray. In spring or summer, you can set out small pots of violets or petunias which could later be planted outdoors. If you're setting a bare wooden table for a period banquet, the centerpiece can be fruits and English cheeses and candles in heavy metal candlesticks.

Armetale makes good reproductions of Old English pewter mugs and serving plates and other dinnerware. Of the several different ways to fold napkins, the Bishop's Mitre would be most appropriate for an English dinner. (Check with your bookstore or librarian for books on how-to-fold napkins.) Silver napkin rings, if you have them, are perfect for those to the manner born. If you have plain wooden napkin rings instead, you can give them a personal touch by adhering on monograms from the leftover letters in your Old English lettering set. You can make "his" and "hers" using appropriate initials, and if the relationship doesn't endure, a razor blade will remove the passé initials.

When using candles, which are almost a necessity for romantic dining, take care when setting a small table. Votive candles in low, broad-based holders are safest, or you can mass your candles on a side table or atop the mantel. When you're using a linen or lace tablecloth for a formal dinner, choose one of the several ways of keeping wax from dripping on the fabric, such as dripless candles, wick protectors like they have in churches or those little glass candlestick fittings called bobeches.

CLOTHING:

For the Tom Jones look, a gentleman might wear an open-necked shirt ruffled down the front with plain trousers of black or some other dark color, For the Mrs. Waters' look, a woman has two choices—"before" and "after". The "before" look (as first glimpsed by the wide-eyed Tom in the woody thicket) would require milady to rip a blouse asunder and leave it hanging in shreds from her waist. The "after" look, only slightly more modest, would call for the type of low-cut gown with a fitted weskit that causes the breasts to spill forth like melons from a cornucopia.

Library reference sections have a lot of information about period costumes that can help considerably in choosing your attire for any of the dinners in this book.

If you're more conservative and it's wintertime, go for tweeds and woolens of all sorts and a Sherlock Holmes pipe (without the opium) and a shot of Scotch whiskey.

MUSIC:

I would imagine Tom Jones and Mrs. Waters listening to the distant strains of chamber music, or a lute being played by a beggar outside the window. Look through your collection of classical music and find something delicate, to counterpoint the vulgarity of your feast.

For another sort of English dinner party, you could do worse than to put on a Beatles tape at low volume. Nostalgia can be a bloody good aphrodisiac.

ENGLISH CHEESE AND CRACKERS

I am going to suggest some English cheese for you to try. A good cheese shop or specialty food store that has bulk cheese will undoubtly let you taste before you buy. I'd suggest trying imported Cheddar, Caerphilly, Cheshire and Stilton. You might find a sage cheese in a city store; so ask about that too. (A couple of small fresh sage leaves, minced with a few stems of chives added to a package of cream cheese is delightful, too.)

When you've decided on the cheeses that you like, get small wedges of each. There is a variety of imported English crackers to accompany cheese. A few names you'll find are: Carr's, Fortt's, Jacob's, and Peek and Frean's.

Stilton is traditionally served after the meal with Port and perhaps fruit, but I feel, that like art, if you know what you like, partake of it as you choose. There is something about a good sherry, cheese and crackers on a winter's eve in front of a fire that cheers me. You may find that it does the same for you.

There is a sherry for every budget and taste. Your local wine merchant will probably be happy to assist you in a choice. By the way, Sherry is an English corruption of Jerez, the town in Spain where the wine is made. It's one of those little sidelights in history that you might want to pursue.

POTTED SHRIMP

Serves 2-4

1 C. tiny, cooked shrimp
½ C. butter, melted
¼ tsp. mace
⅛ tsp. paprika
Dash nutmeg
½ tsp. salt
⅛ tsp. allspice, ground

Melt butter in a small heavy saucepan over low heat. Let it foam and remove most of foam and let butter rest off heat for a moment or two, then decant, leaving the milky solids in bottom of pan. Remove the residue from pan and return the melted butter and hold. Measure spices and have ready. Put butter back on heat and brown lightly. Immediately remove and stir in spices. Stir in shrimp. Pack shrimp in small crock such as cheese comes in, then cover with melted butter. Refrigerate overnight. Serve with toast or crackers.

CHEESE SOUP

Serves 2-4

3 strips bacon, cooked crisp
2 T. green onions, minced
2 T. bacon grease
1 T. flour
¼ lb. cheddar cheese, shredded
Dash Tabasco
1 C. milk
Salt and pepper
Red wine if desired

Cook bacon without burning the fat until bacon is crisp. Reserve. Remove all but 2 T. fat in pan or add butter enough to make 2 T. Sauté the onions in the fat over low heat. Do not let brown. Add the flour and blend, then add milk gradually while stirring constantly. Remove from heat to blend completely. Return to stove and add cheese a bit at a time, stirring constantly while melting. Add Tabasco, salt and pepper. Add wine or more milk to thin to proper consistency. Garnish with crumbled bacon. Serve with crackers.

LEG OF LAMB

Serves 4

1 leg of lamb (spring lamb legs will weigh around 6 lbs.)
1-2 cloves garlic
Rosemary
Salt and pepper

Remove the papery outer covering from the lamb, and excess fat, but be sure to leave a layer to baste the meat as it roasts. Rub with cut cloves of garlic, salt, pepper and rosemary. Slivers of garlic can be inserted in cuts in the meat if desired. Heat oven to 450 degrees. Put roast fat side up on a rack in uncovered pan. Roast at 450 degrees for 10 min. Then reduce heat to 350 degrees and cook 30 min. per pound. Less for slightly pink meat. Serve on heated platter.

ASPARAGUS

Serves 2-4

- 1 lb. bundle asparagus
- Butter
- Lemon juice if desired
- Salt and pepper

Snap woody ends from stalks, making even lengths. Steam or cook in an asparagus cooker until tender. Drain and arrange in serving bowl. Garnish with lemon wedges. If you have any leftover, serve cold with vinaigrette dressing.

BARLEY CASSEROLE

Serves 2-4

- ¼ C. green onion, chopped
- 6 T. butter
- ⅓ C. pearl barley
- 1 C. chicken broth
- ¾ C. fresh mushrooms, sliced
- Slivered almonds, toasted

Sauté onions in half the butter, add barley and brown lightly. Put in casserole with 1 C. chicken broth. Cover and bake 30 min. at 350 degrees, add mushrooms which have been sautéed in the other half of the butter, and more broth if necessary. Bake until barley is tender. Top with almonds.

BIBB LETTUCE WITH LEMON MAYONNAISE

- 1 head Bibb lettuce, washed well, and dried
- 1 recipe Lemon Mayonnaise

Break clean lettuce into bite sized pieces. Arrange in bowl and dress just before serving.

LEMON MAYONNAISE

- 2 egg yolks
- 1 tsp. salt
- ½ tsp. dry mustard
- 2 medium size green onions, chopped
- 1 T. zest from lemon skin (grated skin)
- ¼ C. lemon juice
- 4 T. salad oil
- Pinch dill weed
- ¾ C. salad oil

Blend together for about 30 seconds: 2 egg yolks, the salt, mustard, onion, lemon zest, lemon juice, dill weed and 4 T. salad oil. Remove center part of lid of blender, and with blender on low, pour in a steady stream the remaining oil. If this or any other mayonnaise should curdle, pour mayonnaise out of blender and put in another egg yolk. Add ¼ C. of the curdled mayonnaise and blend briefly, then add remainder of curdled mayonnaise in a steady stream.

This mayonnaise recipe makes more than you need for the above salad, but it will keep refrigerated. It is simply delicious on cold poached salmon and other fish, and makes a memorable tuna salad.

TRIFLE

This dessert has as many versions as there are cooks. It was concocted to use up stale sponge cake, and although it has transcended that purpose, it is still useful. One can use sponge cake such as one buys for shortcakes, or pound cake slices, or ladyfingers. There are options as to the custard filling also. Most recipes for the cream make large quantities; so you'll have to decide what route you want to take if you are cooking for two. I'll take you from the ridiculous to the sublime and let you choose which fits your situation best.

First: The basic ingredients are:

Sponge cake, pound cake or lady fingers
Pastry cream, or vanilla pudding
Sherry, Port, Madiera or other liqueur
Raspberry, apricot, peach or other jam
Whipped cream
Crystalized violets, rose petals, or other decorations

The simplest way for two would be to buy a package of lady fingers, two individual size cans of vanilla pudding, jam of your choice, wine or liqueur of your choice, ready made whipped topping or whipping cream.

To assemble: choose 4 ladyfingers for each dish of trifle. Separate them and spread two with jam, place these two in the bottom of a dessert dish, spoon a little liqueur over them. Spoon on half of the pudding. Repeat this process one more time, then top with whipped cream and garnish. Let stand covered in the refrigerator until well chilled and the flavors are blended. If using crystallized violets, you may want to wait until just before serving to garnish as they will soften and fade into the cream.

To make a larger, simplified version, I have found that Bird's imported pastry cream mix makes a fine filling. Use the same directions for the assembly, except make only one layer of sponge cake in the bottom and along the sides of the dessert bowl.

My grandmother Dibble always made her own pastry cream, but one of the best flavor combinations that I remember is raspberry jam with Creme de Cassis as the liqueur. Do experiment with flavor combinations of your own. How about apricot jam and Amaretto?

TOMATO CHEESE CROUSTADES

Serves 4

8 slices thin white bread, with crusts trimmed
Butter for greasing pan
1 medium tomato, seeded and chopped finely
2 green onions, minced
½ C. cheddar cheese, cubed
½ tsp. fresh basil, or ½ tsp. dry basil, minced
½ tsp. celery seed, ground
Salt and pepper
¼" bits butter

Use a muffin tin that has 8 cups. Butter the sides of each cup and fit the bread into the cups with the four corners sticking up in points. Put in 400 degree oven for about 8 min. Don't worry if they aren't brown as they need to bake again. Remove shells from oven and let dry in tins. Meanwhile, mix filling. Sauté onions lightly in butter left over from buttering tins. Cool. Mix tomatoes, onions, cheese, basil and celery seed. Season with salt and pepper. Spoon into croustades. Dot with butter bits. To serve, bake in 400 degree oven about 10 min.

SWEET AND SOUR CARROTS WITH ONIONS AND PEPPERS

1 8 oz. can tomato sauce
½ C. sugar
½ C. salad oil
½ C. cider vinegar
½ tsp. salt
¼ tsp. Lawry's seasoned pepper
¼ tsp. celery seed, ground
½ tsp. dry mustard
Dash Worcestershire
1 lb. carrots
1 large sweet onion
1 large green pepper

Prepare vegetables by cleaning, then scrape carrots and slice in ¾" diagonal slices. Peel and slice onion into ¼" slices, and slice pepper into ¼" strips. Make marinade from the other ingredients and add the onions and peppers. Cook the carrots until just barely tender and add them to the rest of the vegetables. Let stand in refrigerator overnight. This keeps a couple of weeks or so, and more vegetables may be added from time to time. Serve cold in relish dish.

SOCIAL NOTE: A guest who overstayed his welcome in early England was given the "cold shoulder". In this instance, it was literally a cold shoulder for in those days, meat was spit roasted, and it took a long time for a large shoulder roast to cook all the way through. The part next to the bone was usually underdone and gamey; so that piece was given to the unwanted guest.

LEMON ICE WEATHERWAX

2 eggs
½ C. sugar
¼ C. lemon juice
½ C. corn syrup
1 C. evaporated milk
1 tsp. lemon rind
Pinch salt

Beat eggs until thick and lemon colored. This is best done with an electric mixer as it takes several minutes. Add sugar gradually, beating until custardy. Add the rest of the ingredients and pour into freezing tray. Freeze until partially set, then turn into bowl and beat again at low speed until creamy. Freeze again. At this point, I usually put into individual white porcelain souffle molds. Cover when refreezing. When ready to serve, garnish with whipped cream and crystallized violets or other garnish.

Lemon juice is needed to "cook" the eggs in this recipe, but I cut down on the amount of lemon juice and using piña colada drink mix came up with a nice variation.

FISH AND CHIPS

Serves 2

1 lb. firm, white fish fillets...sole, hake, flounder, cod, etc.
1 12 oz. can flat beer
1¼ C. sifted flour
2 tsp. salt
2 tsp. baking powder
2-3 dashes Tabasco
Oil for frying

2 medium baking potatoes, cut in ½" by ½" by 3" strips or in ½" slices

Pour beer into bowl 2 hrs. before mixing. Batter should rest 2 hrs. before using (at least) so start batter early. Sift dry ingredients into bowl. Make a well in the center. Pour in beer and a couple dashes of Tabasco. Whisk to a smooth batter. Cover and let stand at room temperature for at least 2 hrs. Whisk just before using. Dredge the fish lightly in flour before dipping in batter. Let excess drip off into bowl.

Put 4 to 5" of oil in a deep fryer. Heat to 375 degrees. Batter fried fish puffs up so don't crowd. One or two pieces at a time will be enough. Have a low, flat pan lined with paper towels ready to drain and hold fish. Hold in oven at about 275 degrees while frying chips. Do not use basket for fish as fish will go to the bottom of the fryer then rise. Brown lightly on one side then the other before removing to holding pan.

Fry this amount of potatoes in 4 or 5 batches, in a basket, separating with a wooden fork. Hold with fish until all are done.

If you are a purist, serve fish and chips with malt vinegar in a newspaper cone.

ONION CHEESE PYES

Serves 4

1 T. butter
3 T. green onions, finely chopped
¾ C. Swiss cheese cut in small cubes
2 eggs
¾ C. cream or evaporated milk
Tabasco sauce
Worcestershire sauce
Salt and pepper
Pie crust dough

Using pie crust recipe from page 28, line 8 tartlet tins or muffin cups. Set aside. In a small skillet, melt butter and sauté onions until transparent but not brown. Cool the onions and mix with the cubes of cheese. Meanwhile beat the eggs and milk together lightly and add the seasonings. Divide the cheese mixture among the tarts and spoon the egg mixture over each. Dot each with butter then bake at 350 degrees for 20-25 min. or until brown and bubbly.

CREAM OF CELERY SOUP

Serves 2-4

4 outside stalks celery with leaves, washed and strings removed, chopped
1 C. chicken bouillon
1 T. butter
1 T. flour
½ C. cream or evaporated milk
Salt and pepper
Leaves from heart of celery, chopped for garnish

Put the prepared celery in the chicken bouillon and simmer until celery is very tender. Reserve. In a small saucepan, melt the butter, and blend in the flour. Remove from heat. Pour some of the cooking broth from the celery into the butter-flour mixture and blend thoroughly, then combine the two mixtures. Put over low heat and cook while stirring constantly while it is thickening. Add the cream, salt and pepper and stir to combine. Continue to cook over low heat, stirring until the flour is completely cooked. Transfer to blender and blend smooth. Put back on heat. Add more cream if necessary. To serve, ladle into bowls and garnish.

PARSNIPS WITH BROWNED BUTTER

Serves 2-4

2-3 parsnips, peeled, shredded on medium to large grater or julienned
2 T. butter, browned
Pinch sugar
Pinch onion flakes
Salt and pepper

Either cook parsnips immediately or hold in water acidulated with a little lemon juice. Put drained parsnips in boiling water, add the sugar and onion and simmer until barely tender. They will cook quickly cut in this manner. Meanwhile brown butter, but do not burn. Add drained parsnips to butter and season with salt and pepper.

ROAST BEEF WITH YORKSHIRE PUDDING

- 1 small rolled rib roast
- Salt and pepper
- 1 egg
- ½ C. flour
- ½ C. milk
- 2 T. beef drippings
- Salt and pepper to taste

It is difficult to cook a roast for two but better a rolled than a standing rib. I follow my grandmother's method for roasting: put meat in a very hot oven (450 degrees) for the first 12-15 min. of roasting time. Then reduce heat to 325 degrees. It takes at least 15 min. to pre-heat most ovens to 450 degrees, and I think this is important for sealing in the juices. Use a meat thermometer to achieve the proper degree of doneness. Rare meat -130-140 degrees, Med.-150-160, and well-done (God forbid) 160-170. If you do not have a meat thermometer, allow 12 minutes per pound for rare and 15 min. per pound for well. Remove from oven when done, and hold on a heated platter covered loosely with foil.

Meanwhile, have pudding mixture ready. In blender jar, put 1 egg, flour, milk, and salt. Blend a few seconds, then scrape down jar and blend a bit more. Let the batter rest about 1 hour. To bake, take 2 T. drippings and put them in a baking pan. (When I do a lot, I just use the pan I roasted the meat in, but for two to four people, an 8 by 8 by 2" pan will do.) Put the baking pan on the heat until drippings sputter. Then blend batter briefly and pour into drippings. Bake at 400 degrees for 15 min, then reduce to 375 degrees and bake 15 min. more. Pudding should puff over edge of pan and be golden brown. To serve, take puffed pudding to the table, then cut with serrated knife and lift with spatula.

BRANDIED PEACHES

Serves 2-4

- 4-6 peach halves
- 3 T. brown sugar
- 3 T. butter
- Dash cinnamon
- ¼ C. brandy

Cream sugar, butter and cinnamon together thoroughly. Spread cut side of peach with mixture. Put spread side up in flameproof casserole. Put in broiler 5-6" from heat. Watch carefully until bubbly. Remove from broiler. Flame with brandy.

BAKED HAM

1	3 lb. canned ham, or a cut ham weighing 3 to 4 lbs.
1	tsp. dry mustard
½	tsp. ground cloves
¼	C. brown sugar, honey, preserves or marmalade

If you are entertaining more than two or have plans for left-over ham, do buy a bigger more economical piece, and increase the glaze accordingly. Otherwise, make glaze from mustard, cloves, sugar or honey. (I always seem to have a dab of apricot preserves or orange marmalade in the refrigerator; so I put all the ingredients for the glaze in the jar and blend them well. This not only uses up the leftovers to a good advantage, but is very tasty as well.) To serve a fully cooked ham hot, you need only to heat it through. An attractive way to do this is to score the top of the ham in a diagonal pattern. Put ham in a 350 degree oven for about 20 minutes so the scored area will open up slightly, then glaze will penetrate better. Remove from oven at the end of this 20 min. period. Spread on glaze, return to oven and bake until glaze browns nicely. 15 to 20 min. more. Serve hot or cold.

EGG NOG PIE

3	eggs, separated
⅓	C. sugar
1	envelope gelatin, softened in ¼ C. water
1	C. milk, heated
1	C. whipping cream, whipped
2	T. rum
	Additional whipped cream for garnish
	Nutmeg
	Pie crust/crusts

(See note below) Put egg yolks and sugar in top of double boiler over simmering water and beat with electric beater until thick and pale in color. Stir in gelatin mixture and cup of hot milk. Cook over boiling water, stirring constantly until mixture is smooth. Fill a large bowl almost full of ice. Set top of double boiler containing the custard, into the ice. Stir until custard begins to set. Beat egg whites until stiff, and fold into chilled custard. Next fold in whipped cream and rum. Turn mixture into pie shell/shells. Decorate with additional whipped cream and nutmeg.

This amount of filling will fill two packaged crumb crusts such as Keebler's or Johnston's. Make two, freeze one for later.

BRUSSELS SPROUTS

If there is a national vegetable in Britain, it's Brussels sprouts. Cook them simply, such as steaming, then dress them with salt and butter.

APRICOT SALAD

1 pkg. peach or lemon gelatin, dissolved in 1 C. boiling water plus juice from apricots and water to make 1 C.
1 small can apricot halves
1 3 oz. pkg. cream cheese
¼ C. pecans, chopped

Put gelatin mixture in refrigerator to firm up. Meanwhile, blend nuts into cream cheese, then form into 1" dia. balls. Place between apricot halves. Reserve. When gelatin is slightly thickened, spoon into individual molds until half full. Put in one apricot and complete filling if necessary. Return to refrigerator and set. To serve, unmold on lettuce leaf, and serve with mayonnaise.

DEEP DISH APPLE PIE

English apple pie is a one crust pie. My grandmother used to bake hers in an oval baking dish about 2" deep, and served it warm with Devon cream. In those days she could get unpasteurized cream and put it on the back of her range to work its magic. I've used sour cream mixed with a bit of sugar and vanilla. It's not the same, but it's definitely not bad!

1 pie crust for top, see crust recipe page 32
1-2 lbs. tart cooking apples
Sugar
Cinnamon
Butter
Pinch Salt

Choose a baking dish about 1½ " deep, with a rim that will accommodate a crust around the rim if possible. A Pyrex pie plate will do. Peel and core apples and cut into slices. Butter dish and fill with apples, mounding in center. Sprinkle with sugar depending on tartness of apples...at least 4-5 tablespoons. Sprinkle on about 1 tsp. cinnamon. Dot with butter. Roll crust to fit pan with enough left to crimp the edges. Bake at 450 degrees for 10 min. Then at 350 degrees for 25-30 min. longer until apples are tender. Serve warm with cream.

CREAMED POTATOES

2 medium potatoes peeled and cut in quarters
1 tsp. minced onion
Salt and pepper
1 T. butter
1 T. flour
1 C. evaporated milk
Cheese optional
Dash Worcestershire
Salt and pepper

Simmer potatoes and onion until tender but not mushy. Meanwhile prepare sauce by melting butter in a small pan and stirring in the flour. Add milk bit by bit stirring constantly. Season with Worcestershire, salt and pepper. Add a bit of shredded Cheddar cheese if desired. Cook over low heat until sauce is thickened and has lost its "raw" taste. Combine with cooked potatoes.

FAINTLY FRENCH

FAINTLY FRENCH

Summer Menu
(Avec Argent)
Mushroom Tarts
Jellied Consommé with Caviar
Sole Duglère • Asparagus
Boiled New Potatoes
Crêpes Suzette

Summer Menu
(Sans Argent)
Chicken Liver Pate
Iced Cream of Onion Soup
Salad Nicoise • French Bread
Oranges Riviera

Winter Menu
(Avec Argent)
Escargots Bourguignonne
Cream of Broccoli Soup
Sautéed Tournedos
Potatoes Anna
Tomatoes Stuffed with
Artichoke Salad
French Bread • Peach Melba

Winter Menu
(Sans Argent)
Anchoyade • Crème de Crécy
Carbonnades Monteynard
Green Salad • French Bread
Flambéed Apples

That marvelous landscape of my dream—
Which no eye knows or ever will—
At moments, wide awake, I seem
To grasp, and it excites me still.
"Les Fleur du Mal" (Baudelaire)
Edna St. Vincent Millay translation

So, when I was young, I dreamed of Paris, of France, and of being like the French.

I was first smitten, as I recall, when I went to Girl Scout camp. The counselors taught us the French words of "Frere Jacques", and then later on, in the tent, the older Girl Scouts taught me yet another set of lyrics, even more exotic: "In the southern part of France, where the women wear no pants, and the men go 'round, with their britches hanging down..."

Was it true: How could I get to this place..."France"?

In high school, I had a French boyfriend—or a French pen pal, at least. His penmanship was captivating, like calligraphy, and he wrote his letter on mauve stationery and sealed them in envelopes that were lined with the most delicate tissue paper. However, the sentiments that he expressed—such as, *"I have a brown hair"*—lacked a certain sophistication.

But then I discovered Baudelaire, and he became my private muse—the most mischievous pen pal that a 17-year-old girl could ever have.

Charles wrote to me:

Think, would it not be
Sweet to live with me
All alone, my child, my love?—
Sleep together, share
All things, in that fair
Country you remind me of?
Charming in the dawn
There, the half-withdrawn
Drenched, mysterious sun appears
In the curdled skies,
Treacherous as your eyes
Shining from behind their tears.
Edna St. Vincent Millay Translation

Even more scandalously, Charles sometimes wrote *about* me:

> *Relaxed among the pillows, she looked down at me*
> *And let herself be gazed upon at leisure—as if*
> *Lulled by my wordless adoration, like the sea*
> *Washing perpetually about the foot of a cliff.*
>
> *Slowly, regarding me like a trained leopardess,*
> *She slouched into successive poses...*
> *The whole lithe harmony of loins, hips, buttocks, thighs,*
> *Tawny and sleek, and undulant as the neck of a swan,*
> *Began to move hypnotically before my eyes...*
>
> *Edna St. Vincent Millay Translation*

Enough! Enough! I plotted my escape—as soon as I "grew up", to Gay Paree.

As a freshman in college, while the other girls were listening to Sinatra, I was mooning over the crooning of Jean Sablon. As an aide in the Romance Languages Department, I translated the "Jabberwocky" into French. When I went out on dates I wore Chanel #5. I fell in love with Charles Boyer. I learned in an academic sense about "French Ticklers" and in a more direct sense about French kissing. And of course, I read Baudelaire's "Les Fleur du Mal" (Flowers of Evil) in the original tongue, so to speak.

Finally, at the age of 24, I made my first pilgrimage to Paris. And what a disappointment! I'd imagined that everybody along the Champs Elysees would be breaking into song and dance like Maurice Chevalier himself, but they weren't even smiling! The older women were dour, officious and condescending. The younger women were so chic that I felt frumpy in comparison, straight off the boat from Iowa.

Then there were the men. Sure enough, they all sounded like Charles Boyer, and they were perfectly charming when kissing young ladies' hands, nibbling ear lobes, pinching derrieres, and uttering *bon mots*. But it was my experience (not an in-depth survey, as it turned out) that these initial flourishes were little more than persiflage meant to obscure some rather serious inadequacies that arose (or failed to arise) later on.

I also learned that April in Paris was not what Chevalier, or that airline posters, had promised. April in Paris is usually cold, rainy and dismal. I came to understand that the most rapturous visions of Paris in the springtime are beheld by people who have never been there, and in fact Chevalier expressed this truth most succinctly when he sang: "April in Paris...it's a feeling..." A feeling yes, but not always so enchanting in the material plane.

Over the years, however, I've returned to France many times, both in body and spirit, and my original disappointment has mellowed, especially as I've ventured out of Paris and into the provinces. Particularly, I have to admit, I sense an ambience and kinship with the people of the southern coast of France (where the women wear no pants?).

Consequently, when I think of having a dinner party with a French theme—when I close my eyes and try to see myself there—I never end up standing in the April rain on some back street in Montmartre wondering how to get back to the hotel, but instead I always picture myself sitting at a small cafe somewhere along the Riviera, watching the sun go down and sipping Armagnac from Condom.

Especially if it's wintertime, you might want to do the same.

Many of us have been to Hawaiian luaus or Mexican theme parties, but why not combine the suggestive climate of the Riviera with the superb cuisine of France so that you can jet away from the midwinter blahs in real elegance?

If you like large gatherings, make it a casino party. If you prefer intimacy, make it a beach party around a hot tub. Put travel posters on the walls, plug in the sun lamp, get out your bikini, and make your own waves. In the summertime, make it a pool party.

The French riviera stretches from Menton on the Italian border to St. Tropez, a fairly short strip of coastline that is protected from chilly north winds by the Maritime Alps. The resorts along the road from Nice—at Cap Ferrat, Cap D'Antibes, Juan-les-Pins—are terraced with beautiful flowers, the beaches at Cannes are terraced with beautiful bodies, and the casinos are always spinning with excitement—in my mind, at least.

This was the playground of America's exiled literati in the 1920s. The Fitzgeralds and Hemingway, Gertrude and Alice B (a decadent group if ever there was one), all of them had digs on the riviera. This was also where the Impressionist painters flocked to capture the azure light: Picasso, Matisse, Braque, Chagall, Miro.

It's up to you to decide which era best expresses your mood; which period in past or future history you were meant to join for an evening. Perhaps you and your partner always fancied yourselves as the lost soulmates of Scott and Zelda themselves. Perhaps you see yourselves as Bardot and Vadim. Perhaps you're attracted to the topless bunch, or the bottomless void. Perhaps you know a poetic young spirit, a Baudelaire, who'd like to come along for the ride.

Perhaps some day I'll see you in one of these disguises along the Riviera, strolling the narrow surf-line between certainty and make-believe.

INVITATIONS:

If your budget allows, buy a French cologne for either a lady or a gentleman and send it along with a note proposing, "I'd be delighted if you'd wear this to a small dinner party..."

A much cheaper invitation can be fashioned this way: Go to the library and find a bilingual edition of my old standby, "Les Fleur du Mal", and paraphrase the poem of your choice in French, and send it along with a note explaining that it means, "Please be my guest for dinner along the Cote d'Azur..."

An invitation can be sent on a postcard sized reproduction of an Impressionist painting, such as can be found at art-museum shops. If your town doesn't have a museum, you can write to one asking for a catalogue or list of available Impressionist prints (and enclosing a self-addressed stamped envelope will help the budget-bound museums). If you know your prospective guest extremely well or you're simply very daring, you might send your invitation along with one of the French pleasure devices that can be purchases at adult bookstores. These items are also selling well, I understand, at the sexually oriented home parties (sometimes called F---erware parties.)

SCENTS:

The region around Grasse, France—just a few miles inland from the Riviera—is the world's greatest supplier of perfume. In the heat of summer, a traveler can smell the fields of roses and jasmines and lavendar from miles away. Floral essences from this region are available here in the States and can be used to scent a room by putting a few drops onto an oil ring that sits atop a light bulb. It's best to experiment with this method ahead of time, because it's easy to overpower a small space and leave it smelling like a cheap bordello. It might be fragrance enough to simply buy some fresh flowers of the Grasse* variety and light a few scented candles.

**A perfume maker name Vasse*
Loved a Paris "putain", alas,
But by clever endeavor
He convinced her forever
To retire her asse to Grasse.

TABLE SETTINGS:

If you were to buy your tablewear from one of the boutiques along the Riviera, you could blow your entire annual income in one afternoon. For example, Haviland china, in the "Monceau" pattern, was selling in the U.S. at last report for $175 for a five-piece place setting. Bernardaud patterns cost $100 and more per setting, and some from A. Raynaud et Cie are priced at a sweet $250. Fine crystal from Lalique and St. Louis and Baccarat is equally dear, with wine glasses approaching $100 apiece and goblets even more. The French don't export sterling silver, but Cristofle silverplate can be had for a mere $150 for a five-piece place setting. In little *ateliers* along the Riviera one can find hand-appliqued and embroidered tablecloths for $1,000 and up, or hand-made silk flowers at $50 each.

Obviously, most of us can't afford to get much more than a TV tray at those prices. But, as I've mentioned in another chapter, you can buy fine china or crystal one piece at a time through matching services, which frequently advertise in home-furnishing magazines. You might start by looking through books at the library (in the antiques section) for pictures of patterns that you'd like to collect. Some relatively easy-to-find china patterns in Haviland that you might want to consider are "Ranson", "Alsace", "Clover", and "Autumn Leaf". Antique dealers can help you get started, too. Some plain and gold-bordered china patterns can even be mixed to create a really distinctive table.

In crystal, a line called Cristal d'Arques is much more reasonably priced than Lalique and Baccarat. But by all means search out inexpensive copies of any of these imports. Keep your crystal spot free and never put lead crystal (cut glass) in the dishwasher as the glass tends to fracture on the cut lines. Shiny crystal creates a wonderful effect in candlelight.

Many American stores sell handsome French porcelain cookware by Apilco and Pillivuyt. Some specialty shops have the "Sinceny" or "Nemours" patterns by Longchamps, either of which would set a provincial table. Antique Quimper might be too expensive, but a few pieces of this decorated faience from Brittany would make your table exquisitely French.

For an elegant table, try folding your napkins into fleur-de-lis (See your book dealer or librarian for books on napkin folding.) An arrangement of anemones, baby's breath, roses, carnations, lilies of the valley, or other flowers would be a perfect compliment for a formal table. Either silver or crystal candelabra would complete the centerpiece.

A less formal, typically French provincial setting would start with a plain wooden table, pottery dinnerware, simple glassware, and individual baking or au gratin dishes such as the Apilco or Pillivuyt mentioned above. A clay pot of live flowers, or flowers and herbs, could serve as the centerpiece, and the contents could later be planted outside. Coarsely woven napkins would be suitable for a provincial arrangement, with a matching runner down the center of the table. (I don't think of the Riviera as being "provincial", but when France was divided into provinces, it was known as Provence, from which comes the culinary term à la Provençal.)

As a final suggestion for table settings, let me mention an idea that could be adapted for any of the dinners in this book. Buy some 11-by-14 inch picture frames from Woolco or K-Mart—the kind of flat chromium frames that are used in art galleries—and place reproductions of Impressionist paintings under the glass. Voila! You have attractive place mats that are easy to clean, and you can even use them as lap trays. Some stores carry double-faced art frames so that you could put a different scene on each side, making the place mat reversible. As a variation, glaze the reproduction onto pieces of eighth-inch-thick hardboard by the découpage process. These are great for summer patio parties, especially if you attach a thin railing around the edges to keep the dishes from sliding off.

CLOTHING:

What's your taste? A Dior gown? A G-string bikini?

It's been my observation while in France that the young ladies who appear on the streets looking so chic are really masters of disguise. Those working women who make me so envious aren't actually wearing Paris couturier fashions. They're wearing simple skirts (usually dark and pleated) at exactly the right length; a blouse that's in perfect harmony with a designer scarf, and a piece of handsome jewelry. Many women all over Europe follow this plan, in fact. They buy a few basic clothes of the best quality, and change their appearances from day to day and from season to season by merely switching accessories. American women are now emulating this idea, and I think it's a wonderfully practical step in the right direction.

MUSIC:

You might try to unearth some old Jean Sablon records, if you're old enough to remember him, or some vintage Chevalier.

Also try Debussy's "La Mer" or "Piano Preludes"; Tomita's "Snowflakes are Dancing"; or Ravel's "Daphne et Chloe" or "Bolero" (as in the movie, "10").

MUSHROOM TARTS

Serves 2-4

½ lb. fresh mushrooms
¼ C. green onion minced
2 T. butter
2 T. flour
Dash Worcestershire
Salt and pepper
Milk
Crumbs and cheese optional
1 pie crust (See Page 32)

Wipe mushrooms off with damp paper towel. Trim and slice in thin slices. Melt butter in small skillet and sauté onions until tender but not brown. Add the mushrooms and continue to cook until mushrooms are hot through. Add Worcestershire, salt and pepper. Sprinkle flour lightly over mixture and stir in thoroughly. Gradually add milk, stirring after each addition. It will be a thick gravy. Reserve off heat. Line tart tins or equivalent with pie crust which has been rolled out to a thickness of ⅛". Fill with mushroom filling. Using bits of pie crust, cut fancy shapes for top of tarts or sprinkle with crumbs and grated cheese. Bake at 375 degrees for 12 to 15 minutes, until browned and bubbly. Slip from tins and onto hot serving plate.

JELLIED CONSOMMÉ WITH CAVIAR

Serves 2

1 can consommé, jelled
2 T. red caviar
2 T. sour cream
Chopped dill or chives, fresh

In individual serving bowls put a tablespoon of caviar. Spoon in a serving of consommé, then top with a dollop of sour cream. Garnish with chopped dill or chives and a touch of caviar. Serve ice cold.

SOLE DUGLÈRÉ

Serves 2-4

2-4 fillets of sole
6 T. butter
4 green onions, chopped
2 tomatoes, peeled, seeded and diced
1 T. fresh parsley, chopped
¼ tsp. rosemary ground
½ small bay leaf
1 C. dry white wine
Salt and pepper
1 T. flour
½ C. light cream
Lemon wedges

Choose a heavy skillet with a lid. Put enough of the butter in it to coat bottom. Arrange the fillets in the skillet so they lie flat, and cover them with the onions, tomatoes, parsley, rosemary, bay leaf, wine, salt and pepper. Dot with 2 T. of the remaining butter. Cover pan and bring to simmer. Cook about 10 to 15 min. Fish will flake easily when done. Remove fish to heated platter with a slotted spatula. Keep warm. Reduce the liquid in the pan by about ⅓. Meanwhile cream the remaining butter into the flour and when the mixture in skillet is reduced, add the butter/flour mixture bit by bit to the liquid stirring constantly. When thickened, cook over low heat about 5 minutes longer. Add cream and simmer briefly. Remove from heat and pour sauce over fish. Serve immediately with lemon wedges.

CREPES SUZETTE

I think everyone should experience this classic dish, but I have a theory about European desserts. Crepes, sponge cakes, Genoise, lady fingers, etc.. are used sort of like blotters to absorb and hold rich fillings and additions of sweet liqueurs. Not cheating on the fillings is important, but over the years, faced with baking at high altitudes, I've cheated by using mixes for cakes with good results.

Use your own method for making 4 crepes per person, and hold.

Don't cheat on this part:

8 ½" sugar cubes or 4 loaf sugar cubes
2 bright skinned oranges
¼ C. granulated sugar
½ lb. unsalted butter (only butter)
⅔ C. strained orange juice
Orange peel
3 T. Grand Marnier
2 T. sugar
⅓ C. Grand Marnier
⅓ C. Cognac

Rub sugar cubes over the sides of the oranges making sure to expose each side of the cube to the oils in the skins. Reserve cubes. With a vegetable peeler, peel only the orange part from the oranges. On a clean chopping board (one that doesn't reek of onion.) mash the sugar cubes. Add the orange peel and with a sharp knife mince into a very fine mixture. Remove mixture to bowl and rub the granulated sugar into the mixture with your fingers. Now work the butter into the mixture, then beat with electric mixer until fluffy. Now drop by drop add the orange juice while beating with electric mixer. Next add the Grand Marnier slowly. Cover and refrigerate this mixture.

To serve, place the orange butter in a skillet a bit larger than crepes. Melt until bubbly. Dip both sides of crepe, and fold twice to make a wedge. Place folded crepe in chafing dish, arranging nicely as you go. To flame: Sprinkle with 2 T. sugar, then warm liqueurs, ignite and pour over the crepes, letting it burn out. Serve immediately.

ASPARAGUS

Select enough fresh asparagus for each guest to have about 6 spears. Snap off the tough ends to make the asparagus uniform lengths. Tie the spears in a bundle and cook upright in hot water, or place spears loose in a steamer over water, bring water to boil and steam, covered about 12 minutes or until tender. Serve with butter and salt.

BOILED NEW POTATOES

Choose tiny, perfect new potatoes. About 3 per person, depending on size. Scrub potatoes well, and cook in their skins. When tender, remove from heat and drain. Keep warm. To serve, rub with butter, and sprinkle with parsley or chives bits.

CHICKEN LIVER PATÉ

- 4 strips bacon
- 1 medium onion chopped
- 1 cube butter
- 2 lbs. chicken liver
- ¾ C. white wine
- 2 T. Cognac
- 3 hard cooked eggs
- Salt and pepper

In a heavy 10" skillet render out the bacon over low heat, do not burn, but get crisp. Meanwhile in separate skillet melt half the butter. Pierce livers with darning needle to keep from popping. When butter is hot add livers and sauté until nicely browned all sides. Do not overcook. Meanwhile remove bacon from skillet and add the onions to the bacon fat and sauté until just golden. Turn onions in with livers and add wine, salt and pepper. Simmer until livers are just done. In a blender, blend about half the livers at a time adding the rest of the butter and the hard cooked eggs. Add Cognac, a bit to each blended batch. Pack in buttered mold and refrigerate. Crumble the bacon and refrigerate to add as garnish when serving. To serve, unmold or if using a decorative mold, leave in mold. Add crumbled bacon and parsley. Serve with crackers of your choice.

ORANGES RIVIERA

Serves 2

- 2 large sweet oranges
- ⅓ C. sugar
- Orange rind
- 1 T. Curacao or Triple Sec
- 2 servings ice cream, vanilla or other
- Whipped cream
- Crystallized violets

Rinse off oranges well. Remove stem end if left in, then with small grater grate the top side of the orange. you are going to cut off the top of the orange and use the rest for a "cup"; so only grate down from the top about ¾". Reserve about ½ tsp. of the orange rind. Cut the top off the orange making about a 2" opening. Scoop out the insides. Carefully clean out the inside as smooth as possible. Separate white pulp from orange pulp. Put the orange pulp with the sugar and grated orange peel in a saucepan and, over medium heat, cook until the mixture becomes a thick syrup. Remove from heat and add liqueur. While syrup is cooling, cut the tops of the orange shells in a zig-zag pattern using a pair of kitchen scissors. Refrigerate all until ready to serve. To serve, pack orange "cups" with the ice cream, then with apple corer, remove the center of the ice cream. Fill cavity with orange syrup, letting a bit spill over. Top with whipped cream garnished with crystallized violet.

SALAD NIÇOISE

A variation of this salad is served all along the Riviera, although its name designates it as being from Nice. The basic ingredients almost always include:

green beans, cooked	eggs, hard boiled
potatoes, cooked	vinaigrette dressing
olives	anchovies
capers	tomatoes

Tuna is always an ingredient, and additions might include shredded beets, peas, carrots and peppers.

This is a "composed" salad. The potatoes are cooked with the skins on, then peeled and while hot are cut into cubes, and tossed immediately with an oil and vinegar dressing. I like the following: For 2 medium potatoes:

1	**T. Dry vermouth**	**½**	**tsp. French mustard**
1	**T. white wine vinegar**	**1**	**tsp. green onion, minced**
2	**T. oil**		**Salt and pepper**

Shake the dressing ingredients in shaker and pour immediately over the hot potatoes. While potatoes are cooling, turn them occasionally so that all sides can absorb the dressing. Cool potatoes completely before mixing in with rest of salad.

To compose salad, arrange Bibb lettuce on large salad plate or bowl. Make a base of the potatoes, then top with chunks of cooked (canned) tuna. Arrange green beans like the spokes of a wheel, and between them place slices of hard cooked eggs, olives and tomatoes. Criss-cross anchovies on top and add a few capers if desired. Using 3 parts oil and 1 part white wine vinegar plus a pinch of thyme, basil, tarragon or other herbs, make the vinaigrette dressing. Sprinkle all with salt and freshly ground pepper and add dressing.

ICED CREAM OF ONION SOUP

Serves 2-4

2 medium onions, sliced
1 C. chicken broth
1 egg yolk
1 C. cream or evaporated milk cut in half with water
1 T. catsup
Salt and pepper
Dill, chopped

Cook onions in broth, covered, until onions are very soft. Put cooked onions and broth into blender and purée. Return to saucepan and beat egg yolk into cream and add gradually to the onion mixture. Stir over low heat until mixture thickens. Do not boil. Add catsup for color. Chill. To serve, thin with milk if necessary. Ladle into bowls. Garnish with chopped dill.

ESCARGOTS À LA BOURGUIGNONNE

6 snails per person (canned)
6 mushroom caps per person or snail shells
Snail butter

Scrub the shells and dry them or remove stems from clean mushroom caps.

Snail butter: *(for 4 people—2 dozen snails)*

¼ C. softened butter
1 tsp. onion, finely minced
1 small clove garlic
1 T. fresh parsley, finely minced
Salt to taste
Freshly ground pepper
Pinch thyme
Dash Tabasco

Wilt the onion and garlic in small skillet in a bit of additional butter, then cream all the ingredients together to make a smooth well-blended butter.

To assemble: Put about ¼ tsp. butter in each shell. Push a snail in each shell then seal each shell with additional butter. Set in snail pans and place in pre-heated 450 degree oven for 10 min. Lacking snail pans use a baking pan of some sort with a low side...a pyrex pie plate would be just fine. Put a layer of coarse salt (Kosher salt) in the bottom of the pan and nest the snail shells in salt to hold upright. Mushroom caps can be put directly on a buttered pie pan. Either way snails can be served on toast triangles lacking snail pans. Serve piping hot with either cocktail forks or picks.

SAUTÉED TOURNEDOS

2 ½" thick slices, beef tenderloin per person
Butter
Salt and freshly ground pepper
2 slices toast for filets per person
Red wine
Oil for skillet

Coat a non-stick skillet with oil and bring to high heat. Lift off heat and add a pat of butter for each filet. Do not let skillet get cool during this operation, work quickly. Put filets in pan and onto the heat. Sear quickly on each side. (Meat patted dry with a paper towel on each side, browns better.) If filets are at room temperature these should be ready to serve (rare) when they have browned on each side. Remove to toast pieces, keep warm and add a bit more butter and about ¼ C. wine, salt and pepper to skillet and heat all. Blend and pour over filets. Serve immediately.

ANCHOYADE

Serves 2-4

1 2 oz. can flat anchovy fillets
1 small clove garlic
1 tsp. tomato paste
2 tsp. olive oil
1 tsp. lemon juice or wine vinegar
Freshly ground black pepper
¾" slices French bread
Grated cheese
Parsley

Drain anchovies of all their oil and if you prefer them less salty, soak in warm water 10 min. then drain and dry with paper towel. Put drained anchovies in large mortar, add garlic and tomato paste. Mash with a pestle until mixture is very smooth. Dribble oil in a few drops at a time, stirring constantly until mixture becomes thick and smooth. Blend in lemon juice and pinch of pepper. To assemble: Toast bread under broiler, watching carefully, on one side only. Remove from oven and spread a thin layer of anchovy mixture over untoasted side. (This will make 8 pieces depending on circumference of bread.) Put the spread pieces back on baking sheet, lower oven rack to 8" below broiler coil and toast for about 10 min. or until toasts are bubbly. Remove from oven and sprinkle with grated cheese. Garnish plate with parsley, and serve hot.

CREAM OF BROCCOLI SOUP

Serves 2-4

1 stalk broccoli, or 1 pkg. frozen broccoli
1 stalk celery, sliced or dried celery leaves to taste
1 T. onion minced
1½ C. chicken bouillon
Light cream
Salt and pepper
Thinly sliced lemon

Combine the broccoli which has been washed and trimmed, the celery, onions, bouillon, salt and pepper in a saucepan. Simmer until broccoli is tender. Put the soup in a blender a little at a time and blend until smooth. Return soup to saucepan and add cream for desired consistency. Heat but do not boil. Correct seasoning. Serve hot or cold, garnished with lemon slices.

TOMATOES STUFFED WITH ARTICHOKE SALAD

1 medium size, firm tomato per person
2 cooked artichoke hearts, base only
Mayonnaise
Parmesan cheese, grated
Lemon juice
Salt and pepper, freshly ground

Rinse tomatoes and cut out stem end. Carefully cut the tomato in wedges from top to bottom without severing the skin at the bottom so that you can fan it out like a flower. To mix salad, chop finely the base of the artichoke heart. Sprinkle with lemon juice lightly. Add salt and pepper to taste. For each salad, use about 2-3 T. grated cheese, then bind all with a good mayonnaise. Blend salad and heap in tomato cups. Garnish with snips of chives, dill, or parsley, and place on bed of lettuce.

PEACH MELBA

Here is another classic dessert that should be in everyone's repetoire. (It also gives me an excuse for another limerick):

While sunning at Nice on the beach
In a bikini that didn't quite reach
Mme. Melba got tanned
Much more than she'd planned.
Voila! Mme. Melba's a peach.

1 scoop vanilla ice cream per person
1 peach half, per person, peeled
1 10 oz. pkg. frozen raspberries, fresh raspberries, or raspberry preserves
Currant jelly

The "grabber" in Peach Melba is the flavor combination, and there are several ways to achieve it...some easier than others. Also there are times when you have to improvise with the ingredients at hand. In the summer when fresh peaches and raspberries are available that's the best of all, but do not shy away from the alternates.

Fresh peaches should be poached, as should frozen ones. Make a vanilla syrup from ¼ C. sugar, 1½ C. water and 1 tsp. vanilla. Lower the peaches into the syrup when it comes to a boil and poach at a simmer until just barely tender. (Frozen peaches tend to be underripe so let them cook a little longer than fresh ones. Fresh ones should go no longer than 5 min.) I prefer Freestone peaches to Clings. Let the peaches cool in the syrup.

Thaw frozen raspberries and drain them. Purée in a blender, then put in a saucepan with about ½ C. currant jelly for a 10 oz. pkg. Over low heat let come to a simmer, stir to melt jelly and remove from heat and cool. If using fresh raspberries, mash about a cup with ⅛ C. sugar. Put pulp in a small pan and bring to a boil stirring constantly, reduce heat and simmer until sugar is well dissolved. Remove from heat and cool. Reserve some whole berries for garnish.

You can use raspberry preserves, thinned with a little Kirsch or Raspberry liqueur over low heat, then cooled.

To serve, put a scoop of ice cream in the bottom of sherbet dish, place peach, rounded side up on top of ice cream and cover with raspberry purée.

CARBONNADES MONTEYNARD

I wrestled with my conscience about including this recipe in a chapter supposedly set on the Riviera because this is not a recipe indigenous to that region. My practical sense won out. This is a wonderful way to cook cheaper cuts of beef (and game), and does wonders for the spirit on a blustery night. It can be put together ahead of time and placed in the oven which has been programmed to turn on while you are at work. (Always set it to turn "off", also...just in case.)

- **2 medallions of beef per person each ¾" thick and about 3" by 4" from round, chuck, etc...**
- **4-5 large onions, sliced**
- **1 tsp. mixed herbs such as *rosemary, thyme, marjoram, and parsley**
- **1 bay leaf if desired**
- **1" thick slices of French bread**
- **French mustard of the stone-ground variety**
- **Beer**
- **Bouillon**
- **Salt and freshly ground pepper**
- **Lard for sautéing**

Heat lard in a heavy skillet and sear the medallions on both side, but do not let them cook at all. Lift out meat and set aside. Dispose of the lard in the skillet and wipe out with paper towel. Add about 4 T. fresh lard, heat and add the onions. Wilt the onions but do not brown. In the bottom of a heavy earthenware casserole layer half of the onions. Place the meat on top of onions, overlapping if necessary. Put on rest of onions. Add salt and pepper and sprinkle on the herbs which have been ground together in a mortar. Now pour on about 6 oz. beer and add enough bouillon to just cover. Take enough slices of bread to completely cover the top of the casserole and spread them generously on both sides with mustard. Place the bread on top of onions, then put lid on casserole and seal it as tightly as you can. A piece of foil crimped around the top will help. Cook in a 275 degree oven for 4 hours. Serve from casserole.

** Rosemary should be ground, at least coarsely, otherwise it's like eating pine needles. Do grind it just before using so that it releases its pungency at that moment. (See notes about grinding spices with a mortar and pestle to save money, page 154).*

FLAMBÉED APPLES WITH ICE CREAM

Serves 2

- **2 medium cooking apples**
- **2 T. butter**
- **2 tsp. apricot preserves**
- **Pinch cinnamon**
- **¼ C. applejack or Cognac**
- **Sugar**
- **Ice Cream**

Peel and slice apples in thin slices. Melt butter in heavy skillet and sauté apples over low heat until tender and slightly translucent. Stir in apricot preserves and cinnamon. Hold. Put ice cream in serving dishes, then sprinkle a bit of sugar on the apples, warm the liqueur, flame and pour over the apples and let flame burn out. Spoon over the ice cream. (Apples can be served this way, warm, topped with whipped cream also.)

BIRTHDAY BASH

BIRTHDAY BASHES

SUMMER MENU
(Avec Argent)
Caviar with Sour Cream and Lime
Vichyssoise • Coquille St. Jacques
Snow Peas
Thousand Island Salad
Strawberries Hallelujah
Champagne

Summer Menu
(Sans Argent)
Chipped Beef and
Cream Cheese Cigarettes
Chilled Dilled Cream of Pea Soup
Fondue of Beef
Boiled New Potatoes
Tomatoes with Cottage Cheese Salad
Peach Flambé

Winter Menu
(Avec Argent)
Mushroom Triangles
Cream of Crab Soup
Tournedos - "Birthday Boy/Girl"
Caesar Salad
Pumpkin Cheesecake

Winter Menu
(Sans Argent)
Potato Puffs with Dipping Sauce
Madrilene Cream "X"
Chicken Breasts with
Pimiento Cream
Spinach Salad with Pecans
and Sour Cream Dressing
Cherries Jubilee

Even if you are a modest soul for 364 days of the year—a thinker, a recluse, a poet, a wallflower, a meditator, a ribbon clerk—there is one day on which you should get certifiably reckless, and that is your birthday. It is the one time when it's socially acceptable to announce: "I'm going to celebrate myself. I'm going to get naked and run wild over the news that I've survived for another year. I'm going to gather all of my friends together and hear them deliver a round of testimonials to my great good fortune. I'm going to let everybody know what a hell of a person I am."

It's the healthiest, sanest thing you can do, to give yourself a birthday party. It's an affirmation and a recognition that, after all, you deserve it. You've earned it. So just cast off your adult sense of propriety and—like when you were a kid and could have five pieces of cake and ten scoops of ice cream on your birthday—now feast without shame on worldly desire as a grownup birthday boy or girl. It's more fun that way, and doesn't hurt anybody.

Who knows? The Big One might fall before another year passes. You'd better rejoice about your coming into the world while it's still here.

I, for one, threw a party last summer while the sun was in Leo to celebrate my tenth annual 39th birthday party—and only my hairdresser knows for sure whether that's right (and I didn't invite her). No, I don't think it really matters how many years have passed under the bridge, so long as the river's still flowing. That's why, when people ask me how old I *really* am, I just tell them, "I'm 23 on the Celsius scale, kiddo," and invite them to my next annual revival.

It's equally rewarding to throw a birthday bash for somebody else—a wonderful way to venerate a good friend or lover, especially one who's too shy to throw a party for himself. I wouldn't worry about embarrassing the guest of honor. I haven't met a person yet who (despite protests to the contrary) doesn't enjoy an honest shower of attention once in a while. Besides if it's you who's planning the party, you can be sure that you won't be left off the guest list.

The most momentous parties are those that mark life's sea change—a 21st birthday, or a 30th, or, for those who can handle it with aplomb, a 40th or 50th or 60th. An acquaintance of mine recently observed his 40th by asking 40 friends to a potluck to which they were to bring, according to the invitations, simply "40 of something." The guy suggested publicly that 40 Main lobsters might be an appropriate tribute to his longevity and all-around good nature, or 40 bottles of Nuits-Saint-Georges. But what he ended up receiving, among other things, were 40 back issues of "Modern Maturity" magazine; 40 Chamber of Commerce brochures from Sun City, Arizona; 40 ounces of Geritol ; a 40 inch long cane inscribed: "Old Soldiers Never Die"; and a phony gift certificate for a 40-pound marble gravestone. The birthday boy took it in good spirits, and at 11:25 p.m., the precise minute of his birth, he lined up all of the under-40 guests on one side of the room and all of the over-40's on the other side, and had the juniors pick him up and fling him bodily across the threshold and into the arms of the waiting old-timers. It was a stunning rite of passage, a mockery of all of our fears of growing old, a thumbing-our-noses at death, a very merry exorcism.

Another way to defy the gods of time (temporarily, at least), is to celebrate a birthday in a truly childish manner. I once went to a party for a fellow who was turning 40, and his wife had decorated the house as if it were a 4-year-old's party, with crepe paper streamers and balloons, paper plates and cups, paper hats and kiddie noisemakers, and a game of Pin the Tail on the Donkey. Actually, it was a game of Pin the Diaper on the Little Bill, because the birthday boy's wife had had an old photograph blown up to poster size—a photo of her husband as a newborn lying bottom-up on a bearskin rug—and the guests were invited to take turns sticking it to him. The wife even had a cassette tape of a baby crying which she played at appropriate times, and if it all sounds too ridiculous, you have to understand that the Hawaiian Punch was well spiked.

You say you'd rather not regress all the way to infancy? Then turn the calendar ahead ten years or so and have a teen-age roller skating party. For all of you adults who like costume parties, this is a chance to indulge in the nostalgia for the '40s and '50s and '60s—to get out those bobby sox, those fuzzy sweaters with circle pins, those leather jackets and motorcycle boots, that white sport coat with the pink carnation. While you're at it, memorize the lyrics to "I've Got a Brand-New Pair of Roller Skates, You've Got a Brand-New Key."

The whole idea is to leap out of character for a night, to sneak out of your skin and into somebody else's.

You men: If your lady friend is a little prudish and proper, take her to the race track for her birthday and bet on the daily-double combination that matches her new age; or to the art museum for lunch and a stroll through the galleries; or for a ride on a ferry; or for a walk through the zoo.

You women: If your partner is less than prudish and proper, get a bottle of champagne and a bag of Burger Kings and go to a "friends and lovers" motel to watch x-rated movies from a water bed.

If you are married, take your partner (blindfolded or not) to the place where you met, whether it's for breakfast at Tiffany's or a picnic under the Civil War statue in the park. Or stay at home and cater the entire affair, choosing delicacies that your mate has always wanted to try but has never had money to actually experience. If you live near New

York City, order a birthday cake from a shop on East 51st Street called The Erotic Bakery, or make such a cake yourself. Hire a musician or a whole band. Arrange for a singing telegram or a surprise visit from one of those new "flash-a-friend" agencies.

Have you ever thought of designing a custom-made coupon book for your birthday manchild or womanchild? The coupons might read: "Good for One Chauffered Ride to the Crystal Palace Restaurant for a Dinner of Your Choice," or "Good for Midnight Drinks at the Top of the Mark," or "Redeemable for One-Head-to-Toe Swedish Massage," or "Two Orgasms for the Price of One." Once you start conceiving one of these coupon books, you'll find it hard to stop.

If you're giving a large party for someone else, you might secretly put together a "This Is Your Life" show from old collections of slides or movies, complete with a comic narration à la Ralph Edwards.

Once you know a person's birth date, you can go to the library and snoop through the archives for newspapers published on that same day. Using the library's photocopying machine, you can reproduce headlines, stories, photos and advertisements and make a fascinating collage that could even be framed and hung. If your friend was born in the town where you're living, you might even be able to find the actual birth announcement in the papers, and relatives might be able to give you baby pictures to work into the collage.

In my years of wandering through flea markets and garage sales, I used to collect old magazines that were approximately as well-aged as my friends. Some of my favorites were vintage VOGUE'S, SATURDAY EVENING POST'S and LIFE'S, and when a birthday was approaching I'd look through them for articles and pictures that related to the interests and occupations of the person I had in mind. I arranged the material on a tray that I'd picked up at a second-hand store, and presented it as a memento of the occasion. Trivia Trays (Copyright 1969), I called them. Usually I repainted the trays and then lacquered on the clippings with a découpage process. If this sort of thing appeals to you, I can assure you that the end results make very attractive and long lasting gifts. The materials and instructions for découpage can be found at most hobby shops.

Probably my favorite Trivia Tray was one that I made for a doctor in Cleveland, using ads from a 1929 issue of Physical Culture magazine. I didn't really appreciate medicine until I started pursuing those old classifieds. I especially liked the ad for "The Pandiculator" (it left so much to the imagination), and the "Violetta", which shocked you into good health with it's violet rays, and the device, now lost to the ages, (I hope!) called "The Internal Bath", whose instructions read simply: "Sit on it!"

A book of astrology can lead you into myriad other themes for a birthday party. Take your ideas from the sun-sign symbols (Aries the Ram, Sagittarius the Archer, Aquarius the Water-Bearer) and from the accompanying references to birthstones, favorite flowers, peculiar tendencies and idiosycrasies, and so on. Invite an astrologer to a special friend's birthday party to have his horoscope done on the spot, or give a gift certificate for the same service. You can even get a computer-crafted horoscope sent in the mail, if you plan ahead of time.

Despite all of these clever ideas, and despite the good times I have at my annual-39th parties, I have to confess that one of these years I'd love to observe my birthday by being feted in simple elegance by a perfect gentleman. This is how it would be: He would arrive at my door, on time, with a bouquet of fresh flowers in hand. We would have some champagne and caviar, then we would leave to go to a low-density restaurant with a high-caliber menu, good waiters, and enough time to savor it all. After dinner we would have a drink or two at a cocktail lounge with an aerial view of the city, and soft music in the background. Then we'd go home for a foot massage or back rub while listening to some Debussy or vintage Lena Horne.

Do I hear an offer?

INVITATIONS:

If you decide to make a collage of period magazine clippings, or can find a copy of your friend's birth announcement, these can be styled very nicely into an invitation.

Or how about this one? Put the invitation into a balloon which has just enough air in it to indicate there's something inside. The note will invite the recipient to join you for a champagne flight in a hot-air balloon on his birthday. If you find the right balloonist you can even arrange for him to set you down at a remote and idyllic location where your car will be waiting with a picnic hamper in the trunk.

SCENTS:

A sachet of baby powder, I think, would be most fitting, indeed.

TABLE SETTINGS:

I've already mentioned the idea of using kiddie decorations such as paper plates and streamers, which have the advantage of making for an easy cleanup. Another time-saver is to have the birthday cake made by a bakery, or perhaps more reasonably, by a homemaker whose advertisement you might find on the bulletin board at your local supermarket.

If you make the cake yourself, consider decorating it with miniature souvenirs that represent various aspects of the celebrant's life. These can be bought at specialty shops or made of clay, bread dough and other materials, and can range all the way from toy cars and boats to houses and scenes depicting elaborate orgiastic fantasies.

CLOTHING:

Some people I know who live in the mountains of Colorado — dropouts from the business world, mostly — seem to get the biggest kick out of celebrating birthdays by dressing up in three-piece suits, tuxedos and formal ball gowns. To them it's the heighth of hilarity, and a real turn on to see each other in their previous incarnations as penguins and peacocks (or peahens, as the case may be).

Another idea is to ask the party people to dress as people might have dressed when the birthday child was born. The resulting scene, no matter what the chosen year, will no doubt resemble a convention of Chicago mobsters and their molls.

Finally, of course, in the category of budget clothing, we have the most traditional costume of all: the ever-popular birthday suit.

MUSIC:

At the risk of making the birthday child feel older than his years, you ought to have some vintage music on hand, either from the era of his birth or from his adolescence or some other heyday. A little research will turn up the old standbys (in case you've forgotten). So many classics are being re-recorded nowadays that you shouldn't have any trouble finding what you need in a well-stocked shop.

I comb through the albums at garage sales, Salvation Army outlets and used-record stores and then tape the selections I want on cassettes. This way I can orchestrate my own Golden Oldies programs, and when I'm finished with the albums, I donate them back to the Salvation Army so I won't have to store them.

BIRTHDAY PRAYER

Now I lay me down to sleep.
I pray the Lord my soul to keep.
If I should die before I wake
To see the candles on my cake.
Here is what I want from You.
See that they leave off a few!

BIRTHDAY SYMBOLS AND AFFINITIES

ASTROLOGICAL SIGNS	INFLUENCES	MATE IN	MINERALS FOR LUCK
Aquarius Jan. 21-Feb. 19	Uranus King of Swords	Aquarius	Amethyst Quartz Crystal
Pisces Feb. 20-Mar. 21	Jupiter Page of Cups	Women in Cancer Men in Capricorn or Virgo	Rock Quartz Crystal
Aries Mar. 22-Apr. 20	Mars Queen of Rods	Leo or Saggitarius	Realgar or Orpiment
Taurus Apr. 21-May 21	Venus King of Pentacles	Virgo, Capricorn or Libra	Malachite
Gemini May 22-June 22	Mercury Page of Swords	Libra, Aquarius or Gemini	Geode
Cancer June 23-July 22	Moon Queen of Cups	Women in Pisces or Cancer, Men in Pisces, Virgo or Libra	Chalcopyrite
Leo July 23-Aug. 23	Sun King of Rods	Women in Aries Men in Aries or Saggitarius	Sulphur
Virgo Aug. 24-Sept. 23	Mercury Page of Pentacles	Virgo, Libra or Saggitarius	Fluorite
Libra Sept 24.-Oct. 23	Venus Queen of Swords	Libra, Virgo or Aquarius	Pyrite
Scorpio Oct. 24-Nov. 22	Mars King of Cups	Women in Virgo, Libra and Scorpio Men in Cancer or Virgo	Vanadinite
Saggitarius Nov. 23-Dec. 22	Jupiter Page of Rods	Leo, Aquarius or Libra	Crysacola
Capricorn Dec. 23-Jan 20	Saturn Queen of Pentacles	Libra, Virgo or Taurus	Dogtooth Calcite

CAVIAR WITH SOUR CREAM AND LIME

Caviar...the best you can afford in the size for your appetite
Sour cream
Lime wedges
Pumpernickel bread rounds

Chill caviar thoroughly and serve in a bed of crushed ice. If you can't afford the very expensive imported varieties, as I can't most of the time, try the domestic varieties my way. Put a bit of caviar on the bread, squeeze a bit of lime juice on it, and add a dollop of sour cream. Enjoy.

VICHYSSOISE

Serves 2-4

1 medium leek, white part only
1 medium potato, peeled and diced
3 T. butter
1 C. chicken broth
Salt and pepper
Light cream
Chopped chives or dill

Remove root end from leek, then wash leek thoroughly to remove sand. Cut it into slices and sauté in butter without browning. Add potatoes when leek is transparent and cover with the chicken broth. Cook, covered until potato is very tender. Season and put in blender in small batches, blending until smooth. Thin with cream to desired consistency. Chill thoroughly. To serve, correct seasoning and consistency, and ladle into bowls. Garnish with chives or dill.

THOUSAND ISLAND SALAD

Serves 4-6

1 8 oz. can tomato sauce
1 C. water
1 pkg. Knox gelatin
1 3 oz. pkg. cream cheese
½ C. mayonnaise
1 C. celery cut in ½" dice
½ C. green pepper, diced
3 green onions, minced
½ C. black olives, sliced
2 hard cooked eggs, chopped
Dash Worchestershire and Tabasco Sauces

Soften gelatin in the water and add to tomato sauce in a saucepan. Bring to a boil stirring constantly to dissolve the gelatin. Reduce heat and while continuing to stir add the cream cheese in chunks, blending thoroughly until mixture is creamy. Remove from heat. Add the sauces and whisk in the mayonnaise. Put to cool in refrigerator while preparing the vegetables. When partly set add the vegetables and eggs and pour into buttered mold, or individual molds. Return to refrigerator. To serve, unmold and garnish with parsley and black olives, or save some of the prettiest celery leaves.

COQUILLE ST. JACQUES

Step 1:
¾ C. dry white wine
½ C. water
½ lb. bay scallops or if using sea scallops, ½ lb. cut in quarters
¾ C. fresh mushrooms, minced
1 small onion, peeled
1 small bay leaf
1 tsp. minced parsley
Salt and pepper

Put all ingredients except scallops and mushrooms in shallow pan and bring to a boil. Simmer briefly, then add the scallops and mushrooms and simmer from 2 to 5 minutes until scallops turn milky white. Lift out scallops and mushrooms with a slotted spoon and set aside.

Step 2:
2 T. butter
2 T. flour
⅓ C. cream
1 egg yolk, lightly beaten
Lemon juice
¼ C. Swiss cheese, grated
¼ C. buttered crumbs

Return pan with wine broth to heat and at high heat, reduce about one half. Strain and set aside. Melt the butter and stir in flour. Cook over low heat 2 or 3 minutes. Remove from heat and with a whisk, beat in the hot scallop broth in a slow, steady stream. Return to heat and cook until thickened..a minute or so. Set aside and immediately beat the egg yolk with the cream and spoon in some of the hot sauce, stirring constantly. Combine the egg mixture with the hot sauce gradually while beating with a whisk.

Set back over low heat and cook about a minute or so without boiling, stirring constantly. Season and add lemon juice to taste. Add more cream if too thick. Combine the cooked scallops and mushrooms with sauce and spoon into buttered scallop shells or individual ramekins. Sprinkle with buttered crumbs, and cheese.

At this point you can wrap in plastic for broiling at a later time, or they can go directly under the broiler. They should be placed 5" below heat in the broiler, and browned and bubbly when served...about 4 to 5 minutes.

SNOW PEAS

Serves 2-4

½ lb. fresh snow peas
Butter
Salt and pepper

Wash peas, and pull the strings along edge. Put in a steamer over boiling water and steam 4 to 5 minutes while the Coquille is browning. Remove the peas, butter and season.

CREAM CHEESE AND CHIPPED BEEF CIGARETTES

Serves 2-4

1 3 oz. pkg. cream cheese
1 small jar chipped beef slices
Garlic salt
Dash Worestershire sauce
Cream

Soften cream cheese while blending in the garlic salt, as desired, and the Worcestershire sauce. Use a bit of cream if needed for spreading consistency. Spread cheese on beef as if spreading a piece of bread, leaving a ½" margin around the edges. Roll up like a jelly roll. Put seam side down and repeat until all ingredients are used. To serve, arrange cigarettes on serving dish and garnish with black olives and parsley.

CHILLED DILLED CREAM OF PEA SOUP

Serves 2-4

½ can concentrated green pea soup
¾ C. buttermilk
Juice of ½ small lime
Dash Worcestershire sauce
¼ tsp. dill weed
Salt and pepper to taste
Lime slices to garnish and
Avocado cubes, optional

Put everything but garnish in blender and blend until smooth. Chill until ready to serve, then garnish and serve immediately.

Note: Remember that buttermilk is made from the same kind of culturing process, generally, that sour cream is. The taste in soup is very, very similar, but buttermilk has fewer calories.

STRAWBERRIES HALLELUJA

Serves 2

½ pint fresh strawberries
2 T. sugar
¼ C. strawberry liqueur
2 macaroons crumbled
2 scoops vanilla ice cream
Whipped cream
2 whole berries for garnish

Wash gently, and hull berries. Roll on paper towel to dry. Put in glass bowl and sprinkle with the sugar. Pour on the liqueur, and refrigerate several hours. To serve, put scoop of ice cream in sherbet dish. Sprinkle with crumbled macaroons, ladle on strawberries, then top with whipped cream and garnish.

FONDUE OF BEEF Serves 2

½ lb. sirloin cubes, cut in bite size pieces, per person
Oil for frying
Sauces:
Sour cream and horseradish
Mustard mayonnaise
Bottled chutneys
Bottled steak sauces
Bottled fondue sauces

Put the oil in a fondue pot to a depth of about 2". Be sure pot is on a tray so that oil does not drip on your table or table cloth. Provide each person with a fondue fork with a heat-proof handle. When the oil is boiling hot, each person pierces a piece of meat and cooks it to the desired doneness, then dips it in the sauce of his/her choice. ½ C. sour cream and 1 tsp. horseradish makes a mild sauce. ½ C. mayonnaise with 2 T. mild mustard, or if using a hot mustard start with less and build up. Accompaniments could include tiny pickles, pearl onions, dilled green beans, olives, etc...

TOMATOES STUFFED WITH COTTAGE CHEESE SALAD Serves 2

2 large firm tomatoes
1 C. cottage cheese
¼ C. celery, chopped into ½" dice
¼ C. cucumber, in ½" dice
⅛ C. green pepper, chopped
1 T. green onion, minced
1 T. mayonnaise
Salt and pepper to taste

Prepare tomatoes by removing the top stem end. Cut into 6 to 8 wedges from top to bottom without completely cutting through the bottom; so you can fan out the wedges. Combine all the other ingredients and fill the tomato with the salad. Garnish with an olive if desired, and place tomatoes on a leaf of lettuce on salad plate.

PEACH FLAMBÉ Serves 2

1 C. ripe fresh, or canned peaches, sliced
2 T. butter
2 T. brown sugar
Pinch cinnamon
2 T. brandy,rum ,etc..
2 scoops ice cream, vanilla, peach, red raspberry swirl...

Put the butter and sugar into a skillet other than one with a no-stick lining. Over low heat melt the butter and sugar and let it bubble briefly. Add the peach slices and a sprinkle of cinnamon and turn the peaches to coat all sides. When warm, heat the brandy in a ladle and set the brandy aflame and pour over the peaches. Rotate the pan to cover all and let the flame die out. Spoon peaches over the ice cream and serve immediately.

If you have never flamed a dessert before, practice ahead of time. Treat this flame as you would any other...with caution. It can be done at the table in a chafing dish, but try it ahead of time. Use a ladle, preferably of stainless steel with a long handle. The fumes of the liquor are what ignite, so they sometimes light by themselves if you are warming the liquor over the flame from a chafing dish, a candle or over a gas stove. Just be prepared for that so that you don't get startled and spill flaming liquor over the edge of the ladle.

MUSHROOM TRIANGLES

Serves 2

- ¾ C. fresh mushrooms, minced finely
- 1 T. flour
- 1 T. butter
- ¾ C. milk
- Dash Worcestershire
- Salt and pepper
- Bread
- Butter

Clean mushrooms with damp paper towel, cut off stem end and mince. Put in bowl and sprinkle the flour over the mushrooms, mixing in well. Meanwhile, melt the 1 T. butter in a small skillet. Add the mushrooms and stir, then remove from heat and stir in the milk, Worcestershire, salt and pepper. Return to heat and cook over low heat until thick. This should be a thick paste. To assemble, trim the crusts from firm slices of white bread. Spread the bread with butter on one side. Spread the mushroom paste on the unbuttered side of the bread, and put two slices of bread together to make a sandwich. When you have used up the mushroom mixture, cut the sandwiches in triangles. Cover with plastic wrap and refrigerate until ready to serve. To serve, heat broiler, put sandwiches on cookie sheet 5" from heat and brown lightly one side, turn over and brown lightly second side. Serve hot on garnished tray.

Another delicious hot sandwich is made by substituting finely chopped cooked spinach for the mushrooms in the above recipe, then proceeding the same. You may add some minced onion to taste with the spinach if desired.

CREAM OF CRAB SOUP

Serves 2-4

- 2 T. butter
- 3 medium size mushrooms, fresh
- 1 green onion, minced
- ¼ C. celery diced
- ½ C. cooked crab meat
- Dash Worcestershire sauce
- Pinch of mace
- 1 T. flour
- Lemon juice
- 1 C. evaporated milk
- ½ C. water
- 2 T. sherry
- Salt and pepper
- Finely minced hard cooked egg

In a small skillet, melt the butter and add mushrooms which have been sliced, and the onions, celery, crab meat, dash of Worcestershire sauce, and the pinch of mace. Cook over low heat until the vegetables have become tender. You may cover, but stir frequently. When the vegetables are tender, sprinkle all with 1 T. flour, and blend in well. Remove from heat, and stir in slowly the ½ C. water. Put all in blender and blend until smooth. Pour from blender into the top of a double boiler and stir in the milk, salt, pepper and lemon juice. Continue to cook over boiling water until thickened and flour is cooked thoroughly. Stir in sherry and serve immediately. To serve, ladle in bowls and garnish with chopped egg.

TOURNEDOS

Serves 2

- 2 beef tenderloin filets, 1" thick
- 2 medium baking potatoes, grated and squeezed dry in paper towel
- 2-3 slices bacon
- ½ pkg. (3 oz.) cream cheese, softened
- 3 T. grated Swiss cheese
- 2 green onions, finely minced
- ⅛ C. cream
- Dash Tabasco
- Salt and pepper
- Hollandaise Sauce
- 6 spears, fresh asparagus, cooked tender

Fry bacon over low heat until crisp taking care not to over-brown the bacon grease. Remove bacon and reserve both bacon and grease. Meanwhile, grate the potatoes, squeeze and keep covered. Cream the cheeses, onion, Tabasco, salt and pepper. When well blended mix with the potatoes. Now you will make two patties from the potatoes and fry them in the reserved bacon grease, adding a bit of oil if necessary. Brown the patty on one side, turn and brown on the other. If the patties are very thick. you may want to cover to cook them completely through. Meanwhile have the Hollandaise Sauce made from your own recipe or from a mix, and keep warm. At the same time, broil the filets to the desired degree of doneness.

To assemble, put a potato patty on a hot plate, then top with the steak, then arrange the asparagus on top of the steak and cover with Hollandaise. Garnish with crumbled bacon.

PUMPKIN CHEESECAKE

- 1 8 oz. pkg. cream cheese
- ¾ C. brown sugar
- 1 tsp. cinnamon
- 1 tsp. nutmeg
- ½ tsp. ginger
- ¼ tsp. ground cloves
- 3 unbeaten eggs
- 1½ C. canned pumpkin
- 1 C. evaporated milk
- 1 tsp. vanilla
- ¼ tsp. salt
- 2 8" crumb crusts

Topping:

- 2 C. sour cream
- ¼ C. brown sugar
- ¼ C. white sugar
- 1 tsp. vanilla

Cream the cheese, sugar, cinnamon, nutmeg, ginger, cloves and salt in a large mixing bowl. Add the eggs one at time, beating well after each addition. Blend in the pumpkin, milk and vanilla. Divide filling into two crusts. Bake at 350 degrees for about 40 min. or until center is set. Remove from oven and spread the topping over each. Bake another 5 minutes. Remove and cool. Refrigerate overnight, covered.

(Each serves 6-8)

Ready made crusts which come with a plastic lid can be used, and the extra pie will freeze well, and can be held for later use.

POTATO PUFFS WITH DIPPING SAUCE

Serves 2

- 10 "Tater Tots" by Ore-Ida, per person
- ½ C. sour cream
- 2 T. salad style mustard
- ½ tsp. or more dill weed

Cook "Tater Tots" according to the directions on the package. Blend the rest of the ingredients into a dip. To serve, put the dip in a small bowl in the center of serving dish and surround with potatoes. Furnish picks for dipping the hot potatoes.

MADRILENE CREAM "X"

Serves 2-4

I created this recipe for this occasion so you can name the soup for your guest...MADRILENE CREAM JOHN DOE...Whenever I fête someone on a special occasion, I try to create a dish especially for him/her. I then print the menu on a piece of fancy stationery, and give them the menu with their dish printed on it as a memento.

- 1 can Madrilene, chilled overnight
- 2 T. real mayonnaise
- 1 T. Old El Paso Taco Sauce
- 2 T. sour cream
- Sliced black olives, or green if prefered

Blend mayonnaise, Taco Sauce and sour cream together until well blended. Whisk into jellied madrilene leaving madrilene partly jelled. Garnish with additional sour cream and olives.

CHICKEN BREASTS WITH PIMIENTO CREAM

Serves 2

- 1 chicken breast, boned, per person
- 1 2 oz. jar pimientoes, chopped
- 1 C. evaporated milk
- 1 T. flour
- ½ C. Swiss cheese, grated
- Salt and pepper
- Parsley
- 3 T. butter
- Rice, cooked according to your choice of recipes.

Put 2 T. butter in a small heavy skillet. Over low heat bring it to a bubble and immediately put in the two chicken breasts. Brown lightly on both sides taking care not to burn butter. Remove breasts from the skillet and add the other 1 T. butter. Put the pimientoes in and stir. Sprinkle the flour over the pimientoes and blend. Remove from heat and little by little blend in the milk. Return to low heat and add the Swiss cheese, stirring constantly. Season. Put the chicken breasts in a small casserole or in individual baking dishes. Spoon the pimiento cheese sauce over each breast, cover and bake at 350 degrees for 20 to 25 minutes.

SPINICH SALAD WITH PECANS AND SOUR CREAM DRESSING

Serves 2

Fresh spinach, washed, dried and broken into bite sized pieces, for serving
¼ C. broken pecans
⅓ C. sour cream
1 T. sugar
1 T. cider vinegar
½ tsp. dry mustard
1 tsp. cream style horseradish
Salt and pepper
Blue cheese chunks if desired

Reserve the spinach, pecans, and blue cheese chunks, if desired. Blend the rest of the ingredients into a dressing. To serve, put the spinach, pecans and cheese into salad bowls or on salad plates and top with dressing. Top with a few extra pecans if desired.

CHERRIES JUBILEE

Serves 2

1 can dark, sweet, pitted cherries
1 T. sugar
1 T. cornstarch
2 T. brandy, Kirsch, rum
2 scoops vanilla ice cream

Drain the cherries and reserve the juice. Mix the sugar and cornstarch in a measuring cup and slowly stir in the cherry juice. If there is not enough liquid to make 1 C., add a bit of water. Put the cherries and juice in a small saucepan and over low heat bring to a boil. Cook until the mixture becomes transparent. Hold. To serve, warm the liqueur, ignite and flame the cherries. Spoon over the ice cream in sherbet dishes and serve immediately.

HEARTY BALLBANGER

1½ oz. vodka
½ oz. banana liqueur
4 oz. orange juice
½ oz. Galliano

Shake all but Galliano together and pour over ice cubes. Float Galliano on top.

BUDA & OTHER PESTS

BUDA AND OTHER PESTS

Summer Menu
(Avec Argent)
Ham Puffs
Caraway Soup with Croutons
Transylvania Bandit's Meat
Fried Green Tomatoes
Cucumber Salad
Dark Rye Bread
Pancakes á la Gundel
Coffee

Summer Menu
(Sans Argent)
Cheese Crackers • Spinach Soup
Pan Fried Rostelyos
Summer Squash with
Dill and Sour Cream
Sliced Tomatoes • Crusty Bread
Meringue Tarts with
Whipped Cream
Coffee

Winter Menu
(Avec Argent)
Lipto Cheese and Crackers
Halaszlie • Tokany
Asparagus Pudding
Beet Salad • Crusty Bread
Rum Raspberry Torte
Coffee

Winter Menu
(Sans Argent)
Mushroom Fritters • Potato Soup
Chicken Paprikash
Cabbage Salad • Crusty Bread
Hussar's Kisses • Coffee

Since the history of Hungary is one of invasion and occupation by a succession of foreign tribes, I've always thought it would be interesting to have a Hungarian dinner party to which each guest came dressed as a different conqueror. It would be a large party, I'm afraid—the Scythians, the Sarmatians, the Romans, the Lombards, the Huns, the Magyars, the Mongols, the Habsburgs, the Russians and all. Imagine it...hearing hoofbeats on the front lawn and the butler announcing: "The Ostrogoths are here..."

Having been born under the regal sign of Leo, I think I would have felt right at home among these conquerers. Until recently I even entertained certain fantasies about me and Attilla the Hun, that most ravaging barbarian of all, but then I read somewhere that he was a dwarf.

Another approach to a Hungarian party, in light of the fact that Transylvania was historically part of the empire, would be to host a Count Dracula banquet. Make it on the night of the full moon, and serve a toothsome regional specialty such as braised neck in red wine sauce.

One way or the other, Hungarian love affairs seem to begin and end with food. A couple in today's Budapest might meet at a coffeehouse to share a dainty pastry and then, if they still have an appetite for each other, move on to *gulyas*, sauerkraut and other more solid nourishment. Should the romance fail, it's back to the coffeehouse for both of them to console themselves at separate tables with *dobos torte*.

The foods of Hungary, like the people themselves, are a goulash of mixed ancestry. Because the Danube basin was settled by nomadic horsemen who traveled light, the cooking that evolved favored one-pot dishes such as soups and stews (often laced with fermented horse milk, which later became known as sour cream). When I think of Gypsies, the most homeless of all Hungary's nomads, I imagine them filching or poaching or begging the makings for their meals and then having to cook them up quickly and get their caravans back on the road before the angry townspeople show up. Thus the advantage of simplicity in one of tonight's dinner entrees—Transylvania Bandit's Meat.

However, the influences on the national palate aren't limited to warriors and vagabonds, by any means. For example, ever since Vienna was their capital the Hungarians have been blessed with a fondness for outrageously sweet and heavy pastries. A genetic strain shared with the people of Finland might account for such alien delicacies as the cherry soup that's on one of tonight's menus. The Turks are responsible for the coffee: They brought it with them from the east when they dropped in to occupy Budapest in the

16th Century, and a tourist today can still see them dispensing strong brew from their ubiquitous vending machines in the streets of the capital. (There's a Gyspy saying, by the way, that coffee should be as black as sin, as hot as hell, and as sweet as love.) Nobody is sure who introduced paprika to Hungary, but it has remained as the distinctive spice of culinary life.

So, in the spirit of things, the suggested dinners for our Hungarian affair are a blending, or rather a counterpointing, of different tastes. If Hungary as a nation has had an unfortunate habit of being walked in on by uninvited guests, perhaps in fairness it might be said that the intruders merely wanted to sample the intoxicating cuisine, as we do, and add their few scents worth, and then move on.

The most romantic atmosphere that I can conjure up for Hungary is the image of a Gypsy encampment at night.

Picture it:

You and the companion of your dreams are sitting shoulder-to-shoulder before the crackling campfire. The other Gypsies have gone off to liberate some stray chickens, leaving the two of you alone. A lusty stew is bubbling in a pot on the fire, and the night is seductively warm, and the camp dogs are howling to the moon. You can hear, somewhere in the night, from across the Danube, a trio of violins singing a sweet serenade in old Romany.

The Gypsies have such a sly reputation — the mysteriousness of their customs, the dark sultriness of their faces, the suggestion of licentiousness. In his book "The Gypsies", Jan Yoors describes them as living "in an everlasting Now, in a perpetual, heroic present, as if they recognized only the flow pulse of eternity and were content to live in the margin of history. They are in constant motion, like the waving of branches or the flowing of water."

Gypsies make their living from town to town, as dancers and musicians and horse traders and hucksters, often taking jobs that no one else wants — the hangman, the undertaker, the dog-catcher. But the trade that we associate most with them is fortune-telling. And, as it happens, fortune-telling lends itself perfectly to a romantic dinner party for two.

Invest in a deck of Tarot cards, those medieval tools for divination. If you haven't gotten around to reading the instructions by the night of the party, don't worry, just fake it. Shuffle the cards as if you knew what you were doing, and use your imagination. Maybe you want to hide the "Lovers" card up your sleeve to pull out at the proper moment (and the "Fool" card, as well, just in case). If the evening has been going nicely, you might whip a card out of the deck, any card, and announce with a look of pleasant surprise: "Why this card signifies immediate good fortune in the realm of human relationships." If the evening hasn't been going well, hold the card presciently to your Third Eye and aver: "This card symbolizes sleepiness and irritation and young Gypsies getting on their horses and going home."

If you don't have a Tarot deck, you can always fall back on palm reading. It's a start at holding hands, at any rate.

The best games to play, though, are the ones you invent yourselves — those spontaneous games of role-playing that can last for a few minutes or for an entire evening.

He is the Gypsy violinist and she is the runaway princess.

He is the angry townsman and she is the beautiful begger girl.

Whatever your taste and good sense will permit.

INVITATIONS:

To get into the proper Gypsy mood of mystification, you can begin by sending the invitation in the form of a Tarot card.

Tarot is such a popular distraction nowadays that you shouldn't have any trouble getting a deck at a bookshop or game store or from your local occult-objects dealer. When you look through the deck of 78 cards you'll notice that the 22 cards which comprise the so-called Major Arcana are inscribed with pithy titles such as "The Magician" and "The Hermit" and "The Devil". Select that card which best describes your prospective dinner guest, or which conveys the most appropriate message, and attach your written invitation to the back by means of a pressure sensitive label.

If you want to flatter a male guest you can send the "Emperor" card, which signifies power, protection and perseverance. If you want to be more direct you can choose the "Hierophant", which stands for the possibilitiy of marriage or alliance of some kind. If you're a shy one you can send "Temperance". If you are a man you can send your lady the "High Priestess", which whispers of secrets and mystery and the future as yet unrevealed. If you intend to make this a farewell dinner, then send him "The Fool", which pictures a starry-eyed young prince about to walk off a cliff.

One footnote: You must have your guest bring the card with him to the dinner, because you can't do *anything* properly without a full deck.

Since Gypsies traditionally carry gold coins tied into the corners of their scarves, you could send an invitation along with a scarf that contains some of those chocolate coins wrapped in foil. You might even want to remove one of the candies and slip the invitation into the foil.

For any kind of Hungarian dinner you can enclose your invitation in an empty paprika can.

SCENTS:

From ancient times down through the ages, it has become apparent that man has had certain primitive responses to scent and colors...It has been said that for magic rituals, not only costume, jewelry and hour be appropriate, the perfume must conform as well. It sets the mood, and if properly made will set up specific vibrations.

Hundreds of fragrances are available, and as for colors: gold stands for richness, abundance and self-confidence; red for passion, sex and anger; yellow for warmth, happiness and well-being; blue for protection and spirituality; pink for perfect love, and orange for heat and attraction.

You might use candles that change colors as the flame burns down. I can imagine a candle that begins burning with the orange of attraction, slowly gives way to the red of passion, and finally reaches the pink zone of true love.

You might also consider using bath crystals and body oil made for your Zodiacal sign, then burning a candle dressed with the fragrance representing the sign of your companion.

In general, scented candles with earthy fragrances will complement the kitchen aromas of the peppery cooking suggested in this chapter.

In summertime, settle for a couple of large candles so as not to heat up the room too much. In the winter, however, I recommend lots of candles massed on a tray in the center of the table or dining area, reminiscent of the Gypsy campfires.

TABLE SETTINGS:

A tray of rustic design should be placed under the candles to prevent the wax from dripping on the tablecloth. Around the tray, as a winter arrangement, you can use greens such as magnolia leaves (from the florist) or boughs of fir and spruce and hardy ferns. In the summer, simple flowers such as daisies can be arranged with the greens.

Creating a distinctive atmosphere is the goal, and any visual trick you can think of is fair. Since glittering Vienna was the hub of Hungarian life until World War I, you might prefer to recreate the ambience of that era with fine china and crystal. Herend/Hungary produces china that is too expensive for the average budget, but you can search it out in a specialty shop to get the feel of Hungarian patterns.

However, in keeping with the more basic foods of the nomadic settlers of Hungary, I'm suggesting a less formal table setting. A layered look to the tablecloth would be interesting and could be achieved in different ways. One would be an underskirt of a solid-colored material overlaid with an old fringed shawl. Another might require going to a rummage sale or Goodwill store to find a 1920s or '30s style bridge cloth with cross-stiched flowers, which could then be used with a flowered underskirt.

Simple stoneware and stainless steel flatware would be in order or in some instances perhaps even the marbelized tinware shown for use in picnic baskets.

I suggest dim lighting. To give the impression of being inside a Gypsy encampment or caravan wagon, you could try to do something with draped fabric or bedspreads. Like the Magyars who founded the nation, you could hang woven rugs from the walls and sit on embroidered cushions on the floor.

CLOTHING:

Ethnic clothing is available everywhere these days, and the Gypsy look has been popular with women for years. Remember that you don't have to deck yourself out like a Halloween Gypsy, and in fact you can kill the magic if you overdo it. Jan Yoors, in "The Gypsies" (Simon and Schuster), describes his first glimpse of the women in this way:

"Around the campfires sat women draped in deep-colored dresses, their big expressive eyes and strong, white teeth standing out against their beautiful dark matte skin. The many gold pieces they wore as earrings, necklaces and bracelets sharpened their color even more. Their shiny blue-black hair was long and braided, the skirts of their dresses were ankle-length, very full and worn in many layers, and their bodices loose and low cut. My first impression of them was one of health and vitality."

Married women customarily wear scarves on their heads. Unwed women wear their hair in braids which are loosened on their wedding night.

The Gypsy men that I've seen at fairs in Europe have possessed a dark and charismatic presence, like Valentino. Their standard uniform, as far as I've been able to tell, is black trousers and white shirts open to the chest. Most men wear the traditional scarves knotted around their necks, supposedly a sign of strength and even infallibility.

MUSIC:

My random suggestions: The "Gypsy" album, by Werner Muller. "Hungarian Pictures", by Eugene Ormandy and the Philadelphia Orchestra. "Favorite Melodies of Liszt", by Phillipe Entremont. "Out-of-Doors" (Bartok Opera 14), by Murray Perahia.

HAM PUFFS

Serves 2-4

- ½ C. boiled ham, ground
- 1 egg
- 1 T. sour cream
- Pinch pepper
- Chopped parsley
- Egg wash
- Crust (See Page 32) or
- 1 tube prepared Crescent rolls, cut each roll in half, and roll thinner.

Mix ham, egg, sour cream, parsley and pepper. Put ½ tsp in center of square of dough. Fold in half and crimp edges with fork. If using roll dough, make a crescent by putting filling in center of large end of dough, and rolling up into a crescent shape. Preheat oven to 400 degrees. Brush with egg wash, made by beating egg with 1 T. water. Reduce heat to 350 degrees as soon as puffs are put in the oven and bake 10 to 12 minutes, until nicely brown.

CARAWAY SOUP

Serves 2-4

- 1 T. bacon grease or butter
- 1 tsp. caraway seeds
- 1 T. flour
- 1 pint water
- 1 egg
- ¼ C. sour cream
- Salt and pepper to taste
- 1 C. croutons, either homemade or packaged garlic croutons.

Heat fat and cook seeds 1 minute or so until they "pop". They'll make a crackling sound. Off the heat add the flour, stirring to blend. Return to heat and brown lightly. Add water stirring with a whisk. Cook 15 min. or so. Strain this mixture and return to pot. Beat egg and sour cream until foamy and whip into soup. Add salt and pepper to taste. Serve with warm croutons in individual soup bowls.

FRIED GREEN TOMATOES

My college roommate introduced me to this dish, and I've been addicted ever since. The secret to preparing them properly is to get a fully developed tomato that just isn't red yet. Not the immature, underdeveloped green ones. Those that you see in the market that have just begun to get a tinge of pink are fine. Ask your produce man if you don't see any out as they usually hold green ones back.

- ¼ C. milk
- 1 egg, beaten
- 2 medium green tomatoes cut in ½" slices
- ½ c. flour
- Salt and pepper
- Lard and butter mixed to cover skillet to ½" depth
- Flour on plate
- Sour cream and chives

Dip each tomato slice in flour on plate, then in batter made by beating the ½ C. flour, salt, and pepper into the beaten egg. Fry in hot fat until golden brown each side. Serve on hot platter and put sour cream and chives on the side.

TRANSYLVANIA BANDIT'S MEAT — Serves 2

Bandit's Meat...Robber's Meat...whatever name it gets, in translation, implies that it is quick and could be eaten on the run. Beef tenderloin is the main ingredient; so therefore it fits the expensive meal category...unless of course, you live like the gypsies who made its reputation.

- **1 lb. beef tenderloin**
- **2 tsp. paprika**
- **Salt and pepper**
- **Bacon, thick slices**
- **Mushrooms**
- **Onion, optional, but whole and par-boiled if used**
- ***Bed of hash brown potatoes**

This can be prepared many ways..all cook quickly. To do over charcoal, cut beef in 1" cubes, cut bacon in 1" lengths, wipe off mushrooms with damp towel. Put all in plastic bag with paprika, salt and pepper and shake to coat. String on skewers having bacon on both sides of beef, i.e., mushroom-bacon-beef-bacon-mushroom, etc...You can add onions if you like. (Canned ones will do.) This can be done in a hot skillet by frying out bacon till almost done then adding beef, cut in strips, instead of chunks. Add sliced mushrooms, onions and seasonings at the very last moment, then nest on cooked potatoes of your choice.

*Shred baking potatoes after they are peeled. Immerse in cold water. To fry, press out as much moisture as you can with your hand, then squeeze them in paper towel. Put them in a small non-stick skillet in very hot shortening and fry on one side until crisp and brown, then turn them over. Do not make the layer too thick. When cooking on the second side, season to taste and cover them partially so they cook through.

CUCUMBER SALAD — Serves 2-4

- **2 medium cucumbers cut in thin slices**
- **1 tsp. salt**
- **1 medium onion sliced very thin**
- **Pinch sugar**
- **Sweet paprika**
- **¼ C. cider vinegar**
- **½ C. water**
- **Sour cream if desired**

Sprinkle cucumber slices with salt and let stand in glass bowl as long as 2 hours, turning to be sure each slice is salted. Add more salt if needed. Meanwhile marinate onion slices in vinegar, water, sugar and paprika mixture. To combine, squeeze water from cucumbers with hand, then turn out and press between paper towels. Add to onion mixture and correct seasoning. If you want sour cream dressing, drain the mixture reserving some of the liquid to blend with sour cream, and add back to the cucumber-onion mixture. Serve as a relish. Keep refrigerated.

PANCAKES À LA GUNDEL

1 egg
⅓ C. plus 1 T. flour
⅓ C. milk
½ tsp. sugar
Pinch salt
⅓ C. carbonated water
Sweet butter, clarified for frying pancakes

Mix all ingredients except carbonated water and let rest for 1 to 2 hours. Meanwhile, clarify butter and prepare filling. To prepare pancakes, add carbonated water and fry crepes in hot crepe pan with clarifed butter. Cover and keep warm.

Walnut filling:

½ C. ground walnuts
1 T. chopped raisins
1 tsp. orange rind, grated
1 T. rum
¼ C. sugar
1-2 T. light cream
Butter for sautéing filled pancakes
Hot chocolate sauce of your choice with rum to taste

Put sugar and cream in a small heavy skillet. Let bubble gently over low heat, then add raisins, orange rind, walnuts and rum. Stir thoroughly and let this mixture cook a minute or so over low heat. Adjust consistency by adding a bit more cream if necessary, or more of the ground walnuts. Should be a spreadable mixture.

To assemble: put a heaping spoonful of walnut filling in center of each of 4 pancakes (if serving 2). Spread out slightly and fold into quarters, making a wedge shaped piece. Sauté each in butter for a few minutes. Overlap on serving plate. Pour on chocolate sauce, garnish with whole or chopped nuts and serve immediately.

SPINACH SOUP

Serves 2-4

2 strips bacon, chopped
3 green onions, chopped
¼ lb. fresh spinach, washed well
1 T. flour
1 C. chicken bouillon
½ C. sour cream
1 hard cooked egg, sliced

Fry out bacon over low heat, until crisp. Lift out bacon and reserve. Add onions to grease and sauté lightly over low heat. Add washed spinach with water clinging to leaves. Cover and let cook until spinach is wilted and tender. Meanwhile blend flour into sour cream. Reserve. When spinach is tender, put into blender with chicken bouillon and purée. Put back into pan over heat and add sour cream mixture. Cook until slightly thickened. Remove from heat and chill. To serve: correct consistency with milk or buttermilk. Garnish with bacon and egg slice.

PAN FRIED ROSTELYOS

Serves 2-4

- 1 Rib eye steak weighing 1 lb. cut in thin strips across the grain
- Salt
- 1 T. flour
- 2-3 T. lard
- 1 medium onion, peeled and sliced in ⅛" slices
- 1 small clove garlic, crushed
- ⅛ tsp. caraway seeds
- 1 tsp. paprika
- 2 small potatoes, cubed
- 1 small green pepper, diced
- 2 small tomatoes, diced
- Water
- Salt and Pepper

Heat lard in heavy skillet. Rapidly brown meat on all sides. Remove meat to bowl and while still hot, sprinkle the flour over it and toss to coat. In the same skillet, adding more lard if needed, sauté the onions 4-5 minutes on low, then add the garlic and spices and cook 4-5 minutes more. Remove garlic, add the tomatoes, peppers and potatoes with enough water to barely cover. Cover pan and simmer until potatoes are tender. Add meat back into pan and stir gently and cook until the mixture is slightly thickened. Season. Correct consistency with a bit of hot water if necessary. To serve: put in heated tureen.

SUMMER SQUASH WITH SOUR CREAM AND DILL

Serves 2-4

- 1 lb. zucchini or other summer squash peeled, seeded and cut in julienne strips
- Salt
- 1 T. butter
- 1 T. flour
- ½ C. sour cream
- Pinch sugar
- 1 tsp. vinegar
- 1 tsp. dill freshly minced or ½ tsp. dry dill weed
- Salt and pepper

Sprinkle zucchini with salt and let stand 1 hour or more under cover. Squeeze moisture from squash and pat dry with paper towel. Meanwhile, melt butter in sauce pan, add squash and toss in butter until well coated. Cover pan, turn down heat and simmer until almost tender. Don't overcook. Meanwhile, whisk flour into sour cream. Pour sour cream over squash, stirring gently until sauce is thick. Stir in sugar, vinegar, dill, salt and pepper to taste. To serve: Turn into heated bowl.

ATTILLA'S REVENGE

1½ oz. dry gin
dash dry Vermouth
1 drop Tabasco
twist of lemon peel

Shake with ice and serve with lemon twist.

MERINGUES WITH FRUIT

Meringue shells are very versatile and if kept stored, air tight, will last a long time for a variety of desserts. They can be filled with a scoop of ice cream with your choice of toppings or with various creams topped with whipped cream or with fruit fillings.

There are some basic facts you need to know about beating egg whites. They will not beat up if they come in contact with any grease, or broken egg yolk. Further, if anything greasy comes in contact with the beaten egg whites, they will break down. Plastic acts the same as grease; so don't use plastic bowls, scrapers, lined pastry bags or plastic coated cooky sheets. With that in mind follow the directions below.

4 egg whites
½ lb. superfine sugar (not confectioners)
Pinch cream of tartar

Fresh raspberries, strawberries, peaches, etc...sweetened slightly
Whipped cream, sweetened

Beat egg whites in a deep bowl with electric beater until foamy. Add the cream of tartar and blend then start adding the sugar a bit at a time. Do not overbeat...whites should stand up in stiff peaks. Cut a brown paper bag to fit cooky sheets, then using a pointed tipped tablespoon, spoon out a mound of meringue onto the baking sheet. Using the tip of the spoon, spread in circular motion from the center, creating a 3" "nest". A pastry bag with decorating tip can be used, but it must be a cloth bag uncontaminated with grease. Put sheet of meringues into pre-heated 200 degree oven for 1 hour. Turn off heat, and let cool in oven. Remove from paper and store air tight. To serve, fill with sweetened fruit and top with whipped cream.*

THE PURPLE HICKEY
(Count Dracula's Favorite Drink)

1 glass (3 oz.) blackberry brandy
1 oz. cream floated on top
dash nutmeg

HUN'S HONEY

1¼ oz. Bourbon
dash Angostura Bitters
½ tsp. honey
1 tsp. Maraschino liqueur
Shake with ice and serve on the rocks.

LIPTO CHEESE AND CRACKERS

Serves 2

- ¼ lb. Lipto cheese, or Brindza or cottage cheese, sieved
- ½ cube butter
- ½ tsp. paprika
- ½ tsp. salad mustard
- ¼ tsp. caraway seeds, crushed
- 1 T. onion, grated
- ¼ tsp. anchovy paste

Lipto or Brindza cheese should be put through ricer. Blend in all other ingredients until light red throughout. Refrigerate. To serve: mound in a small bowl and serve with your choice of crackers or crusty bread. To make a dip, add sour cream to desired consistency.

HALASZLIE (Fish Soup)

Serves 2-4

- ⅛ C. butter
- 1 small onion, minced
- 1 stalk celery, chopped
- 1 carrot, chopped
- 1 tsp. paprika
- Bouquet garni (1 clove garlic, 1 bay leaf, few peppercorns, sprig thyme, few sprigs parsley) tied in cheesecloth bag.
- ½ C. dry white wine
- 2 C. water
- Fish trimmings or cut tail pieces from fillets
- 1 whitefish fillet, cubed and floured (½ lb.)
- ¼ C. each diced carrot, onions, green beans and peas

Melt butter and slowly sauté the onion, celery and carrots. Stir in paprika and cook 2-3 minutes. Add bouquet garni, fish trimmings and water to cover, salt and pepper to taste. Bring to a boil, then reduce heat, skim carefully then cover and simmer for 1 hour. Strain through dampened cheese cloth about 3 layers thick. Return broth to clean kettle. Add vegetables and simmer about 15 minutes. Add fish cubes which have been shaken in flour. Simmer gently 7 to 8 minutes. Serve hot.

BEET SALAD

Serves 4-6

- 2 C. cooked beets or canned, julienne cut
- ½ C. white wine vinegar
- 1 T. sugar
- 1 tsp. salt
- 1 tsp. mustard
- Pinch caraway
- 1 T. horseradish, fresh, grated or drained salad style horseradish

Put beets in glass or stainless steel bowl. Bring all other ingredients, except horseradish to a simmer. Mix beets and horseradish and pour hot marinade over them. Cover and let stand overnight. This keeps well; so chill and serve the leftovers as a relish for several meals.

TOKANY

Serves 2-4

- ½ C. stewing beef, cubed
- ½ C. lean pork, cubed
- 3 strips bacon, heavily smoked, cut in 1" pieces
- 1 medium onion, chopped
- 1½ tsp. Hungarian paprika
- ½ C. water
- Pinch caraway seeds
- Pinch marjoram
- ¼ C. dry white wine
- 1 T. butter
- ¼ lb. mushrooms, sliced
- ½ C. sour cream mixed with 1 T. flour

Cook bacon over low heat then add onion and wilt. Add paprika and ½ C. water. Simmer briefly to cook paprika. Add beef, caraway, marjoram, and wine. Cook 30 min. at a simmer, covered. Add pork and ¼ C. more wine or water as desired. Cook over lowest heat until meat is tender. (Can also be cooked in oven at 300 degrees.) 10 min. before serving, sauté mushrooms in butter. Add to meat. Stir in sour cream and bring to simmer over direct heat, but do not cook further. Serve with noodles.

ASPARAGUS PUDDING

Serves 2-4

- 1 10 oz. pkg. frozen asparagus tips or cooked fresh
- 1 slice bread
- ¼ C. milk
- 2 T. butter
- 2 eggs separated
- 2 T. sour cream
- Butter for baking dish

Thaw asparagus and squeeze out moisture. Steam 5 minutes, then drain. Meanwhile soak bread in milk and squeeze dry. Butter a 1 qt. baking dish well. Whip butter until light, then add bread, egg yolks, sour cream, salt and whip until fluffy. Whip egg white and using RUBBER (not plastic) spatula, carefully fold egg whites into yolk mixture. Combine carefully with asparagus. Put in baking dish, not over ¾ths full. Cover baking dish. Set dish in pan half full of water and cook 325 degrees 1 hour.

RUM RASPBERRY TORTE

Serves 4-6

- 1 Jiffy Cake Mix, yellow or equal 8" square cake
- ½ C. water
- ½ C. sugar
- ½ C. light rum
- ½ C. raspberry jam
- 1 cube butter
- 4 oz. semi-sweet chocolate
- ½ lb. powered sugar
- 2 T. rum

Bake cake in 8" square pan. Line bottom of pan with wax paper. Cool cake on rack and remove layer carefully. Cut in half. Then cut each half into two layers. On a cookie sheet, put a piece of wax paper and lay the 4 layers side by side. Put cut sides down. Pierce each layer with tines of a fork in several places. Meanwhile bring the sugar and water to boil and boil 1 minute. Cool and add rum. Spoon syrup over cake, cover and reserve. Melt chocolate and butter in top of double boiler. Blend. Remove from heat and add the 2 T. rum and beat in butter alternately with powered sugar. Beat until fluffy. To assemble: Put cake layer cut side down on serving dish. Spread with jam, add next layer and repeat. Leave jam off top layer and frost cake completely with chocolate-rum frosting. Wrap loosely and chill several hours.

MUSHROOM FRITTERS

Serves 2

½ lb. mushrooms
1 T. lemon juice
1 pint water
Salt and pepper
Flour for dredging
½ (scant) C. flour
1 egg separated
1 T. vegetable oil
½ C. milk
1 C. lard or more for frying

Remove stems from caps (Save them for other purposes.) Wipe caps clean with damp paper towel. Put water and lemon juice in saucepan and bring to boil. Lower mushrooms into boiling liquid and boil two minutes. Drain and wipe mushrooms with a paper towel. Shake mushrooms gently in bag with seasoned flour. Make a thick batter with flour, egg yolk, oil and milk. Whip egg white until stiff. With RUBBER spatula fold whites into batter. Dip mushrooms into batter. Fry in hot oil, 375 degrees a few at a time until golden brown. Remove to drain with slotted spoon.

POTATO SOUP

Serves 2-4

1 medium baking potato, peeled and diced
2 T. butter
¼ C. celery, chopped
1 small parsnip, diced
¼ C. onion finely chopped
¼ C. carrot finely chopped
1 T. flour
2 C. chicken bouillon
Pinch marjoram
Salt and pepper

Melt butter in 2 qt. saucepan. Add all the vegetables and cook uncovered, stirring until vegetables take on a golden color. Sprinkle flour over vegetables stirring to coat, then add the bouillon while stirring to blend. Add seasoning to taste. Bring to boil, but reduce heat immediately and barely simmer, partially covered until vegetables are all tender. Serve hot in soup bowls.

CHICKEN PAPRIKASH

Serves 2

- 2 pieces chicken per person
- 2 T. lard
- ½ C. onion, chopped
- 2 tsp. Hungarian paprika
- 1 C. chicken broth
- 1 T. flour blended in ¾ C. sour cream
- Noodles or Dumplings, cooked

Wipe off pieces of chicken and put into skillet with heated lard. Be sure each piece lies flat and brown lightly on each side. Remove browned chicken. Set aside. Pour off fat from skillet, leaving a light covering. If lard is too brown, wipe out skillet and replace with fresh lard. Add the onion and cook over medium heat until lightly colored. Off the heat, stir the paprika into the onions. Return to heat and add chicken broth. Bring to a boil and scrape down any browned bits. Put chicken in broth. At a simmer, cover pan and cook 20-30 minutes or until chicken is tender. Remove chicken, and add sour cream—flour mixture to broth using a whisk. Simmer 8 to 10 minutes. Put chicken back into sauce and coat each piece. To serve, put chicken on a nest of noodles or in a bowl of dumplings and cover with sauce.

CABBAGE SALAD

Serves 2-4

- ½ small head cabbage, shredded
- 2 T. onion grated
- 1 tsp. sugar
- 1 tsp. salt
- ¼ C. salad oil
- 1 T. vinegar
- ½ tsp. caraway seeds

Shred cabbage and put in large bowl. Cover with hot water and let stand about half an hour. In a separate bowl mix dressing. To assemble, drain cabbage and press out moisture with hands and paper towels. Toss with dressing. Cover and chill salad at least 10 minutes before serving.

HUSSAR'S KISSES

- ⅔ C. butter, must be butter
- ⅓ C. sugar
- ½ tsp. vanilla (or use vanilla sugar)
- 1 egg yolk plus 1 egg
- 1⅓ C. sifted flour
- ½ C. pecans, chopped finely
- ½ C. raspberry jam
- Egg wash (1 egg beaten with 1 T. water)

In mixer bowl cream with electric beater, the butter and sugar. Beat until light and fluffy. Add egg yolk and egg and beat again until fluffy. Add the flour. Blend. Chill dough. Pinch off ¾" balls of chilled dough and put on ungreased baking sheet. With thumb make a depression in the center of each ball. Brush cookies with egg wash. Sprinkle with nuts. Bake in pre-heated 350 degree oven for 15 minutes or until golden. Cool. Fill centers with jam.

Made in Japan

The ritualistic order of serving a Japanese meal is having, first, something from the mountains; then something from the sea, then from the fields, and last something from the towns. Tea, of course, is from the mountains, and serving tea at the beginning of your meal will fulfull that requirement.

Following are various categories of food, and with some experimentation, you can put together a Japanese menu to suit your own taste.

Whatever you choose to cook, please be aware of the beauty of Japanese food. Its visual appeal is unequalled in my estimation.

Inscribed on the entrance to the Yoshiwara, ancient Tokyo's fabled red-lantern district, was this timeless legend: "Lust Will Not Keep...Something Must Be Done About It!" And so it was. For centuries, Japanese men came to the Yoshiwara to surrender to a ritualistic satiation of their most animalistic senses. (So much for the inscrutable Oriental!)

The Yoshiwara was a city within a city, built upon a reedy marsh in the 17th Century and surrounded by a moat. Yoshiwara was the Japanese word for "reed moor", but with a slip of the brush it could be translated as "joyful moor", and that turned out to be a more appropriate meaning, and the one that stuck. In time Yoshiwara became a sort of generic term for "city of pleasure".

To get to the Joyful Moor, a gentleman crossed a bridge that arched the moat. At once he was in a fantasy land where cherry blossoms, bathing in the glow of hanging lanterns, cast a delicate aura of pink over gardens and tea houses and chambers of delight. This scene was so enchanting that on special holidays men sometimes brought their wives or girl friends along. But when the men came alone they turned their bodies over to the care of exotic women who pampered them, powdered them, bathed and massaged them, and entertained them with a sophisticated sensuality unknown to the Western world.

The prevailing morality was open-minded. The married men who frequented the Yoshiwara weren't considered to be infidels, and weren't necessarily being starved for pleasure at home. Even proper young ladies, after all, were given "Pillow Books" at their weddings which gave them liberal and graphic educations in the many positions of conjugal bliss. No, their husbands simply subscribed to the proverb of the day: Why use the familiar pot at home if you can delight in a fancy vessel in the Yoshiwara ?" And don't feel too sorry for the wives, because high-born ladies often had their own outside lovers, not to mention their dildoes of jade and ivory and a fascinating variety of other sex toys.

In the hierarchy of the Yoshiwara, the elite charmers were the geishas. A geisha began her training at around the age of 5 at an early Oriental version of charm school. She studied floral arrangement, the tea ceremony, folk singing, dancing, manners, the art of conversation—everything that might be necessary to make her the ultimate gentleman's companion. And yet the geisha wasn't expected to be the man's sex partner, unless she wanted to be. Courtesans and several classes of prostitutes satisfied the baser need.

It was a status symbol for a gentleman to maintain his own geisha, a distinction that only the wealthy could afford. The custom was for a man of standing to invite his male friends and acquaintances to the house of his geisha, where she would entertain and converse with them until they'd had all the food and drink they desired, and then she would arrange through her staff for sexual appeasement all around. The geisha might satisfy her own appetites through an entirely different arrangement, because, although she was a kept woman, she wasn't *owned* by anyone.

Historically, in fact, geishas seem to have drawn the most criticism—not for their slavishness to men, which has only recently become an unpopular habit—but instead for their choice of extracurricular playmates. Apparently, geishas liked to hang around with sumo wrestlers and Kabuki actors, the former being so fat that they had logistical problems with sex and were inclined to have atrophied gonads, and the latter tending towards narcissism and homosexuality.

In short, the geisha had a mind of her own.

Japanese erotic art, which has a long and proud tradition of its own, provides a provocative glimpse into the libertine past. Artists were turning out those helpful little "Pillow Books", or "Bride's Scrolls", as early as the 11th Century. Later on, from the early 1600s to the late 1800s, artists were allowed inside the Yoshiwara itself—inside the very brothels—to paint from live action. It was the original Insta-Cam, but without instant replay. The artists weren't voyeurs, either, but the eminent artists of the day—Utamaro, Hokusai, Hiroshige, Shigemasa. The works that they thus produced are known as the shunga, or Spring Pictures.

Artistically, the shunga are masterpieces. Anatomically, they are textbook Freud. In the backgrounds are exquisitely painted screens, floral arrangements and sumptuous bed clothing. The human figures are always dressed in luxuriant kimonos (and in fact the Japanese characters for foreplay mean "trembling silk"). The kimonos are conspicuously parted in front, with brilliantly colored sex organs protruding gigantically, and the lovers are depicted in ludicrous positions that could be achieved only if their bodies were made of silly putty.

There are many redeeming features of Japanese erotic art, but I find humor to be high on the list. The shunga even remind me faintly, in their grotesqueries, of those pornographic comic books I once found hidden in my parents' bedroom. One painting in particular amuses me, and reminds me of the old Cole Porter song about, "Birds doin' it, bees doin' it, even educated fleas doin' it..." For there on the couch are the kimono-clad lovers in furious copulation, while in the foreground dogs do it, mice do it, and a cat watches on like Dr. Kinsey.

An engrossing selection of these Japanese woodblock prints can be found in "The Complete Book of Erotic Art", by Drs. Phillis and Eberhard Kronhausen (Bell Publishers).

In any case, the history lesson is now over.

It was intended, naturally, to get you into the mood to arrange a Japanese dinner party for two. For you women who are offended by the image of the geisha fussing over her partner like a Las Vegas madam at a Legionnaires' convention, let me remind you that the last game of the evening is lady's choice. Anyway, it seems to me that we women have ample opportunities to prove our independence from men; I don't see any particular reason for having to prove ourselves romantically independent as well. We have as much to gain from truly passionate situations as men do—maybe more, since we've been repressed for so long. So I say: Take yourself very seriously...until the sun goes down. And remember that God gave man football so that She'd have Sundays as a day of rest.

Besides, this fantasy can be turned around. There were geisha men, too, back then, called *hokan.*

A deluded male geisha from Edo
Belived he was a loaded torpedo,
And this Freudian notion
Caused quite a commotion
When he gave in to his lively libido.

The Yoshiwara itself is long gone, having been succeeded in Tokyo by the Ginza, night baseball and roller disco. But that can't stop us diehards from bringing back the old ways. It's quite easy to turn a living room in, let's say Lincoln, Nebraska, into a Japanese tea house for the evening, and easier yet to slip into a silk kimono.

Going with custom, you can greet your guest at the front door with a steaming hot perfumed towel, which the guest can use to wipe off his or her hands before donning the kimono. (An ice bucket, by the way, will keep a towel hot for several hours.) If you are preparing this party for the person you live with, a steaming towel is a wonderful token of greeting when your mate walks in the door after a hard day's work.

Another friendly way to say hello in Japanese is to give your guest a few minutes of Shiatsu (accupressure) foot massage. Actually, any kind of foot massage will do, and will have approximately the same relaxing effect on your guest as two dry martinis.

Stretch the evening out. Make everything a ritual.

A leisurely soak in a hot tub would be stunningly appropriate, as would later on, a more general body massage, which is one of the geisha's specialties. A formula for homemade massage oil can be found in the Scandinavian chapter of this book, or you might want to purchase one of the scented oils that are on the market.

Finally, the two of you might want to, as they say in the Orient, "throw the bones". But wait—before you jump out of your kimono—all that means is to practice the ancient method of divination known as the I Ching. It was a Chinese custom that was later adopted by the Japanese, and involves the casting of bones, sticks or coins to foretell the future. (see notes)

I have to confess that, although I love Japanese floral arrangements, Japanese gardens, Japanese clothing, Japanese lacquerware, Shinto shrines, bonsai specimens, origami, kirigami, and my little Sony clock-radio, I do not happen to be fond of Japanese cooking. The beauty of its presentation notwithstanding, I find it difficult to embrace a cuisine that does not recognize cheese or chocolate. So I have called upon some fellow decadents who really adore Japanese food, and they've helped me put together some tantalizing recipes for your evening on the Joyful Moor.

INVITATIONS:

The Japanese have turned the simple act of folding paper into an elaborate art form known as origami. Packages of origami paper can be purchased at import shops, along with instructions for folding it into intricate and myriad shapes. I'd suggest writing your invitations on the white side of the paper, then folding it into a design that delights you, and mailing it off.

With a little more ingenuity you can make up a scroll with Japanese characters and pseudo Japanese artwork, with your own translation at the bottom.

Or buy a paper parasol and paint on the invitation so that it pops into view when the parasol is opened.

SCENTS:

Many people, for some strange reason, have an Oriental incense burner languishing around the house somewhere—one of those tiny, tarnished brass tureens, or a fat-bellied Buddha sitting in full lotus with the incense holder in his lap (ouch!). Well, now is the time to fetch that curio out of the junk drawer, dust it off, and put it to use. Buy some incense and burn a bit before the night of the party to get a feeling for how much you'll want to use, and in which locations around the house.

Joss sticks can be stuck in potted plants and vases. A little experimentation with these before the party can insure that the ashes from the stick don't drop into your guest's *sake.*

TABLE SETTINGS:

It's true in Japan, as nowhere else, that small is beautiful. In centuries of relatively crowded living on four narrow islands, the Japanese have learned to use space to it's best advantage, and to miniaturize. Thus the dwarf bonsai trees, and the meticulous care that is bestowed on the placement of each pebble in a Japanese garden, and the developement of the high art of Ikebana, or flower arrangement. Ikebana, especially, I think, reflects this people's sensitivity to natural beauty in its eloquent arrangement of the most ordinary materials such as branches, flowers, pods and grasses. A single blossom coupled with a bare branch becomes a thing of wonder following the principles of Ikebana.

So this is a good place to start in arranging a Japanese table. Books on Ikebana can be found in stores and libraries, and the materials are probably available for picking right in your own back yard or in the nearest vacant lot. Chances are that you already have suitable containers in which to arrange the found materials.

If you want to be authentic you'll make two Ikebana arrangements: one for the dining table and one for the tokonoma. A tokonoma is an integral part of the traditional Japanese home—a low platform decorated with fine art objects and reminders of the season, set against the wall beneath a painted scroll that also depicts the season. On the platform will be an Ikebana arrangement, perhaps some small statuary, an incense burner, carved jade or ivory, and maybe a beautifully lettered haiku poem. The lady of the house usually is the one who keeps the tokonoma current, and sometimes at the end of an arduous winter she'll force a branch of cherry blossoms or forsythia as a harbinger of spring.

You can build your own tokonoma fairly easily and make it a permanent part of your home, if you've got the space and the yen. The platform should be eight to ten inches off the floor, and could be finished as simply as with a can of black spray enamel. Oriental scrolls and wall hangings can be found at import shops. Choose one that will compliment the rest of your furnishings, and the flowers that you pick for the Ikebana can fall into the same harmony. Add a lovely paper fan, or a geisha doll, or a Kwan-Yuen figurine. The Metropolitan Museum of Art, the Pacific Mercantile Company at Sakura Square in Denver and The Denver Art Museum are all sources of tasteful Japanese accessories.

The dinner table should also be low—about 10 inches off the floor—and in fact it could be placed beneath the wall scroll to double as a tokonoma platform. (See illustration.) You might be able to eat off a low coffee table, or you can set a board or folded card table on top of discreet piles of bricks, books or ballasted coffee cans. A ball of floral clay on top of each leg will help to keep the tabletop from slipping. You might cover the table with a piece of black vinyl that is folded under at the edges and held in place with thumbtacks or duct tape. Or you might prefer bright red felt, a piece of brocade from the remnant counter, or some other material that strikes you as Japanese.

Add sofa cushions, pillows or low stools, and you can proceed to setting the table.

Lacquered tableware would be most authentic—and least practical. I was once at the home of a friend who had lived in the Orient for 25 years, and she served lunch on 200-year-old lacquerware plates. They were very pleasing to the eye, of course, but we were all required to eat with chopsticks because the edges of the silverware would have scratched the lacquerware and ruined it forever. If you want to be a purist and serve out of a lacquered *koban* and eat with sticks, more power to you! Be as authentic as suits your fancy. Fortunately, Japanese dinnerware imports come in an amazing array of materials and patterns, that allow for great flexibility, Noritake, alone, has dozens of patterns from the "Sheer Ivory" bone china to the "Concept 1" stoneware.

You should feel free to mix and match pieces according to your eccentricities. But buy something of good quality to begin with. A plain white china that is cook-and-serve, oven-safe, microwave safe and freezer-safe is eminently suited to today's casual life styles and I can see it being used on various occasions with Dansk "Bistro", or with Italian pottery salad plates shaped like leaves, or with individual French casserole dishes in terra cotta.

By the way, I should mention that all of the trademarked items that I suggest are drawn from my own experience. My pockets haven't been lined by any manufacturer, distributor or retailer. I should also add that I can't vouch for the durability or any other qualities of the products that attract my eye.

U.S. manufacturers of china turn out an enormous range of internationally flavored patterns. "Temperware" by Lenox is one of those strong dinnerwares that's meant to go from freezer to oven to table, and the "Coral Blossoms" pattern would be just right for a Japanese meal. If you don't want to invest in a complete set of such a defined pattern, then accent what you already have with bowls, teapots and cups and saucers of Oriental design.

I'd suggest giving your guest a choice of using chopsticks, silverware and/or porcelain soup spoons. After all, it's really tacky to have seaweed hanging down your chin.

CLOTHING:

We should try to please all of the senses, and so in choosing clothing we ought to consider how a garment feels as well as how it looks. For this reason, you might shop around for a silk kimono. But if your budget is small don't worry, synthetic-fabric kimonos feel alright, too—to the right touch. Many colors and designs are available, with prices starting from $25. Some import shops have antique kimonos in heavier fabrics. You can also find kimonos in lingerie departments.

Gentlemen who are more conservative might prefer a *happi* coat in more subdued tones.

Tabi (socks) and *zori* (straw slippers) are inexpensive enough that you might want to furnish them for your guest(s) in true Japanese style. Another touch for a man could be a lavendar scarf tied around the forehead, but be aware that this was the fashion for actors who were female impersonators.

MUSIC:

One more confession: I'm not wild about Japanese music, any more than I am for Japanese food. But any well-stocked record store should have some *samisen* music, zen-meditation music, and even made-in-Japan *rock and roll.

**A seductive maid from Taipan*
Played "come-on" games with her fan,
So a daimyo *from Kobe*
Loosened her obi
And she was instantly "Made in Japan".

The creator of the music for the "Shogun" TV series, Osamu Kitajima, has albums available, as does a group called Kitaro. You might also check the ethnic-records file at your public library.

As far as I'm concerned, Sarah Vaughn's "Live" in Japan album would be a perfectly mellow start to an evening in your tea house.

SWEET COOKED CLAMS

Serves 2

12 small littleneck clams, shucked, (or shrimp or mussels)
¼ C. sake (rice wine)
3 T. sugar
3 T. soy sauce

Combine the sake, sugar and clams in small skillet. Bring to boil and cook, stirring for 3 min. Stir in soy sauce and cook for one min. Remove clams and set aside. Boil liquid in skillet over high heat for 10 min.—until it forms a syrupy glaze. Add clams and stir gently to coat, about 1 min. Serve cold.

STEAK AND GREEN ONION ROLLS

Serves 2

2 slices beef tenderloin, each about ¼" thick, pounded gently to flatten to ⅛" thick
2 medium green onions
¼ C. teriyaki sauce

TERIYAKI SAUCE

½ C. sweet sake (mirin)
½ C. Japanese, all purpose soy sauce
½ C. chicken bouillon
Sugar to taste
½ tsp. fresh ginger root, scraped
MSG if desired

Meat pieces should be 4-5" long and 3" wide. Aim to have pieces long and narrow. Marinate meat in sauce at least 1 hr. Cut onions to equal length of meat, then cut them in half vertically. Place each half going in opposite direction in center of meat. Beginning at wide side of meat, roll meat and onion into tight roll. Secure seam with toothpicks. Broil in broiler or over hibachi or pan fry for about 3 min. Remove with tongs and dip in sauce again. Return to fire and cook on other side for 3 min. Cut into 1" lengths and serve with sauce for dipping.

GINGER PORK CUBES

Serves 2

½ lb. pork tenderloin
½ C. shoyu (soy sauce)
¼ C. sake
2 T. sugar
1 clove garlic
½ oz. ginger root, grated

Cut meat in 1" cubes. Make marinade from remaining ingredients. Marinate meat at least 1 hr. String meat on skewer. Broil over charcoal, turning to cook all sides, or pan fry and baste with sauce. Serve on skewers or with picks. Reduce sauce slightly to serve with meat as dip.

CHICKEN SOUP

Serves 2

½ chicken breast, boned and cut in bite size
3 green onions, trimmed and cut diagonally
Fresh mushroom slices
1½ C. dashi one
¼ C. soy sauce
1 small piece ginger root

Put chicken in small pan with soy sauce and ¼ C. dashi. Simmer until tender. Remove. Divide chicken, green onions and mushrooms between two small bowls. Using a garlic press, squeeze two drops ginger juice into each bowl. Bring rest of dashi to boil and pour over ingredients in each soup bowl. Serve immediately.

MISO SOUP

2 C. dashi
2½-3 T. miso, to taste, for type of miso...red takes less
MSG
Appropriate garnish or additional ingredients

Thin miso with part of dashi and press through a fine sieve. Blend and bring to a boil. Add MSG. Have ready any and all ingredients to be added immediately before or after adding broth to bowl, depending on their purpose. See list below.

daikon	tofu	carrots	bean sprouts
leeks	Chinese cabbage	mushrooms	peas
green onions	potato	turnips	clams
wakame	spinach	lotus root	shrimp
cabbage	snow peas	celery	nuts

SUNOMONO

Serves 2-4

1 medium cucumber
1 can crabmeat, drained
Salt

VINEGAR SAUCE

2 T. vinegar (rice vinegar if desired)
2 T. soy sauce
2 T. dashi or bouillon
Sugar to taste
MSG

Pull the tines of a fork firmly from one end of cucumber to the other, making a regular pattern as you proceed. Then slice the cucumber into thin slices. Sprinkle the slices with salt and set aside in a strainer. Remove membranes from crabmeat and rinse meat in a strainer. Press cucumbers between paper towel and then combine with crabmeat. Dress with the sauce. Keep cold until ready to serve.

CAULIFLOWER

1 small cauliflower
1 small green pepper, sliced thinly
1 small green onion, sliced
½ tsp. salt
1 stalk celery, cut in ⅛" diagonal slices
½ C. vinegar
2½ T. sugar
MSG

Separate cauliflower into flowerets, then blanch, drain and reserve. Dip peppers in boiling water, remove and put with cauliflower. Put celery in a bowl and sprinkle with salt. Let stand, then drain. Put vinegar, sugar, water and MSG in a saucepan and bring to boil. Cool. Put vegetables in a glass bowl. Pour vinegar mixture over them. Place a plate on top of vegetables, so it will hold vegetables under liquid. (A clean Mason jar full of water on top of plate will hold vegetables under liquid.) Allow to stand about 5 hours, then chill before serving.

CHINESE CABBAGE PICKLES

2 lb. head, Chinese cabbage
4 green onions, chopped
1 red or green bell pepper
½ lemon, cut in strips, seeded
¼ C. vinegar
4 tsp. soy sauce, or to taste
¼ tsp. MSG

Cut the cabbage, starting at the top edge in circular slices about ¾" wide. These will be parallel to the circular base of the cabbage. Put in a large bowl and pour boiling water over cabbage. Let stand about 5 min. Then drain. Chop the green onions, sliver the pepper, then mix with the lemons and add to the cabbage. Add the vinegar, soy and MSG. Place a heavy weight (about 1 lb.) on top of salad and let stand for at least an hour before serving. (This can be kept refrigerated for several days.)

EGG SOUP

Serves 2

1½ C. dashi
1 tsp. soy sauce or more
1 egg, beaten
2 green onions, sliced

Heat dashi and shoyu together to boiling. Turn off heat, and gradually stir in egg. Immediately pour into two bowls and garnish with onions.

BROCCOLI MUSTARD RELISH

½ lb. broccoli, coarsely chopped
Dash salt
½ C. vinegar
MSG
1 T. prepared mustard
2 tsp. sugar

Bring broccoli to boil in salted water to cover. Remove from heat and pour off water. Cover broccoli with cold water to cool rapidly. Drain. Mix remaining ingredients and mix with broccoli. Let stand covered two days before serving.

GOMA-ZU

(Sauce for Vegetables)

½ C. cider vinegar
2 tsp. soy sauce
½ tsp. salt
1 T. sugar or to taste
Pinch MSG
Toasted sesame seeds
1 T. mirin or sherry

Mix all together except sesame seeds. Most Japanese recipes call for seeds to be ground into paste, but I like the crunch and added them whole. This sauce is used on bean sprouts, spinach, cucumbers, pea pods, watercress, etc...It is served as a salad.

RICE AND NOODLES

On Pearl S. Buck's authority, I state that the Japanese prefer their rice bland to permit other flavors to penetrate the grains. It is cooked, therefore, without anything but water. According to Miss Buck, it is also slightly sticky. My feeling is: cook rice the way you find it most successful to insure the overall outcome of the meal.

BUCKWHEAT NOODLES (Soba)

These are a fine accompaniment to many Japanese meals. I found them tasty as a "nest" for the GINGER PORK CUBES (see Appetizers). I must admit I added some salt and butter along with some of the sauce from the cubes.

Cook according to the directions found on the package or:

Drop the noodles in boiling water, then when the water starts to boil again, stir and add about ½ C. cold water. When the water boils again, stir and add another ½ C. water. Do this for a total of 4 times. Cover the pan. Turn off the heat and leave for about 15 minutes. Rinse well. These can be served hot or cold; so determine which way they are to be served. Rinse with cold water if serving cold and with hot water if serving hot. The usual sauce is soy.

SEAFOOD TEMPURA

Batter:

1 egg yolk
1 C. flour
1 C. ice water
1 tiny pinch baking soda
Pinch salt

Dipping Sauce:

1 C. dashi
⅓ C. mirin
1 tsp. sugar
⅓ C. plus 1 T. soy sauce
MSG

All brought to boil in saucepan, and held until needed.

Batter is made immediately prior to use. Mix lightly beaten egg, ice water, soda and salt in mixing bowl. Sift flour in and blend lightly with whisk..DON'T OVERBEAT. Batter will be lumpy and thin. To keep ice cold, put batter bowl in another bowl containing ice. Heat oil to about 375 degrees (constant temperature is important). Dip each piece in batter, fry both sides until golden and immediately serve that piece. Serve with dipping sauce in individual bowls.

Note: An electrically controlled pot for frying at the table allows the host/hostess to fry the pieces and pass them around immediately upon browning.

A wide variety of vegetables and fish may be used in this traditional dish. The only criterion being that they are very, very, fresh, cut in the proper size, and at least 6 in number...although there may be as many as 14.

shrimp	lobster	zucchini	peas
scallops	mussels	mushrooms	green beans
clams	flounder	green peppers	broccoli
oysters	sole	onions	carrots
squid	whiting	eggplant	lotus root
eels	tuna	cauliflower	potatoes

SALMON TERIYAKI

Serves 2

¼ C. soy sauce
2 T. mirin or sherry
⅛ C. sugar
MSG
2 salmon steaks

These are best done 7" above hot coals. (An hibachi is fine.) Marinate steaks about an hour, turning a couple of times. Put over hot coals for about 5 minutes per side, basting with sauce once or twice.

PORK WITH BAMBOO SHOOTS

Serves 2-4

- ½ lb. pork, cut in strips
- 1 small can bamboo shoots, drained
- 1 C. fresh snow peas, or sugar snaps
- 3 T. oil
- 2 T. soy sauce
- 1 T. sugar
- 2 T. sake
- MSG

Sauté pork and shoots in hot oil until nicely browned all sides. Reduce heat and add remaining ingredients except peas. Simmer until meat is tender and add peas. Cover so that peas steam through just a bit. Serve immediately with hot rice.

BEEF TERIYAKI

Serves 2-4

- 1 lb. beef tenderloin, cut in 1" cubes
- 1 tsp. or more grated, fresh ginger root
- ¼ C. Japanese soy sauce
- 1 small clove garlic, mashed
- ¼ C. mirin
- 2 T. peanut or sesame oil

String cubes of meat on individual skewers. Mix the rest of ingredients into a marinade and brush all sides of meat with it. Lay skewers in the remaining sauce and turn a couple of times, letting stand for an hour or more. Cook over hot coals until cooked to proper doneness. Baste with marinade while cooking. Serve with rice, noodles, etc...

RICE DISH WITH CHICKEN AND EGG

Serves 2-4

- 1 C. cooked rice (warm)
- 1 large chicken breast, cooked, boned, sliced
- 1 C. chicken broth
- ¼ C. soy sauce
- ¼ C. sake or sherry
- ½ C. mushrooms, sliced
- ¼ C. green onions, sliced diagonally
- 2 eggs lightly beaten

Simmer broth, soy sauce and sake. Add chicken, mushrooms and onions and simmer until mushrooms are just tender. Meanwhile, divide rice in two serving bowls. (Little "lotus" bowls are perfect.) Add beaten eggs to simmering chicken, stirring until eggs are nearly set. Ladle chicken mixture over rice. Garnish with carrot "flowers" and cashews. Serve immediately.

STEAM BROILED SHRIMP WITH CHICKEN, GINKGO NUTS AND MUSHROOMS (a la Mama-san Ewalt)

Serves 2

Anyone who knows me will not be surprised that in the face of centuries of tradition, I have seen fit to do it "my way". First off, this dish called for a cooking utensil that has been impossible to find...a "horoku". After a brief analysis, and a discussion with a local brickmaker, I decided there was no reason why I couldn't use commercially made clay saucers..of the type used to put under clay flower pots to catch the water.

This dish is made by putting the ingredients in a bed of hot coarse salt, which has been sprinkled with a little water; so, when covered, the dish "steam-broils". Instead of one big "horoku" for the assembled guests, I used 8" saucers for individual servings. It is necessary to scrub the saucers well before and after use because being unglazed, they are quite porous. (Mine went through the dishwasher nicely.) Instead of using any kind of lid, I used heavy-duty aluminum foil. (Whew! Now on to the recipe)

4-6 large shrimp or prawns, raw, with tail section on
8 medium mushrooms, scored with an "X" on the top
1 small can ginkgo nuts, drained
1 chicken breast, cut in 1" cubes
2 sprigs pine needles, washed
Several onion rings
Several strips green pepper
Coarse salt (Kosher salt)

Ponzu (Dipping Sauce)

½ C. soy sauce
½ C. lime juice
Garnishes to pass:
Grated ginger root
Minced green onion
Grated daikon (or icicle radish)

After cleaning clay saucer, put a ½" layer of salt on the bottom of dish. On that put a few sprinkles of water. Put saucers on baking sheet, cover with foil and set them in a preheated 400 degree oven to heat the salt. Remove hot saucers from oven. Arrange all ingredients, equally divided, in a pleasant pattern in the two dishes. Drop on a few more drops of water, cover with aluminum foil and seal well. Put back in oven and leave undisturbed 12 to 15 minutes. Remove from oven and carefully remove foil. Serve in the clay saucers. Use chopsticks if possible, or cocktail forks to lift the food from the salt and to dip in sauce and garnishes.

Author's note: I've experimented with cubes of steak, etc...and have had a lot of fun (and good food) with this method of service.

INDEX

C

D

E

F

N

O

P

R

S

T

V

Y

Z

Liquid Measure Conversions

Cups and Spoons	Liquid Ounces	Approximate Metric Term	Approximate Centiliters	Actual Milliliters
1 tsp	1/6 oz	1 tsp	½ cL	5 mL
1 Tb	½ oz	1 Tb	1½ cL	15 mL
¼ c; 4 Tb	2 oz	½ dL; 4Tb	6 cL	59 mL
⅓ c; 5 Tb	2⅔ oz	¾ dL; 5 Tb	8 cL	79 mL
½ c	4 oz	1 dL	12 cL	119 mL
⅔ c	5⅓ oz	1½ dL	15 cL	157 mL
¾ c	6 oz	1¾ dL	18 cL	178 mL
1 c	8 oz	¼ L	24 cL	237 mL
1¼ c	10 oz	3 dL	30 cL	296 mL
1⅓ c	10⅔ oz	3¼ dL	33 cL	325 mL
1½ c	12 oz	3½ dL	35 cL	355 mL
1⅔ c	13⅓ oz	3¾ dL	39 cL	385 mL
1¾ c	14 oz	4 dL	41 cL	414 mL
2 c; 1 pt	16 oz	½ L	47 cL	473 mL
2½ c	20 oz	6 dL	60 cL	592 mL
3 c	24 oz	¾ L	70 cL	710 mL
3½ c	28 oz	4/5 L; 8 dL	83 cL	829 mL
4 c; 1 qt	32 oz	1 L	95 cL	946 mL
5 c	40 oz	1¼ L	113 cL	1134 mL
6 c; 1½ qt	48 oz	1½ L	142 cL	1420 mL
8 c; 2 qt	64 oz	2 L	190 cL	1893 mL
10 c; 2½ qt	80 oz	2½ L	235 cL	2366 mL
12 c; 3 qt	96 oz	2¾ L	284 cL	2839 mL
4 qt	128 oz	3¾ L	375 cL	3785 mL
5 qt		4¾ L		
6 qt		5½ L (or 6 L)		
8 qt		7½ L (or 8L)		

To convert: *Ounces to milliliters:* multiply *ounces* by 29.57

Ounces to Grams

Ounces	Convenient Equivalent	Actual Weight
1 oz	30 g	(28.35 g)
2 oz	60 g	(56.7 g)
3 oz	85 g	(85.05 g)
4 oz	115 g	(113.4 g)
5 oz	140 g	(141.8 g)
6 oz	180 g	(170.1 g)
8 oz	225 g	(226.8)
9 oz	250 g	(255.2 g)
10 oz	285 g	(283.5 g)
12 oz	340 g	(340.2 g)
14 oz	400 g	(396.9 g)
16 oz	450 g	(453.6 g)
20 oz	560 g	(566.99 g)
24 oz	675 g	(680.4 g)

To convert: *Ounces* to *grams:* multiply *ounces* by 28.35

Pounds to Grams and Kilograms

Pounds	Convenient Equivalent	Actual Weight
¼ lb	115 g	(113.4 g)
½ lb	225 g	(226.8 g)
¾ lb	340 g	(340.2 g)
1 lb	450 g	(453.6 g)
1¼ lb	565 g	(566.99 g)
1½ lb	675 g	(680.4 g)
1¾ lb	800 g	(794 g)
2 lb	900 g	(908 g)
2½ lb	1125 g; 1¼ kg	(1134 g)
3 lb	1350 g	(1360 g)
3½ lb	1500 g; 1½ kg	(1588 g)
4 lb	1800 g	(1814 g)
4½ lb	2 kg	(2041 g)
5 lb	2¼ kg	(2268 g)
5½ lb	2½ kg	(2495 g)
6 lb	2¾ kg	(2727 g)
7 lb	3¼ kg	(3175 g)
8 lb	3½ kg	(3629 g)
9 lb	4 kg	(4028 g)
10 lb	4½ kg	(4536 g)
12 lb	5½ kg	(5443 g)
14 lb	6¼ kg	(6350 g)
15 lb	6¾ kg	(6804 g)
16 lb	7¼ kg	(7258 g)
18 lb	8 kg	(8165 g)
20 lb	9 kg	(9072 g)
25 lb	11¼ kg	(11,340 g)

Inches to Centimeters

Inches ("in")	Centimeters ("cm") (Nearest equivalent)
1/16 in	¼ cm
⅛ in	½ cm
3/16 in	less than ¼ in/¾ cm
¼ in	¾ cm
⅜ in	1 cm
½ in	1½ cm
⅝ in	1½ cm
¾ in	2 cm
1 in	2½ cm
1½ in	4 cm
2 in	5 cm
2½ in	6½ cm
3 in	8 cm
3½ in	9 cm
4 in	10 cm
5 in	13 cm
6 in	15 cm
7 in	18 cm
8 in	20 cm
9 in	23 cm
10 in	25 cm
12 in	30 cm
14 in	35 cm
15 in	38½ cm
16 in	40 cm
18 in	45 cm
20 in	50 cm
24 in	60 cm
30 in	75 cm

To convert: *Inches* to *centimeters:* multiply *inches* by 2.54

Flour and Sugar Measurements

Flour equivalents are for flour scooped and leveled. Level even with lip using knife edge.

Flour Measurement	Ounces	Nearest Equivalent
1 Tb	¼ oz	7½ g
¼ c; 4 Tb	1¼ oz	35 g
⅓ c; 5 Tb	1½ oz	50 g
½ c	2½ oz	70 g
⅔ c	3¼ oz	100 g
¾ c	3½ oz	105 g
1 c	5 oz	140 g
1¼ c	6 oz	175 g
1⅓ c	6½ oz	190 g
1½ c	7½ oz	215 g
2 c	10 oz	285 g
3½ c	16 oz; 1 lb	454 g
3¾ c	17½ oz	500 g

Sugar Measurement	Sugar Ounces	Nearest Equivalent
1 tsp	⅙ oz	5 g
1 Tb	½ oz	12-15 g
¼ c; 4 Tb	1¾ oz	50 g
⅓ c; 5 Tb	2¼ oz	65 g
½ c	3½ oz	100 g
⅔ c	4½ oz	125 g
¾ c	5 oz	145 g
1 c	7 oz (6¾ oz)	190 - 200 g
1¼ c	8½ oz	240 g
1⅓ c	9 oz	245 g
1½ c	9½ oz	275 g
1⅔ c	11 oz	325 g
1¾ c	11¾ oz	240 g
2 c	13½ oz	380 - 400 g

Temperatures

Fahrenheit degrees are converted to the most convenient Celsius term with Celsius degrees in parentheses.

Fahrenheit °/ Celsius °	(Actual Celsius °)
—5 °F/—20 °C	(—20.6 °C)
32 °F/0 °C	(0 °C)
37 °F/3 °C	(2.8 °C)
50 °F/10 °C	(10 °C)
60 °F/16 °C	(15.6 °C)
70 °F/21 °C	(21.1 °C)
75 °F/24 °C	(23.9 °C)
80 °F/27 °C	(26.7 °C)
85 °F/29 °C	(29.4 °C)
100 °F/38 °C	(37.8 °C)
105 °F/41 °C	(40.6 °C)
110 °F/43 °C	(43.3 °C)
115 °F/46 °C	(46.1 °C)
120 °F/49 °C	(48.9 °C)
125 °F/52 °C	(51.7 °C)
130 °F/54 °C	(54.4 °C)
135 °F/57 °C	(57.2 °C)
140 °F/60 °C	(60 °C)
150 °F/66 °C	(65.6 °C)
160 °F/71 °C	(71.1 °C)
165 °F/74 °C	(73.9 °C)
170 °F/77 °C	(76.7 °C)
180 °F/82 °C	(82.2 °C)
190 °F/88 °C	(87.8 °C)
200 °F/95 °C	(93.3 °C)
205 °F/96 °C	(96.1 °C)
212 °F/100 °C	(100 °C)
225 °F/110 °C	107.2 °C)
228 °F/109 °C	(108.9 °C)
238 °F/115 °C	(114.4 °C)
250 °F/120 °C	(121.1 °C)
275 °F/135 °C	(135 °C)
285 °F/140 °C	(140.6 °C)
300 °F/150 °C	(148.9 °C)
325 °F/165 °C	(162.8 °C)
350 °F/180 °C	(176.7 °C)
375 °F/190 °C	(190.6 °C)
400 °F/205 °C	(204.4 °C)
425 °F/220 °C	(218.3 °C)
450 °F/230 °C	(232.2 °C)
475 °F/245 °C	(246.1 °C)
500 °F/260 °C	(260 °C)
525 °F/275 °C	(273.9 °C)
550 °F/290 °C	(287.8 °C)

To convert: *Fahrenheit* to *Celsius:* subtract 32, multiply by 5, divide by 9.

BIBLIOGRAPHY

Longstreet, Stephen and Ethel, YOSHIWARA, City of the Senses, New York, David McKay Co. Inc. 1970

Yoors, Jan, THE GYPSIES, New York, Simon and Schuster, 1967

FOODS OF THE WORLD, Time/Life Books, New York, 1969

Montagne, Prosper, LAROUSSE GASTRONOMIQUE, New York, Crown Publishers, Inc. 1961

THE SAVOY COCKTAIL BOOK (Revised Edition), New York, Arno Press, 1976

HORIZON COOKBOOK, Vols. I and II, New York, American Heritage Publishing Co. 1968.

Campbell, Carol, SERVE IT FORTH and QUITE A MATTER OF FANCY, Oberlin, Ohio, Camcote House

Buck, Pearl S., ORIENTAL COOKBOOK, Simon and Schuster New York, 1972

Millay, Edna St. Vincent and Dillon, George, (Translation of:) LES FLEUR DU MAL (FLOWERS OF EVIL) by Charles Baudelaire, New York, Harper & Brothers, 1936

Fettner, Ann Tucker, POTPOURRI, New York, Workman Publishing Co., 1977

Chappell, Helen, A GENTLE GUIDE TO MAGICK, New York, Links Books, 1974

To Purchase Additional Copies of

DECADENT DINNERS & LASCIVIOUS LUNCHES

Consult your favorite bookseller
or order direct from the publisher

Remit $11.95 plus 75¢ postage per book to:

RENAISSANCE HOUSE
PUBLISHERS

A Division of Jende-Hagan, Inc.
541 Oak Street • P.O. Box 177
Frederick, CO 80530